296.0904
G65
a
Gordis, Robert.
Judaism in a Christian world.

JUDAISM
IN A
CHRISTIAN
WORLD

BOOKS BY ROBERT GORDIS

THE BIBLICAL TEXT IN THE MAKING

THE JEW FACES A NEW WORLD

THE WISDOM OF ECCLESIASTES

CONSERVATIVE JUDAISM

KOHELETH: THE MAN AND HIS WORLD

THE SONG OF SONGS

JUDAISM FOR THE MODERN AGE

A FAITH FOR MODERNS

THE ROOT AND THE BRANCH:
JUDAISM AND THE FREE SOCIETY

THE BOOK OF GOD AND MAN—A STUDY OF JOB

ROBERT GORDIS

JUDAISM IN A CHRISTIAN WORLD

McGRAW-HILL BOOK COMPANY

NEW YORK   TORONTO   LONDON   SYDNEY

For Fannie

PROVERBS 31:31

The present volume is, in part, based upon various studies and papers that have previously appeared in print. I acknowledge with thanks permission to utilize, in modified form, material originally published under the auspices of the Leo Baeck Institute, B'nai B'rith, the Religious Affairs Committee of Federation, Sheed and Ward, and Syracuse University Press, and in the pages of *Congress Weekly* and *Jewish Frontier*.

It is a pleasure once again to express, however inadequately, my gratitude to my devoted and learned friend, Dr. Abraham I. Shinedling, who gave the book the benefit of a meticulous proofreading and who prepared the Index.

JUDAISM IN A CHRISTIAN WORLD

Copyright © 1966 by Robert Gordis. All Rights Reserved. Printed in the United States of America. This book; or parts thereof, may not be reproduced in any form without permission of the publishers.

Library of Congress Catalog Card Number: 66-23275
First Edition   23777

CONTENTS

v

FIVE

Judaism and Freedom of Conscience 96

SIX

Judaism in the Christian World View 125

SEVEN

The Judeo-Christian Tradition—Illusion or Reality 149

EIGHT

Intermarriage and the Jewish Future 181

NINE

Directions of the American Jewish Community 209

NOTES 235

INDEX 246

THE PERIL
AND THE PROMISE

NEARLY FORTY CENTURIES AGO Judaism began as the faith of a minority of one. Never since has it attained to a position of numerical superiority. To be sure, the prophet of the Babylonian Exile sought to encourage his dispirited brothers by declaring, "Look to Abraham your father ... for he was but one when I called him and I blessed him and made him many" (Isa. 51:2). But this statement is true only relatively. In absolute terms, the words of *Deuteronomy* were more accurate, "It is not because you were more in number than any other people that the Lord set his love upon you and chose you. For you are the fewest of all peoples" (*Deut.* 7:7).

To leap across the centuries to modern times, no nation has sustained anything like the mass destruction wreaked upon the Jews. Six out of sixteen million—nearly two-fifths—have been brutally done to death in a single decade. Today Jews constitute only six-thousandths of one percent of the world population.

The perils confronting the Jewish people in its struggle for survival derive not only from its small numbers but from the difficult conditions of its existence. During the period that its life was centered in its homeland, the Jewish people clung precariously to a narrow strip of land along the eastern shore of the Mediterranean. Because of its geographical position, perched on a thin ledge at the crossroads of Europe, Asia, and Africa, Palestine resounded to the march of conquerors more than any other land in recorded history. It was its position rather than its natural resources that made it desirable. For the country could scarcely be called a land "flowing with milk and honey" except by contrast with the sands of the surrounding desert. As the frequent references in the Bible to famines make clear, the Promised Land could not compare in fertility to the Nile and the Euphrates valleys, in which Egyptian and Mesopotamian civilization came to flower.

Moreover, the Jewish people lived in its homeland for only a small fraction of its history. The period from the conquest of Joshua until the destruction of the First Temple lasted a little over six hundred years. After the Babylonian Exile came the age of the so-called Second Commonwealth. This era began with the proclamation of Cyrus, King of Persia, in 538 B.C.E., permitting Jews who so desired to return to Palestine. It ended with the destruction of the Second Temple by the Romans in the year 70 C.E. —another period of six hundred years. To this may be added a further one hundred and fifty years, during which Palestine continued to be the spiritual center of world Jewry, until it was eclipsed by Babylonia.

Brief as was the period of Jewish residence in Palestine, Jewish independence was even more short-lived. In the biblical era, Jewish independence lasted only four centuries, from the days of Saul to the destruction of the First Temple, and in the post-biblical era, a little less than eighty years, from the proclamation of Jewish independence by Simon the Maccabee in 142 B.C.E. until the seizure of Palestine by the Roman general Pompey in 63 B.C.E. In sum, the

Jewish people lived in its homeland for less than one-third of its history, and enjoyed independence—if that is the proper term—for less than one-eighth of its career.

Even during the period of the First Temple there were large Jewish communities in the Diaspora, notably in Egypt, Mesopotamia, Syria, and the Greek "islands of the sea," as *Isaiah* (11:11) and other biblical sources indicate. In all these lands, the Jewish inhabitants obviously constituted but a small minority of the general population. During the period of the Second Commonwealth there were far more Jews living outside the borders of the Holy Land than within it. Jews left their native land in substantial numbers because the Roman empire facilitated travel and trade throughout its vast territories. Yet nowhere did Jews dominate any city in the Greco-Roman world, not even Alexandria, the center of Jewish Hellenistic culture and religion.

Following the burning of the Temple and the destruction of Jewish independence by the Romans, there began the nineteen-hundred-year era of dispersion and exile. This condition has been dramatically altered, but not ended, by the establishment of the State of Israel in 1948. Despite the extraordinary figure of two million Jews ingathered in the State of Israel, it still remains true that five-sixths of world Jewry live in the Diaspora. The conclusion is clear that the abnormal status of a minority has been the norm for Jewish life for most of its existence.

The nineteen centuries of exile since the destruction of Jerusalem by the Romans in 70 c.e. fall into two unequal and totally different periods. Until the French Revolution in 1789, Jews in Europe lived under medieval conditions. Though there were Jews in Spain long before there were Spaniards, Jews in France centuries before the emergence of a French national group, and Jews in Germany for fifteen centuries before the creation of the German Empire,

they were a foreign body everywhere and citizens nowhere. Juridically they were "slaves of the royal ex-
chequer," and their residence was by sufferance and not by
right—at the pleasure of kings, nobles, or the Church, and
only as long as their presence seemed useful to the ruling
powers.

Thus the Jews of France suffered such calamities as massacre at the hands of the Crusaders in the eleventh and
twelfth centuries, the burning of the Talmud and other
sacred books in the thirteenth, and mass murder and pillage
by mobs in the fourteenth. In addition, they were expelled
from the royal domains in 1182, recalled in 1198, driven
out in 1306, readmitted in 1315, expelled once more in
1322, brought back in 1359, and finally driven out in 1394.
From England the Jews had been driven out in 1290. Two
hundred years later, in 1492, came the tragic expulsion of
the Jews from Spain. Even before the final blow de-
scended, the life of Spanish Jewry was punctuated by a
succession of acts of discrimination and persecution, spolia-
tion and massacre. It is customary to speak of the miracle of
Jewish survival. More soberly, the process may be described as one of imperfect Jewish annihilation.

The full extent of this extermination emerges from a
comparison of the estimates by scholars of the number of
Jews living in 70 C.E. and eleven centuries later, in 1173.
Thus the famous New Testament scholar, Adolf von Har-
nack, estimates that the world Jewish population in the
year 70 C.E. was four million, with at least one-half living
outside the confines of Palestine. More recently, the contemporary Jewish historian, Salo W. Baron, has suggested
even a higher figure. He believes that in the first century
C.E. there were two million Jews in Palestine, with a world
Jewish population of eight million Jews being "fully within
the range of probability."

On the basis of the data given by the Jewish traveler

Benjamin of Tudela, who died a thousand years later in 1173, scholars estimate that the Jewish population of the world had fallen to one million. Thus, after thirty-five generations of natural increase, it had fallen to one-fourth or one-eighth, mute but graphic evidence of the hazards confronting Jewish survival.

This peril was twofold in character. During the seventeen centuries preceding the French Revolution the danger was primarily physical and secondarily spiritual. To apply modern terms not yet known, medieval Jewry was exposed to anti-Semitism as a major threat, and to assimilation as a minor one. There were, to be sure, many examples in the Middle Ages of defection from Jewish ranks, sometimes compulsory, sometimes voluntary. History knows of Jews converting freely to the dominant faith, throwing in their lot with the majority, and thus avoiding for themselves and their descendants the liabilities of Jewish affiliation. Primarily, however, the hazards confronting the medieval Jewish community were material—persecution, expulsion, expropriation, massacre.

Even after the French Revolution, the physical peril remained all too real. When the forces of reaction triumphed over the spirit of the Revolution they expressed themselves in attacks upon Jews, who had been newly emancipated by the French Revolution and Napoleon. Anti-Jewish riots in which the medieval cry "Hep" (*Hierosolyma est perdita,* "Jerusalem is destroyed") resounded through the streets of Germany, occurred frequently during the first half of the nineteenth century.

Indeed, in the second half of the century Jew hatred was now dignified with a "philosophic" name, anti-Semitism, concocted by a Frenchman and adopted by Germans with alacrity. Decked out in all the trappings of pseudo-science, anti-Semitism became a respectable political "movement" in the closing decades of the century. The German court preacher, Stöcker, launched a party which polled several million votes on a program calling for the removal of Jewish rights in Germany. Even the hoary lie of the blood accusation, the vicious charge that Jews used the blood of Christian children for the Passover, which had first appeared in Norwich, England, in 1144 and had spawned untold massacres throughout Europe during the ensuing centuries, was revived in the modern era. In 1882 Jews were accused of ritual murder in Tisza-Eszlar, Hungary.

In the East, where Jews continued to live under medieval conditions until the overthrow of the Czarist regime, pogroms like those of Kishinev in 1903 and the infamous trial of Mendel Beilis (1911–13) on the charge of ritual murder, demonstrated the reality of the physical peril to Jewish survival. The horrible climax was reached in the Nazi holocaust which exterminated six of the seven million Jews of Europe, brutally torturing and murdering men, women, and children without pity, by the most efficient and scientific methods.

Genuine as the physical peril has been—and it can hardly be exaggerated—the threat it poses to the preservation of the Jewish heritage and the Jewish identity has become secondary to the spiritual danger confronting modern Jewry.

It derives from the processes set in motion by the French Revolution. These new forces could be hindered or even halted, but they could not be permanently reversed. The slogan of "Liberty, Fraternity, Equality" was applied not only to the various classes in society but to the Jews as well, and it brought in its wake the "emancipation" of the Jews. With many hesitations and evasions the Jews of Western Europe were admitted to political citizenship in the lands of their sojourning, and were given opportunities to participate in the national life—political, civic, economic, and cultural.

Now the relative roles of the twin perils of anti-Semitism

and assimilation have been reversed. It is the danger of assimilation that has become primary. In an age of growing mass pressures, conformity becomes the goal and individuality increasingly difficult to maintain. Both under the democratic political order and under Communist rule, the liabilities of being a Jew continue to be genuine and widespread. There is every temptation, particularly for able and ambitious young people, to cast off the ties that constrict their progress in their chosen career by binding them to "a despised faith," to use Judah Halevi's phrase. When some modern Jews desert their people in response to the call of convenience and the drive of ambition, they have at hand various high-sounding ideological formulas, such as scientific enlightenment, social justice, internationalism, tolerance, and brotherhood, to disguise and help justify their defection.

In addition, traditional religion as a whole is being challenged by a series of revolutions in human thought that have undermined the belief in the truth of Scripture and the teachings both of Church and Synagogue for millions of educated men and women.

In the ancient world man was the center of the universe. The earth was regarded as flat, surrounded by the great sea on all sides. Arched above the earth like an inverted bowl was the sky, in which the sun, the moon, and the stars had been placed to illumine man's path and to serve his needs. To Jews and Christians alike God had created the world, the earth was its center, and man was its crown and glory.

This view was shaken to its foundations by Copernicus. This obscure Polish monk in the seventeenth century demonstrated what had long been suspected, that the world was heliocentric and that the planets, of which the Earth was one of the smallest, revolved around the sun. To his successors the solar system was revealed as but one small element in the vast expanses of space. The earth was a tiny clod and man a speck of dust upon it. The process of downgrading man had begun.

In the nineteenth century came the Darwinian revolution. The English biologist Charles Darwin assembled a mass of evidence, much of which had been known before, which demonstrated that all life was part of a single process of evolution and that man, far from standing apart from the lower animals, represented only one more link in the evolution of species.

Centuries before, the biblical sage Koheleth had speculated whether man was more than a beast. Now science seemed to have given the final answer: Man was simply an animal, a more agile and certainly a more cunning ape than his brothers, the baboon and the gorilla.

The ultimate blow to man's self-esteem was dealt by the Freudian revolution in the twentieth century. The father of psychoanalysis, Sigmund Freud, was a veritable Columbus of the mind, discovering continents undreamt of before. He revealed unsuspected levels of consciousness in man and sought to trace their impact upon his behavior, both during his waking and his sleeping states. In his psychoanalytic theories Freud emphasized the power of irrational impulses and frustrated desires in molding and at times perverting the human psyche. The popularizers and the vulgarizers of Freud went even further in the downgrading of man, declaring that man was nothing but a collection of abnormalities, with only a thin line separating the so-called normal from the neurotic and the psychotic. The gift of reason, in which man had gloried through the ages as the mark of his superiority over the beast, was now discounted as a delusion. His conscience was no longer the voice of God, but the mechanism of the super-ego. Biology had demonstrated, or so it appeared, that man was no better than the beast. Now psychology seemed to show that man therefore all the more devastating. Most modern Jews are the children of East European Jewry, where the Emancipation and the Enlightenment of the eighteenth century scarcely penetrated. It was only when they emigrated to Western Europe and America, at the end of the nineteenth and the beginning of the twentieth century, that they found themselves catapulted from the medieval world into the atomic and space age virtually overnight. There was scarcely time or opportunity for them to meet these challenges and respond to them adequately. For all these reasons, the so-called "modern spirit" poses a far greater challenge to Judaism than it does to Christianity.

In the face of the varied perils threatening the survival of Judaism several distinct responses have emerged. A highly prevalent reaction, which continues to gain in strength, is the path of assimilation and total separation from Judaism and the Jewish community. This approach—or more precisely, this escape—is rarely formulated in theoretical terms or justified in words. Nonetheless, assimilation has continued to make headway, taking on countless forms under varying conditions. All too often the most creative members of the Jewish group adopt this negative response to their ancestral heritage. They soon discover that if they remain Jews, their advancement in their chosen field of endeavor, be it science or art, commerce, industry or government, will be hindered through the subtler forms of anti-Jewish prejudice still operating in the Western world, and that their total acceptance in the upper echelons of "society" will be severely limited. The remedy seems clear and easy. Generally the many gifted Jews who succumb to the temptation to desert their Jewish patrimony find the process of assimilation facilitated by their ignorance of the content of Judaism in any meaningful sense. They are therefore honestly unable to see any value in Judaism or find in it any insights relevant to the concerns of modern man.

Assimilation is the perfect, the logical answer to their problem of advancement and acceptance.

Yet in spite of the façade of intellectual conviction that they have set up to justify their defection, assimilated Jews frequently betray their emotional unease by an overt attitude of hostility to the heritage they have spurned. Their attitudes toward Judaism and the Jewish community are, as often as not, a reflex of the prejudice and ignorance of Judaism which is still rampant in Western culture. Defection from Jewish tradition is obviously "practical"; rationalization makes it "right."

The right to alienate oneself from one's heritage is inalienable in a free society. When Hitler prohibited the assimilation of Jews in Germany, he was denying their freedom. Yet it cannot be denied that there are grave moral issues involved in the process of defection. It is scarcely a mark of moral courage or of intellectual integrity to surrender one of the great religio-cultural traditions of mankind without having made any genuine effort to understand it. That the process of alienation from Judaism is generally motivated by practical considerations rather than by lofty ideals will be passionately denied. But the evidence is undeniable. If two groups, one Christian, the other Jewish, of successful and creative people in the arts, sciences, business, or government, who are similar in education, interests, and economic level are compared, one will find a far greater degree of defection from their religious tradition among the Jews than among their Christian counterparts. Studies have shown that the percentage of Jews included in *Who's Who* who give no information as to their religious affiliation is much higher than among Christians listed in the same work. Similarly, surveys have indicated that attendance at public worship is far lower among Jews than among Christians of the same cultural and economic level.

This is not all. The ethical indignity involved in most

forms of assimilation produces psychological traumas among many modern Jews. The phenomenon, which was studied by Theodor Lessing in his important work *Juedischer Selbsthass*, takes on countless forms. Like all forms of psychopathology, Jewish self-hate runs the gamut from minor, scarcely noticeable "tics," through neuroses of ever-increasing severity, to the extreme of total psychosis and mental collapse.

A striking instance is afforded by the tragic life of Otto Weininger, a gifted Viennese student of philosophy and psychology. His book *Sex and Character* appeared in 1902 when he was only twenty-two years old. Though marked by a pathological hatred of Judaism, the work bore obvious signs of brilliance and evoked the interest of Sigmund Freud. Weininger, who was born a Jew, had converted to Christianity that same year. Even this step did not suffice to allay his hatred and contempt for Jews and Judaism. A year later he came to Beethoven's home in Vienna and put a bullet through his head.

A few other instances out of many may be cited. Max Beerbohm is the subject of a highly perceptive and sympathetic study by the English writer and editor, Malcolm Muggeridge. Muggeridge insists that the key to the limitations of Beerbohm's life and achievement lies in his lifelong attempt to hide and deny his Jewish origin.[1]

An American counterpart to the Weininger tragedy took place recently. An enterprising newspaper reporter discovered that the Kleagle of the Ku Klux Klan in New York, a violent apostle of anti-Semitism and anti-Negroism, was actually a young Jew named Daniel Burros. When the young racist learned of his imminent "exposure," he threatened to kill the reporter, but instead committed suicide.

These are admittedly extreme instances, but only in degree. A few years ago there was the case of a distinguished

[1] *New York Review of Books*, Nov. 25, 1965, pp. 31–33.

American research scientist who had won the Nobel Prize for his epoch-making discoveries in biology and medicine. When he discovered that the publishers of *Who's Who in American Jewry* were planning to include his biography, since he was born of Jewish parents though he had been converted to Christianity, he sued in the courts to prevent the inclusion of his biography. He contended that his children would suffer great psychological damage if they discovered his Jewish background, which had been kept a secret from them.

There are, of course, many less severe and much more common manifestations of the same sense of Jewish inferiority. American Jews are moved by a widespread tendency to change characteristically "Jewish" surnames such as Cohen, Goldberg, Levy, Horowitz, and Shapiro, each of which has been borne by many distinguished figures both in the past and the present. Some truth—but not much—inheres in the contention that less obviously "Jewish" names may minimize initial manifestations of prejudice. In some instances, the argument is advanced that the names are difficult to pronounce and spell. Curiously, Christian Americans with difficult surnames of Dutch, Welsh, or Slavic origin are rarely as solicitous about the comfort and ease of those whom they meet. Other, less severe manifestations of Jewish self-hatred are legion. It has been noted by sympathetic and perceptive Christians that some Jews will hide a knowledge of Yiddish, will publicly flout Jewish practices, and will take delight in telling anti-Jewish stories in an imaginary Jewish accent. These are all instances of maladjustment brought on by the desire to assimilate with the majority and thus cut the nexus of Jewish belonging.

In sum, there are grave moral issues involved in the process of self-alienation from the Jewish heritage. The effort to break with one's past, whether superficially successful or not, often creates grave psychological traumas induced by inescapable guilt feelings. These factors are sufficient to validate the judgment that, from the standpoint of individual well-being, assimilation is an unsatisfactory response to the challenge confronting Jews and Judaism in the modern world.

That is, however, by no means all. Because assimilation is especially tempting to talented and creative men and women, its results are particularly unfortunate in several other respects. By totally obliterating Jewish values and attitudes from their lives, these gifted assimilationists impoverish their own richly endowed spirits, which could gain immeasurably from the resources of the Jewish tradition. In addition, their alienation from the Jewish community robs Jewish life of great sources of strength and creativity. Finally, the world is deprived of significant Jewish values and insights that they could have introduced into the mainstream of modern civilization.

Had assimilation been the only response to the perils confronting Jewish existence in the modern world, this book would not have been written. The Jewish group would have moved so far along the road to total extermination beyond the point of no return that the end would have been clearly in sight.

However, in spite of its apparent attractiveness, assimilation did not capture the field. Most modern Jews were either unwilling or unable to accept this philosophy in practice. They were far from being of one mind with regard to the specific response to be adopted, but they were united in rejecting overt or covert assimilation as the answer to the Jewish problem. Most modern Jews are incurably survivalist. They may not know what they want, but they are agreed on what they do not. The various motivations, both internal and external, that are at work in the Jewish com-

munity and the competing philosophies that offer a rationale for Jewish existence will be examined in detail later in
this volume.

Most modern Jews would not express themselves with
the eloquence and the conviction of the distinguished
American Jewish leader, Cyrus Adler, who wrote in 1894:

> I will continue to hold my banner aloft. I find myself born—
> ay, born—into a people and a religion. The preservation of my
> people must be for a purpose, for God does nothing without a
> purpose. His reasons are unfathomable to me, but on my own
> reason I place little dependence; test it where I will it fails me.
> The simple, the ultimate in every direction is sealed to me. It
> is as difficult to understand matter as mind. The courses of the
> planets are no harder to explain than the growth of a blade of
> grass. Therefore am I willing to remain a link in the great
> chain. What has been preserved for four thousand years was
> not saved that I should overthrow it. My people have survived
> the prehistoric paganism, the Babylonian polytheism, the
> aesthetic Hellenism, the sagacious Romanism, at once the bland-
> ishments and persecutions of the Church; and it will survive the
> modern dilettantism and the current materialism, holding aloft
> the traditional Jewish ideals inflexibly until the world shall
> become capable of recognizing their worth.

Jews today may lack the simple piety of an earlier generation and would differ as to the specific Jewish ideals to
be cherished, interpreted, and held aloft in the modern
world. But they would insist on maintaining the Jewish
identity and on preserving those aspects of the tradition that
they believe to be viable and significant. Moses' injunction
to the Israelites at Sinai, "Ye shall be a kingdom of priests
unto Me and a holy nation," may sound too pretentiously
sacral for modern tastes. The prophetic formulation of Israel's role in history as a "covenant to the peoples, a light to
the nations," may carry too cosmic a ring for modern ears.
Yet the conviction continues to persist among Jews that the

Jewish tradition contains precious truths and that the Jewish way of life possesses sources of beauty and meaning that must not be permitted to die.

For modern Jews, Israel's race is not yet run because its work is not yet done. The many-faceted Jewish contribution to civilization is not limited to the achievements in the past but is rich with meaning for the future. It is this vision of the promise which supplies the dynamic for fighting the perils confronting Jewish existence today. But this incurably individualistic and stiff-necked people has not arrived at any measure of agreement as to the measures to be employed.

Nowhere does this faith in the eternity of Israel burn more intensely than in certain right-wing Orthodox groups that are at the furthest possible remove from assimilation. With unremitting fervor they urge total isolation from the contemporary scene. Being acutely conscious of the temptations of the modern world and the threat it poses to the preservation of ultra-Orthodoxy, these groups advocate and seek to practice a voluntary re-ghettoization of the spirit.

This return to the ghetto may take the form of the physical creation of self-sustaining communities which are both colorful and touching in their single-minded devotion to an ideal. Several such settlements now exist or are projected in suburbs near New York City. It should not be necessary to point out that like the Amish communities, such settlements, which incidentally add color and variety to the American scene, have every right to existence within the framework of our democratic order. In addition, there are concentrations of ultra-Orthodox Jews in certain neighborhoods of Brooklyn and Queens where they dominate the landscape, in spite of the presence of other elements in the population.

Generally, physical re-ghettoization proves impractical,

because of the cost, the necessity for economic contact
with the general population, and various social and political
pressures. Instead, a determined effort is made to create a
spiritual ghetto. The ultimate heresy, to be opposed at all
costs, is the effort to bring the Jewish tradition into contact
with the ideas of modern science and philosophy. Efforts
are made to insulate themselves, and especially the youth,
from contact with non-Jews or with Jews of different
views—beyond the usual amenities. Above all, any meaningful dialogue on the issues of contemporary religious
thought is strongly opposed as likely to undermine faith.
Secular education is regarded as an unfortunate necessity,
either in order to earn one's livelihood or in deference to
the law of the land. Nevertheless, secular education is to be
avoided wherever possible, and minimized where it cannot
be totally eliminated. In these circles even Orthodox institutions of more modern cast, such as Yeshiva University in
New York City, are looked upon askance as representing a
dilution, if not a betrayal, of "authentic" or "Torah-true"
Judaism.

It is undeniable that for those willing and able to adopt
these techniques of isolation the survival of Judaism is guar-
anteed—except for those individuals who, rebelling against
the rigors of the system, break with the entire pattern and
surrender its structure of values *in toto*. Intransigent atheism is all too often an inverted Orthodoxy. There is an unmistakable psychological link between the fanaticism of the
Greek Orthodox Church under Czarism and the absolutism
of atheistic Communism which succeeded it as the religion
of Soviet Russia.

The basic drawback of the formula of isolation as a
recipe for Jewish survival lies elsewhere. The devotees of
spiritual isolationism manifest a passionate and profound
sense of commitment to their faith, which is admirable in its
single-mindedness and capacity for sacrifice. Yet paradoxi-

cal as it seems, it is tragically true that these isolationist groups represent a violation of the essence of Judaism. For their outlook represents the petrifaction of the living Jewish tradition, which has survived through the ages precisely because it was able to meet the challenge and react to the stimulus of other cultures and peoples.

The evidence for this conclusion is abundant in every period of Jewish history. One can scarcely imagine a poorer habitat for a tradition of spiritual isolationism than Palestine, which at the crossroads of three continents was always exposed to all the cultural and intellectual influences of the Middle East. As modern archaeology and research make increasingly clear, every page in the Hebrew Bible reveals the close and intimate contact of ancient Israel with the cultures of Egypt, Syria, Assyria, and Babylonia, accepting, rejecting, modifying, and enriching these various sources of influence.

As for the Talmud, the second great monument of the Jewish genius, the notion that it represents an "indigenous" product of the Jewish genius "uncontaminated" by contact with the surrounding environment must be stigmatized as a myth. The process of creative interaction between Jews and the environment in the Greco-Roman era is evident in the vocabulary of the Mishnah and the Talmud, which contains hundreds of Greek and Latin words. The rabbis were familiar with the literature, the folklore, and the way of life of the Hellenistic world in which they lived, as the researches of Saul Lieberman and other scholars have abundantly documented. The affinities between the Talmud and Roman law have been explored by David Daube, Boaz Cohen, and other scholars, and the surface has scarcely been scratched.

With regard to medieval Jewish culture, the lines of influence were always clear and undeniable. Medieval Hebrew poetry consciously modeled itself upon Arabic poetry. Jewish philosophy, which sought to reconcile the Jewish religious tradition with the truths believed to inhere in Plato and Aristotle, was the counterpart of Islamic and Christian scholasticism, intimately associated with them and exerting a great influence upon them. Hebrew philology and biblical exegesis were the direct consequence of Jewish contacts with medieval Arab linguistics and exegesis.

How is it possible for the advocates and practitioners of Jewish isolationism in the contemporary world to dismiss the massive record of creative contacts between Judaism and the world? They are able to do so by ignoring the incontrovertible evidence for the biblical and the Talmudic eras, and by denigrating the medieval philosophic and scientific contribution as "un-Jewish" and "unauthentic." They disregard the historical experience of Alexandrian and Babylonian Jewry in the ancient world and of medieval Spanish and Italian Jewry, all of which were marked by close contact with the general culture of the age. Instead, they adopt as their model of "true" Judaism the East European Jewish community of the past few hundred years, which was isolated from the surrounding environment and which found neither challenge nor stimulus in the low cultural level of the general population.

The preservation of the Jewish tradition on isolationist terms, however, is unworkable in the free society of the West. It is true that the genius of the free society lies in granting every religious and cultural group the widest possible latitude in the development and maintenance of its specific tradition and way of life. Basic to the free society is the liberal faith that all legitimate ends are in harmony with one another. Hence it believes that if all men are free to cultivate their own gardens, the entire countryside will blossom like the rose. Out of its devotion to liberty, the free society can even tolerate within its borders small enclaves that are devoted exclusively to their own special goals and are little concerned with the common weal. But it cannot permit this type of exclusivism to become general. For no society—and the free society is no exception—will assent to its own destruction. The free society endows its members—and the voluntary groups they create—with inescapable duties as well as with inalienable rights. It cannot permit itself to be torn asunder and fragmented into alien and hostile sectors, lacking any common universe of discourse or any overarching set of loyalties.

Jewish isolationism, like that of any other religious, ethnic, or cultural group, may be legally defended under the provisions of the American Constitution, but it cannot be regarded as being spiritually at home in American society. Isolationism creates a caste of permanent, voluntary aliens who enjoy the benefits of American civilization but do not contribute to it in accordance with their potentialities. Voluntary self-ghettoization can therefore appeal only to a tiny minority, however picturesque and articulate.

Isolationism is not merely impractical in the free society. It is, in the deepest sense, unworthy of the Jewish tradition, as revealed in its greatest and most creative periods. The widespread adoption of the isolationist pattern for Jewish life would mean a tragic narrowing of intellectual perspective and moral vision for the Jewish people. Isolationism would preserve the shell but not the spirit of the people that gave the Bible to mankind, whose prophets saw Israel as the Servant of the Lord proclaiming the basic religious and ethical truths to all men, whose faith has served as the source of the two great monotheistic religions of Christianity and Islam, and whose sons, in Heine's words, have "fought and bled on every battlefield of human thought." The path of isolation might conceivably preserve Judaism, but at a tragic cost to Judaism, to Jews, and to the world. If it succeeded, it might overcome the peril; but it would obliterate the promise.

The present work is written in the conviction that there is both vitality and value in the Jewish tradition and that the potential service of the Jewish group to mankind is far from ended. The preservation of Judaism without Jews, or of Jews without Judaism, would be a major tragedy. For if the insights and values of the Jewish tradition are to have a significant impact upon the human condition, it is not enough for them to survive as a field of antiquarian research; they must be embodied in a living community.

Conversely, it is not enough to preserve the Jewish identity through a body of men and women recognized as Jews. What is important is *meaningful* survival. The Jewish community can derive meaning and purpose for its life and sacrifice only if it is attached to a vital tradition and if it strives to expound and adhere to its values and standards.

In this endeavor the Jewish community, the bearer and heir of the Jewish tradition, is confronted by major challenges which derive from its position as a minority culture in a non-Jewish world. The present work seeks to deal with these challenges to meaningful Jewish survival. In the process, we hope to illumine some of the values which Judaism can contribute to the world.

As we strive to grapple with the perils threatening Judaism and the Jewish people today, our goal will not be survival for its own sake, however legitimate this claim may be. The *raison d'être* for the struggle derives from the promise and the vision that have been the hallmark of the Jewish tradition in its greatest hours. In opposing both isolation and alienation, the present work is dedicated to the goal of *integration without assimilation, acculturation without absorption.*

Chapter 1 presents the historical background needed for an understanding of the status of the Jewish people and the problems confronting the Jewish tradition in the twentieth century. They have their origin in the eighteenth century when the two great movements already referred to, the Enlightenment and the Emancipation, shattered the structure of the Jewish community and undermined the authority of the Jewish tradition. These factors of dissolution led to widespread defection from Jewish ranks in Central and Western Europe. The process of escape from Judaism was brutally interrupted by the Nazi holocaust. But far from being halted, assimilation in its various forms is marching on with seven-league boots everywhere in the world today.

Chapter 2 analyzes the historical and psychological reasons which prevented the disappearance of Jews and Judaism. The various types of positive response to the challenge of the modern era which arose in the Jewish community of Central and Eastern Europe are described. This search for meaningful Jewish existence was pursued in various areas. In the field of culture it produced such phenomena as the Science of Judaism, the revival of Hebrew, and the flowering of Yiddish. But for most Western Jews, Judaism was primarily a religion. The various religious movements—Reform, Neo-Orthodoxy, and Conservatism, which originated in Germany, were destined to be transplanted and modified in the American environment. Finally, the most dramatic response to the challenge of dissolution lay neither in culture nor in religion but in Jewish nationalism. Zionism laid the foundations for the rebirth of the modern State of Israel and has had important consequences for the life of Diaspora Jewry, the full implications of which are yet to be revealed.

For over two millennia the genius of "the people of the Book" revealed itself preeminently in Jewish learning. In the modern era the traditional concept of Torah proved unable to retain the loyalty and interest of Jewish youth who had come into contact with the Western world. The

desire to win their loyalty for Judaism and the need to validate the Jewish position in modern Europe led to the rise
of the Science of Judaism. The history of this significant
movement is briefly traced in Chapter 3. An analysis is
offered of the very genuine achievements as well as the limitations of the Science of Judaism. It is maintained that both
the traditional ideal of Torah and the modern ideal of the
Science of Judaism are needed today in order to cross-
fertilize each other and to aid the modern Jew in his task of
self-discovery. A modern revitalized Jewish scholarship can
also serve two other great purposes. It can help to forge a
meaningful bond of unity between Israeli and Diaspora
Jewry and to reveal "the light in Judaism" to contemporary man.

Chapter 4 deals with a theme so frequently discussed that
it can scarcely be described as novel or exciting. Yet the
subject cannot be avoided. The difficulty which many Jews
and non-Jews experience in finding a proper role for the
Jewish community in Western society stems, in large measure, from a deep-seated confusion regarding the nature of
Jewish identity. From widely varying standpoints the
effort is made to subsume the Jewish group under some
such familiar category as "religion," "nationality," or even
"race." This inability to comprehend aright the nature of
Jewish identity leads into a mass of distortions and inner
contradictions on the part of the advocates of one or another "solution." If we begin with any of these conventional answers regarding the character of Jewish belonging,
we shall find that an entire series of major issues remains in-
soluble. We cannot hope to find a valid approach to such
problems as the attitude of Jews living in the Diaspora to
the State of Israel, or the key to their deep sense of identification with their native or adopted land. We are unable to
understand the relationship of Israeli Jews to world Jewry
on the one hand and to their Arab fellow citizens on the

other. The confusion was dramatically highlighted in the case of a Catholic priest of Jewish birth who sought to be recognized by the State of Israel as a Jew in nationality and a Christian in religion.

In this chapter it is maintained that the key to Jewish identity lies in reckoning with two fundamental aspects: the uniqueness of the Jewish people and the organic character of Judaism. Properly apprehended, these principles offer a theory for answering such basic questions as those we have referred to above, as well as such issues as the status in the Jewish tradition of Jewish converts to Christianity and of non-Jewish converts to Judaism.

Chapter 5 is concerned with one of the most significant values of the Jewish tradition—its concept of religious liberty and its development in Judaism. It is pointed out that there are three aspects to this ideal. The first, the claim of each religious group to practice its faith without interference from others, is, of course, widely held. Far less deeply entrenched within each religious community is the recognition of freedom of conscience for dissidents within its own ranks. It is the third aspect of religious liberty, the attitude toward those professing other creeds—in which Judaism developed a unique outlook—that has the largest measure of significance for modern man. Such a theory of religious liberty is of basic importance for the free society of today. It will be of even greater significance in the emerging world community of tomorrow.

Since Judaism is a minority religion everywhere in the world, its survival, particularly in meaningful terms, is impossible without a substantial measure of understanding and acceptance on the part of the dominant culture. In spite of extensive areas of prejudice and misunderstanding still in existence, there is an unmistakable growth in the quest for brotherhood and interfaith understanding both within the denominations of Christianity and beyond. In

Chapter 6 the unique importance of Judaism for the Christian world is highlighted. It is suggested that the Christian world must be ready to seek a deeper grasp of Jews and Judaism than has heretofore been achieved. The chapter also discusses several major roadblocks on the path of mutual understanding. These must be cleared away in order to advance the cause of intergroup amity and true mutuality of influence.

Chapter 7 considers the validity of the now familiar concept of a Judeo-Christian tradition. Because of the age-old burden of antagonism between Judaism and Christianity and the existence of significant differences between the two faiths, some thinkers have been led to deny the truth of the idea. In this chapter the origin and history of the concept is treated, as well as the reasons for the reluctance in certain quarters to accept the doctrine. The criteria for evaluating the truth of the concept are presented.

Far more significant than the mere affirmation or negation of the idea is the analysis both of the differences and of the points of similarity between the two components of the Judeo-Christian tradition. Their points of contact make mutual interaction possible; their points of difference make their independent survival necessary.

Chapter 8 treats the phenomenon of Jewish intermarriage in the modern world, which is arousing increasing concern. Because of the growing extent of the intermarriage of Jews and non-Jews in the Western world, there are substantial grounds for looking upon the phenomenon with grave disquiet. Not only does it pose the major threat to Jewish group survival but it frequently has unfortunate consequences for the personal happiness and the moral and psychological well-being of the human beings involved. After an analysis of the various causes underlying this complex phenomenon, some possible courses of action for the

Jewish community are presented, designed to minimize this basic threat to the Jewish future.

Chapter 9 surveys the contradictory trends characteristic of Jewish life in America. On the one hand, the factors making for assimilation, often impersonal and virtually unconscious, continue to make headway. On the other, the present American Jewish generation, both youth and adult, manifests a far greater measure of acceptance of one's Jewish background. For a growing minority there is also a conscious desire to establish meaningful identification with their heritage. This goal is often hindered by some practical difficulties encountered by young people seeking affiliation with the organized Jewish community. The steps needed to improve the situation are outlined.

In conclusion, it is contended that the peril confronting Judaism can be met and the promise it possesses can be fulfilled only by a renaissance of the Jewish heritage. If Judaism is to survive as a significant factor in a predominantly non-Jewish world, it will be necessary to re-create the organic Jewish community in which all phases of Jewish life, religion, law, music, literature, art, recreation, and social cohesion will reenforce and enrich one another. This type of Jewish community existed from ancient times, through the Middle Ages, to the period of the French Revolution and the Emancipation. There will, however, be one crucial and far-reaching difference—the Jewish community of the future will be voluntary in character. Thus it will not depend on persecution or coercion to hold the loyalty of its members but on its innate resources of the spirit. In a voluntary community dedicated to organic Judaism the Jewish tradition, contentful and multiform, will enrich the lives of its devotees and enable contemporary Jews to make their most significant contributions to the free society of today and the world community of tomorrow.

The two hundred years that separate the French Revolution from the Nazi onslaught on civilization have been freighted with greater promise and peril for Judaism and the Jewish people than any similar period of time in history. The massive achievements and the colossal failures of the modern era should teach us that only that society is truly free which is dedicated to the maximum development of each human being. This goal requires not only liberty for the individuals, but the right of spiritual self-determination for the group. For it is from their various voluntary associations, social, religious, and cultural, that men derive the ideals and values which make them human.

CHAPTER ONE

JEWISH TRADITION
IN THE MODERN WORLD—
FACTORS OF
DISINTEGRATION

IN ITS ORIGINS the Jewish tradition goes back to antiquity, but it is not simply part of the dim past. The cultures of its earliest contemporaries, the Babylonians and the Canaanites, and even the civilizations of the Greeks and the Romans, who appeared later on the stage of history, survive today only in books and works of art. The nations that created and sustained these treasures are gone. Not so the Jews, who have time and again disproved and often irritated the prophets who had announced their inevitable disappearance. Nevertheless the tradition has never been so gravely threatened with dissolution as in the twentieth century. If we seek to understand the contemporary status of Judaism and the problems it confronts in the modern world, we must relate it to the millennial experience of the Jewish people, which has been the creator and exemplar of the tradition for thirty-three centuries.

During the long expanse of Jewish history, three major types of Jewish communities emerged: [1]

The first category was the *natural community*, of which ancient Palestine during the First and Second Commonwealths offers the most striking illustration. This community, which was rooted in its own soil, may be described as both exclusive and inclusive. It was exclusive in the sense that a Jewish child born in Palestine during the period of national independence or autonomy could join no other community except the Jewish, unless he chose to dissociate himself by means of a violent act of apostasy or treachery.[2] Barring such extreme and infrequent departures from the norm, a Jewish child grew naturally into the institutions of Jewish life, which he regarded as his natural environment.

The natural community, too, was all-inclusive, embracing every area of human experience. To be a Jew was to be a member of a group which shared in common all aspects of human life, such as geographical contiguity, economic interdependence, and political unity. Moreover, all the religious and cultural values of life were created and shared in common.

Another characteristic which the natural community possessed is that it was largely *self-determining*, to the extent to which any people living upon its own soil may be described as being the master of its own destiny. Even during the periods of Jewish subjection to foreign powers— Persian, Greek, Egyptian, or Roman—Palestinian Jewry possessed local autonomy, which included religious and cultural activity and its own legal and judicial system.

With the Roman Exile and the rise of the Diaspora after the year 70 C.E., another type, the *compulsory community*, appears on the stage of Jewish history, taking on varied forms in ancient Babylonia, in Christian Spain, and in medieval Poland. In the later Middle Ages it developed the now familiar pattern of the ghetto throughout Europe. The basic distinction of the compulsory community is that it is not self-determining. Juridically speaking, the basis for the participation of Jews in Jewish community life was not their own volition but the organized pressure of the state. It is not to be imagined for a moment that there were no inner sanctions in Jewish life, universally felt and deeply rooted. But irrespective of whether the individual Jew wished to associate himself with the Jewish community or not, he was compelled to do so by the "host" community in which he lived.

The implications of this fact are far-reaching. In the medieval state the Jew as an individual had no official existence; he was a cell of the Jewish community. In levying taxes upon Jews, the government would place the assessment upon the Jewish community as a whole, which in turn would allocate the shares to each individual member. The most important consequence was that the Jewish community had the power to enforce taxation upon its members. The significance of this function can scarcely be exaggerated, for the right to tax means the right to govern, and therefore to organize and influence every area of life, not merely the economic. The Jewish community legislated for its members, maintained a system of courts with power to enforce decisions in civil, criminal, and ritual cases, and supported the synagogues, schools, bathhouses, and slaughtering houses. This was true of the Babylonian Exilarchate, of the Spanish *Aljama*, and of the Polish *Vaad Arba Aratzoth* (The Council of the Four Lands). By virtue of these functions, the Jewish community became the all-inclusive agency for all group needs and activities.[3]

Not only is this type of community inclusive; it is, to all intents and purposes, also exclusive. While it is true that some Jews, especially of the wealthier and more privileged classes, might be lost to their people through assimilation or conversion, either voluntary or forced, escape for the Jews as a group was impossible. Indeed, for most of them it was unthinkable, since the Jewish community was the only one with which they had any real contact.

More important than the differences between the "natural" and the "compulsory" types of community were their far-reaching similarities. In reality the natural community was compulsory for the average Jew because no other was within reach, and the compulsory community was natural because no other was conceivable.

Even more significant is the fact that both the natural and the compulsory community were *organic*.[4] The activities that we are accustomed to categorize today as religious, cultural, educational, civic defense, charitable, and administrative were maintained by and for all the members of the Jewish community within a single pattern of organization.

Finally, neither type of community was troubled by what might be described as the hallmark of the modern Jew, the problem of his status and the character of his group life. Nowhere in the Bible or in the Talmud do we find any discussion as to whether the Jews are a religion, a nationality, or a race. Even the medieval Jewish philosophers did not concern themselves with this issue. Until modern times it sufficed to recall the classic formulation attributed to the *Zohar*, "God, Israel, and the Torah are one," [5] which emphasized the organic relationship linking religion, culture, and peoplehood.

With regard to the hierarchy of values among these three fundamentals, one could go a step further. The Talmud had not hesitated to declare that God Himself said, "Would that men forsook Me but kept My Torah." [6] The tenth-century philosopher Saadia had enunciated the view, "We are a people only by virtue of our Torah." [7] By juxtaposing these statements, one might derive the conclusion that of the three elements of God, Israel, and the Torah, it is the Torah—the tradition—which is *primus inter pares!* Indeed, normative Judaism as a whole may be described as Torah-centered. Torah, which means "teaching, guidance, discipline," encompasses the entire law, lore, and learning of Judaism. Its foundation is the five books of Moses and the Bible. Its elaboration is to be found in the Talmud and rabbinic literature, and its extension in the Responsa, the Codes and the religio-ethical literature of post-Talmudic Judaism.

To be sure, there were variations in religious practices among Jewish communities in different parts of the world, as there were in their political and economic status. Yet the basic pattern was one of uniformity. In 1565 the great rabbinic scholar Joseph Karo published his compendium of Jewish law intended for the layman, which he called *Shulḥan Arukh*, "the Prepared Table." In it he codified the practice of the Sephardim, or Spanish Jewish communities. His work was soon enlarged by the glosses of Rabbi Moses Isserles, who in his *Mappah* ("Tablecloth") added the practice of the German-Polish communities. In this augmented form the *Shulḥan Arukh* became the standard guidebook to Jewish traditional practice. For a variety of historical reasons the *Shulḥan Arukh* superseded all its predecessors, including even the great *Mishneh Torah* of Maimonides, and became the ultimate arbiter of traditional Judaism everywhere. For all Jews segregated within the ghettos, the Jewish community constituted the authoritative government, the Jewish tradition the normative way of life, and the *Shulḥan Arukh* its code of practice.

To an outsider, it might seem unbelievable that within these dark and forbidding walls ghetto life could be tolerable and even joyful. Yet that was emphatically the case. Jewish life in the Middle Ages was vital and beautiful, informed by a sense of unity and a triumphant faith. Everywhere the Jew followed the same pattern of life as laid down in the Law of Moses and interpreted by the Rabbis. The Torah governed his work and his festivals, his food and his family life, his culture and his recreation, and spiritualized it all. Though he was physically weaker than his neighbor, the Jew was conscious of his distinction in possessing this "precious treasure." Each morning he rose to thank God for having made him a member of Israel, and to reaffirm his conviction that the Torah and the command-ments were his life and the length of his days. His lot was hard to bear but never beyond endurance. His oppressors possessed might, but he had patience. In God's own time redemption would come, and Israel would be restored to its homeland. Meanwhile he concluded his daily prayers by proclaiming his perfect faith in the coming of the Messiah, for whom he waited daily, however much he might tarry.

Thus life went on behind the dark walls of the ghetto, which served as a barrier, to be sure, but also as a bulwark. Then a mighty rumbling arose, and the French Revolution undermined those hitherto impregnable walls. As the vic-torious French legions carried the slogan "Liberty, Frater-nity, and Equality" to every corner of Europe, those ideals were applied, slowly and hesitatingly, even to the Jews. The civil Emancipation of the Jews proclaimed by the French Assembly on September 28, 1791, was no all-conquering tide. On the contrary, it varied with the ebb and flow of liberalism and reaction in the various states of nine-teenth-century Europe. With each wave of liberalism Jews were enfranchised and admitted to citizenship; each return of reaction sought to restore the status that had existed be-fore the Revolution. But each receding wave of reaction was unable to undo completely the fruits of the Emancipa-tion. In this piecemeal fashion the Jews of Germany, Italy, and France were given substantial political rights and civic equality, though the army, "high society," and even the uni-versities gave scant practical recognition to the new ideals.

Almost universally eighteenth- and nineteenth-century Western Jews greeted the Emancipation with enthusiasm and severed their relationship to the Jewish community in the ghetto with relative ease. This reaction was not due merely to the promptings of personal advantage. Another

influence called them to the brave new world outside: the
intellectual impact of the Enlightenment. The philosophers
of the Age of Reason in France and England, as well as in
Italy and Germany, adopting reason as the instrument of
human redemption, had rediscovered the fundamental
truth of the unity and equality of mankind. With reason as
their touchstone, they subjected every element of the social
and cultural structure of their times to rigorous analysis.
The state, education, religion, the family, the status of
women, the criminal code, and the moral system, all came
under their critical scrutiny and were found wanting.

The impact of the ideas of the Enlightenment upon organized Christianity was severe. Upon Judaism it was cata-
strophic, for behind its ghetto walls Judaism had all but lost
touch with contemporary life and thought. Judaism in the
eighteenth century was far narrower in compass and far
more thoroughly isolated from the philosophy and science
of its day than it had been in the twelfth or thirteenth century. The Enlightenment constituted a far more powerful
challenge to Judaism than did medieval Aristotelianism or
Platonism, and its defenses were now infinitely weaker.
When therefore the Emancipation demanded the destruction of the organic Jewish community and the diminution
of the Jewish tradition as the price for political and civil
equality, the Jews of Central and Western Europe were
more than willing to pay it. There were a few exceptions,
to be sure, like the Jewish community of Holland, which
asked to be permitted to retain its autonomous, segregated
status and preserve its traditional pattern of life. Such devi-
ations were rare. By and large, Jews found in the Enlightenment the necessary intellectual support for the conviction that the transaction was a bargain.

From the vantage point of the twentieth century the limitations of the Emancipation and the Enlightenment are
clear. The Emancipation was a great step forward in the

progress of mankind toward freedom, but it was not the
final step. It represented the collapse of the feudal system,
the coming of age of the middle class, and the transfer of
power to the *entrepreneurs* of the Industrial Revolution. Its
viewpoint on government and economics was succinctly
summed up in the philosophy of *laissez faire* and in the doctrine of "freedom of contract," by which a factory hand in
Manchester, competing for a job against a thousand other
workers, was on a par with the mill owner, with equal
rights that were not to be "compromised" by social legislation or collective bargaining. The Emancipation was a consequence of the spirit of individualism.

Moreover, and this is directly germane to our theme, the
Enlightenment advocated by the Age of Reason lacked a
sense of historical development and of the slow growth of
institutions and practices among men. It did not appreciate
the importance of the nonrational elements of human life,
the deposit of customs and attitudes created by human experience, both individual and collective. Hence it failed in
another crucial respect. In emphasizing the individual rights
of man, the thinkers of the eighteenth century looked upon
the group relations of man as external, insignificant, and ar-
tificial. They did not understand that a man's economic position, his cultural interests, his ethnic roots, his religious
loyalties, and his social ideals all constitute essential elements of his personality without which he is scarcely
human. For the advocates of the Emancipation, the Jewishness of Jews was accidental and therefore expendable.
Hence the Emancipation, for all its positive achievements,
failed to accord to Jews the basic right of spiritual self-
determination.

These drawbacks of the Age of Reason, with their negative effects on Judaism, have led, particularly in the post-
Hitler period, to widespread expressions of scorn for both
the Enlightenment and the Emancipation. We are told in

some quarters that the century and a half of Jewish history extending from the French Revolution in 1789 to the Nuremberg Laws in 1935 has been a tragic aberration. Quite aside from the debatable proposition that a period of a hundred and fifty years in the life of a people can be dismissed as a blind alley, it is noteworthy that there have been few applications by the eloquent *laudatores temporis acti* for reghettoization and for the surrender of their civic, political, and economic positions in Western society. Moreover, it is interesting to note that these glorifiers of the ghetto tend to use German, English, French, Yiddish, and modern Hebrew as the literary media for their discontent, all of which are products of the modern age they are castigating.

There is an even more basic objection to this denigration of the eighteenth century. In our day the menace of unbridled nationalism has been immeasurably heightened by the threat of aggressive totalitarianism. All the more reason for jealously guarding the concept of the inherent and inalienable rights of man proclaimed by the Age of Reason, which remains a bulwark of humanity that we abandon at our peril.

To revert to our theme, most Western Jews welcomed the Emancipation as ushering in the Messianic Age. As the ghetto walls were breached, Jews streamed into Western society, leaving the age-old Jewish tradition a shambles behind them.

A homely parable may illustrate the process. Traditional Judaism may be compared to a vase, handed down as a precious heirloom from father to son and set up in the family homestead in a place of honor. An earthquake breaks out, the home is shaken to its foundations. The vase is hurled to the ground and is smashed to bits. Each jagged piece is no longer beautiful, for it is without shape or form. Many of the children now see no reason to cherish the broken potsherds. For them, the only wise course is to sweep the debris out of the homestead.

Thus the first and decisive answer to the challenge of the new age was assimilation. Judaism was no longer a joy but rather a burden and an embarrassment. Heinrich Heine summarized the attitude of his entire generation when he declared: *Das Judentum ist ein Unglück,* "Judaism is a misfortune." Hitler was to offer a bitter parody of Heine in his cry: *Das Judentum ist unser Unglück,* "Judaism is *our* misfortune."

It is often assumed that this wholesale rejection of Judaism was solely a matter of convenience. Actually there was a considerable element of conviction, at least on the conscious levels of thought. The eighteenth century with its emphasis on reason, and the nineteenth with its great scientific discoveries, particularly the theory of evolution, seemed to undermine religious ideas and sanctions and make religious practices distasteful and irrelevant. Patriotism, tolerance, internationalism, and science—all the lofty ideals of the modern age—were invoked to justify total absorption in the majority group. For once, intellectual conviction agreed with practical convenience in urging abandonment of the sinking ship. Those who were logically consistent sought release by outright conversion or through intermarriage, so that their children at least might be free. Fortunately for their peace of mind, they could not foresee the fate of their "non-Aryan" grandchildren.

Total assimilation was, however, not the universal answer of modern Jews. To revert to our parable, most of the children were unwilling to part even with the misshapen fragments of the vase. Each one snatched at a bit of clay and guarded it jealously. He clung to it proudly as the patent of his nobility, the emblem of his origin. There was little or nothing he could do with it, but he refused to do without it.

The majority of Jews were unwilling or unable to surrender their Jewish distinctiveness *in toto*. Often they felt a deeply rooted emotional attachment to familiar Jewish ideals or practices. Many Jews were kept within the Jewish fold by a sense of loyalty to parents, grandparents, or other kinsmen—impulses which they often could not justify on rational grounds and of which they might even be ashamed. In many instances the motive was a sense of *noblesse oblige*. Thus the German Jewish leader, Gabriel Riesser, declared that it was ignoble to desert the sinking ship of Judaism merely for the sake of personal advantage or convenience.

In many other cases Jews found themselves unable to accept the dogmas of Christianity, while their sense of honor and self-respect forbade their entering the portals of the Church with tongue in cheek. Thus David Friedländer, the acknowledged leader of the Berlin community, addressed an anonymous Epistle to Pastor Teller in 1799 on behalf of "several heads of families of the Jewish denomination," offering to accept Protestantism on condition that they be excused from subscribing to the belief in the divinity of Jesus. When Pastor Teller replied that a form of Christianity without Christ was meaningless, Friedländer surrendered the plan and became active within the Jewish community.

Subtle inner factors such as these were immeasurably strengthened by far from subtle external conditions, particularly the rise of modern anti-Semitism.

As though arranged by a cosmic dramatist, a series of tragic incidents during the nineteenth century reminded most Western Jews that they were united by an ineluctable Jewish destiny. In 1840 a Capuchin monk disappeared in Damascus, Syria, and the old cry of ritual murder was raised by the French consul, Ratti-Menton, who proved his charge by torturing Jewish prisoners until they died or "confessed." In 1858 modern Jews were again rudely shaken out of their complacency by a crisis nearer home. Edgar Mortara was a six-year-old Jewish child who was secretly baptized by his Catholic nurse during an illness. He was then forcibly carried off by Papal gendarmes and the Church refused to surrender him to his heartbroken parents, in spite of remonstrances from all quarters of Europe and America. The next great blow to assimilation was the Dreyfus Case in France in 1894, which shocked Theodor Herzl into Jewish consciousness and led to the creation of political Zionism. In the interim, however, the Russian pogroms of 1881 and the six ritual murder trials held in Russia, Bohemia, Hungary, and Germany between 1882 and 1911 demonstrated that the millennium had not yet dawned and that anti-Jewish prejudices were still powerfully entrenched.

Modern Jews also had other reminders that lacked the sensational character of these major events but were far more influential because they affected their daily lives. Such were the countless forms of discrimination, both petty and gross, that the average Jew encountered in academic, social, and economic circles.

It goes without saying that not all those causes affected all Jews or operated with equal force. Collectively, however, they created a powerful refutation of the argument that total assimilation was the answer for most modern Jews. There were also inner motivations at work. Many possessed a deeply rooted desire to perpetuate the Jewish identity, an attachment to cherished observances and practices, and a streak of stubborn determination not to surrender Judaism merely because it was the butt of prejudice and ill will. Many Jews could not in good conscience assent to the dogmas of Christianity, which generations of their ancestors had found totally unacceptable. As a result of these external and internal factors, the majority of Jews living in Western Europe, of which America was a cultural dependency, espoused two goals. The first was the retention of political citizenship with its concomitants of civic equality, economic opportunity, and cultural acceptance; and the second, the retention of some form of Jewish identity. *From the days of the French Revolution to the present, the ideal which most modern Jews have sought, and not always found, is integration without assimilation and acculturation without absorption.*

JEWISH TRADITION
IN THE MODERN WORLD—
FACTORS OF REGENERATION

ANALOGIES ARE convenient but rarely adequate. In tracing the tragedy of the modern Jew, we have compared Jewish life since the Emancipation to the jagged and shapeless fragments of a once-beautiful vase. These bits of clay were all that remained to the children of the glory of their father's house, and they therefore insisted on preserving them with obstinate zeal.

Beyond this point, however, the parable fails us. For Jewish life is best compared not to clay but to protoplasm. It is not inert matter but rather a living organism, possessing a will to survive and often unsuspected powers of recuperation. Hence a better analogy for Jewish life would be those living creatures which have the gift of replacing lost or injured organs by growing new parts or by having their bodily functions taken over by those remaining. As Jewish life was smashed into countless fragments, various schools of thought arose, each determined to preserve one or another element which it regarded as indispensable for Jewish survival. Nay more, each school tended to insist that its own chosen aspect could be developed and extended, so that it would serve perfectly in place of the older integrated pattern of Jewish living that had prevailed before the Emancipation and the Enlightenment.

The earliest attempt at reconstruction was made by a group of young German Jewish intellectuals who had received a university training. In 1819 they banded together to create *der Verein für die Wissenschaft des Judentums* ("The Society for the Science of Judaism"). Their revolutionary hope was that the scientific study of Jewish history, literature, and institutions would bolster the wavering loyalty to Judaism of the younger Jewish generation and win the respect of the larger community for the Jewish heritage and its values. But the high hopes of Eduard Gans, Moses Moser, Heinrich Heine, and their colleagues turned to dust and ashes. Within a few short years virtually all the members of the group lost heart in the enterprise and abandoned Judaism completely in order to advance their personal careers. There was one towering exception, Leopold Zunz, who remained loyal, in Heine's words, to "the great caprice of his soul." Virtually single-handed, he founded the modern Science of Judaism.[1] In the century and a half which has elapsed since Zunz's pioneering works began to appear, the Science of Judaism, which we shall consider at greater length below, has become a multi-faceted and far-reaching area of research. It is today being carried on with zeal and ability by means of journals, monographs, and books appearing regularly throughout the world. The religion, history, literature, law, institutions, folklore, and languages of the Jewish people during three and a half millennia continue to be the subject of dedicated and gifted research by Jews and non-Jews in every civilized country.

By its very nature, however, modern Jewish scholarship was directed to the past rather than the present. It was a method of research, not a philosophy of life. Moreover, the early masters of the Science of Judaism, Luzzatto, Rappaport, Graetz, and Weiss, whether they wrote in Hebrew or in other languages, were accessible to broad sections of the Jewish people and their works found a place in every cultured Jewish library. The more recent scholarly works, on the other hand, which are often marked by exhaustive and exhausting erudition, are read only by specialists.

The importance of this type of research can scarcely be overestimated. It has, however, proved wholly inadequate as a Jewish way of life or even as a direct factor in Jewish survival. A culture can help preserve a people only if it be a popular culture, drawing its sustenance from the great masses, dealing with their problems and aspirations, and ministering to their needs. That the Science of Judaism never became. As the defection of its earliest protagonists proved, it could not generate the necessary loyalty for a great renaissance of Judaism. It was perhaps enough that it supplied the tools for the various positive philosophies of Jewish life that arose in the nineteenth and twentieth centuries.

Such a cultural renaissance did take place during the middle and closing decades of the nineteenth century and was concentrated almost entirely in Eastern Europe. It was basically a literary efflorescence, with Hebrew and Yiddish as its vehicles of expression. The Jews of Poland, Russia, and Rumania, unlike their Western brothers, lived in large compact masses and had never been exposed on a large scale to the opportunities and temptations of political equality. They had, therefore, never lost the sense of Jewish nationhood. Even they, however, had felt the impact of modern ideas upon traditional Judaism, and many of the youth were losing their religious moorings under the influence of the "Enlightenment," which characteristically bore a Hebrew name in the East, the *Haskalah*. Its leaders declared, in effect, that the Jewish religion had grown weak and unsatisfactory, and was incapable of safeguarding the life of the Jewish people. On the other hand, they felt that Judaism could still be preserved as a modern secular culture.

With regard to the medium of this culture, there was no unanimity. Some preferred to make Yiddish, which was the language of the masses, the vehicle of modern Jewish culture. Within a few decades a rich literature, a powerful drama, and a living press came into being. S. J. Abromowitch, I. L. Peretz, Sholem Aleichem, Sholem Asch, Menahem Boraisha, I. B. Singer, and H. Leivick are some of the leading figures in the Yiddish cultural renaissance.

What the future of Yiddish is, is difficult to say with assurance. Indications point to its gradual elimination as a living tongue. In the United States, Poland, and South America, the younger generation tends to speak the language of the country and therefore has no need, and often no knowledge, of Yiddish. Nevertheless it seems clear that for years to come Yiddish will still survive, especially in large centers of Jewish population, and vigorous efforts are being made to preserve it in Latin America and even in Israel. All that can be predicted about its future is that it is unpredictable.

Another highly influential group in Eastern Europe espoused Hebrew and succeeded in bringing the ancient tongue back to life. During the past century a group of gifted writers, P. Smolenskin, J. L. Gordon, Ch. N. Bialik, Ahad Ha'am, S. Tschernichowsky, and Zalman Schneur, created a vital literature in prose and poetry, and demonstrated that the language of Isaiah and Akiba, enriched by its medieval and modern developments, could serve to express every nuance of human thought and emotion.

Today the creative future of the Hebrew language is assured, since it has a flourishing present as the official tongue of the State of Israel. There is an extraordinary literary, scholarly, and scientific output in Israel with significant contributions from the Diaspora, all written in Hebrew. So vital is this influence radiating from the State of Israel that many of its leading spokesmen insist that the Hebraization of Jews living outside of Israel is all that is required to guarantee the Jewish survival of the Diaspora and the maintenance of its relationship to the Jewish homeland.

The value of this modern cultural renaissance is enormous as a creative and quickening force. Yet it is clear that culture alone cannot constitute an enduring pattern of Jewish living. The cultural revival in Yiddish and Hebrew began in those lands where Jews were excluded from general life. As Jews became integrated into the dominant culture of their native lands, Hebrew and Yiddish were either crowded out completely or, at best, accorded a secondary position. It may be possible to spread a reading knowledge of Hebrew among increasing numbers of American Jews. Yet, at the most, they will constitute only a small fraction of American Jewry. It is hardly likely that Hebrew can ever be made the spoken everyday tongue of American Jews. For Yiddish the prospects seem even less hopeful. One conclusion is clear: for the meaningful survival of the Jewish tradition, culture is a necessary but not a sufficient condition.

At the same time that small groups of Jewish intellectuals were attempting to extract the facet of culture from the totality of Jewish life, far more intensive and extensive efforts were made to isolate and preserve the aspect of religion from the pattern of the Jewish tradition. Early in the nineteenth century a logical formula was evolved— designed to achieve the two goals of citizenship and Jewish identity. All that was necessary was to reduce Judaism to the dimensions of a religious denomination and eliminate all those elements of the tradition that were not specifically "religious." Thus by the side of the German citizens of Catholic faith and the Protestant persuasion, there would be a third category of *Deutsche Staatsbürger juedischen*

Glaubens, "German citizens of the Jewish faith." This phrase was actually incorporated into the name of the central organization of German Jewry.

The first movement to reflect the impact of the new age and to seek to reckon with its demands and attitudes was Reform Judaism.[2] As classical Reform evolved in Germany during the first half of the nineteenth century, it represented a synthesis between the practical demands of the laity and the theoretical formulations of the rabbis. The laymen, such as David Friedländer, Israel Jacobson, and Jacob Herz Beer, the father of the composer Meyerbeer, were concerned with "beautifying" the service by eliminating the traditional Jewish cantillation and by the introduction of the organ. On the other hand, the scholars sought to establish guiding principles for reform. Thus Samuel Holdheim (1806–60), who had been trained in Talmudic dialectics, was concerned with the problems of Jewish law and sought to justify the changes he desired by evolving a distinction between "religious" and "nonreligious" observances and between biblical and Talmudic enactments. Abraham Geiger (1810–74), perhaps the most brilliant Jewish scholar of the era, validated his Reform outlook by tracing the growth of religious ideas and institutions in Judaism as reflected in the pages of the Bible and the Talmud.[3]

Ultimately a theory of Reform Judaism emerged, which rested upon four cardinal principles: The first was the *separation of the religious and national elements in the Jewish tradition.* By the surrender of its national aspects Judaism would parallel Christianity as a religious sect pure and simple, so that Jews, like their Catholic and Protestant neighbors, would be recognized as patriotic Germans, Frenchmen, or Englishmen, differing from their fellow citizens only in religion. To prepare for this delicate operation upon the organism of Judaism, the national elements were declared to be transitory and hence expendable, now that the national life of the Jewish people was ended. Only the religious and ethical aspects were held to be timeless and binding. Samuel Holdheim, son of the Age of Rationalism, was the most consistent exponent of this doctrine, rarely flinching in applying this principle to the Jewish heritage. Geiger, who had a profound sense of history and a deeper appreciation of Jewish tradition, was considerably less consistent in giving up the particularist practices in Judaism. Thus he opposed the transfer of the Sabbath to Sunday, the practice of intermarriage, the surrender of circumcision, and other logical consequences of the attempted elimination of the national elements from Judaism.

At all events, Reform insisted that of the complex regimen of Jewish practices only the ethical law was binding, and this, by its very nature, was not enforceable by synagogal authority. As for ritual, the hallmark of Judaism, it was essentially a private affair. Only such ceremonies were to be retained as possessed edifying value, or were in conformity with the esthetic standards of Western Europe. Since much of Jewish ritual was Oriental and exotic, many elements within it were stigmatized as unattractive. Hence there followed the surrender of the varied traditional modes of chanting the service, the cantillation of the Torah, the Prophets, and the Megillot, the use of phylacteries and the prayer shawl, and the Oriental custom of covering the head at worship. The dietary laws, which tended to separate Jews from non-Jews and which posed practical problems in modern society, were felt to be unnecessary, if not downright objectionable.

The second pillar upon which Reform rested was the maintenance of the principle of the reality of growth and the legitimacy of change in Judaism. Here again Holdheim, as a Talmudist, sought to validate the changes he favored by the citation of passages in rabbinic literature which suggested less rigorous observance. Geiger, as a theologian and historian, enunciated the doctrine of progressive revelation to serve as the foundation for the reforms he felt necessary. He cited the changes in the biblical text and in the interpretation of Scripture, as well as the stages in the evolution of Jewish law as evidence for his views. In fact, the entire Science of Judaism supplied the scholarly proof for the principle of development in Judaism.

Third was the surrender of the concept of the binding authority of Jewish law. Reform leaders recognized that the separation of the national and religious elements in Judaism and the far-reaching changes in personal observance and synagogue ritual they favored could not be achieved within the framework of the Jewish tradition, no matter how liberally it was interpreted. This was true whether these changes were accomplished by the decision of rabbinical synods or, as was usually the case, through a process of nullification by the laity.

It was therefore necessary for Reform to declare that the traditional Jewish Halachah, which included civil, criminal, and ritual law, and which had been accepted as binding for centuries, no longer had authority in the modern world. The dietary laws were surrendered, as was the strict observance of Sabbath rest. In the field of domestic law, Jewish divorce was abolished, though Jewish marriage was retained through the creation of the untraditional concept that marriage was a sacrament, while divorce was purely a civil matter.

From these principles there flowed the fourth characteristic of Reform: *the establishment of a Jewish religious regimen eclectic in character.* Every rabbi, layman, and congregation was free to retain or reject rituals *ad libitum.* To minimize the confusion of such a state of affairs, Geiger and his successors in Germany, like Isaac Mayer Wise in America, attempted to create a synod or rabbinical council as a supreme legislative authority for modern Judaism, but with no success. In the strongly individualistic atmosphere of the nineteenth century such efforts were doomed to failure.

The most comprehensive statement of the philosophy of Reform Judaism in its classic phase was embodied in the *Pittsburgh Platform* of 1885 and the most consistent application of the theory of Reform was made in the United States.[4] In Germany, for a variety of reasons which need not detain us here, Reform lost much of its momentum in the second half of the nineteenth century and reverted to a more traditional pattern.

The rapid rise and growth of Reform during the first half of the nineteenth century evoked a spirited reaction which crystallized as neo-Orthodoxy.[5] One of the most gifted of the newer rabbis, who had been trained in German universities, was Samson Raphael Hirsch (1808–80). Deeply mystical in temperament, while conversant with modern thought, Hirsch was as acutely aware as Geiger of the contradictions between the modern world and traditional Judaism. However, he came to a diametrically opposite conclusion. Instead of modifying the tradition to the times, Hirsch called for "bending the times to the Torah." Hirsch was quite willing to concede the truth of the principle of growth and development in all human institutions. But Judaism was divine and, as such, immutable. Biblical and Talmudic Judaism, the product of Divine revelation, constituted one unchanged and unchangeable unit derived from the absolute source of truth, which is God.

As for those practices which seemed to be meaningless or distasteful to the modern temper, Hirsch insisted that they needed only to be given a spiritual or symbolic meaning in order to win the allegiance of men. He first presented his views in a brilliant and moving volume which appeared in 1836 entitled *The Nineteen Letters of Ben Uziel*.[6] His subsequent rabbinical and literary career was dedicated to expounding these basic doctrines and establishing separate congregations dedicated to neo-Orthodoxy.

Unlike other teachers of traditional Judaism who favored retaining a great measure of unity and cooperation with the larger Jewish community, Hirsch felt that the purity of his doctrine could be maintained only through separatist congregations with their own houses of worship, schools, abattoirs, ritual bathhouses, and cemeteries. Though the adherents of *Austrittsorthodoxie* ("separatist Orthodoxy") of Samson Raphael Hirsch were never numerous, they became an articulate and significant minority in the German culture sphere, which included not only the German states, Austria, and Hungary, but outposts in Great Britain and the United States as well. Their unflinching loyalty to all the minutiae of Jewish observance and their readiness to sacrifice for their convictions served as a countervailing force to the onsweeping tide of Reform.

A larger and far more influential challenge to Reform came from a third direction. In response to the same issues as Reform, a third tendency arose, called the "positive-historical school" in Germany and Conservative Judaism in the United States.[7] Zechariah Frankel, its leading spokesman (1801–75), was a modern rabbi in training and outlook. Thus his opinion was solicited with regard to the new and radical Reform prayer book created by the Hamburg Temple, and he attended the Rabbinical Conference convened by Geiger in Frankfort in 1845. Unlike Samson Raphael Hirsch and the other defenders of Orthodoxy, who denounced the prayer book because they denied the legitimacy of ritual change *ab initio*, Frankel defended the right of modification on the basis of his historical studies. He insisted, however, that the changes made in the Hamburg prayer book were not in accord with the spirit of Judaism. The elimination of all references to the restoration of Zion meant obliterating the sense of national loyalty which was integral to the Jewish religion. As he wrote, "A people without a center or government of its own can never attain to honor among the nations of the world. We must therefore demonstrate that the desire for rebirth still lives within us. Is not this hope better than the undignified efforts to imitate and assimilate ourselves to our neighbors?" [8]

At the Frankfort Conference Frankel listened without enthusiasm to many proposals advanced for changes in the Sabbath, the dietary regulations, and the laws of marriage and divorce. Nevertheless he remained in attendance until the discussion turned to what seemed a comparatively minor matter. When the delegates voted that the Hebrew language was not "objectively" essential to Jewish prayer but should be retained only to meet the "subjective" needs of the older generation, Frankel walked out of the Conference. Frankel, who was a distinguished Talmudist, did not need to be reminded of the rabbinic dictum, "You may recite the *Shema* in any language you understand." [9] It was not a matter of law, but of the entire approach to the Jewish tradition. Frankel was no theologian; he lacked the taste and probably the capacity for the formulation of principles which Geiger possessed in preeminent degree. Yet his reaction to the Hamburg prayer book and the Frankfort Conference, which were both landmarks in the history of Reform, are highly revelatory of the new trend of which he became the acknowledged leader.

It was a foregone conclusion that he would be accused from both the right and the left. Both Geiger and Hirsch regarded him as a temporizer, lacking either the courage to implement his secret Reform convictions or the self-sacrifice to adhere to his stubborn Orthodox prejudices. Actually, however, the positive-historical school had a point of view or, what is at least equally important, a climate of attitude with very respectable antecedents. In the judgment of a distinguished contemporary Jewish historian, Conservative Judaism, both in its positive attitudes and in its omissions, is most directly in the mainstream of traditional Judaism. To cite Professor Salo W. Baron: "Neo-Orthodoxy, equally with Reform, is a deviation from historical Judaism. No less than Reform, it abandoned Judaism's self-rejuvenating historical dynamism. For this reason we may say that . . . the 'positive-historical' Judaism of Zechariah Frankel and Michael Sachs and the 'Conservative' Judaism of America have been much truer to the spirit of traditional Judaism. By maintaining the general validity of Jewish law and combining with it freedom of personal interpretation of the Jewish past and creed, Frankel and his successors hoped to preserve historical continuity. . . . It is Conservative Judaism which seems to show the greatest similarities with the method and substance of teaching of the popular leaders during the declining Second Commonwealth, inasmuch as clinging to the traditional modes of life, it nevertheless allows for the adaptation of basic theological concepts to the changing social and environmental needs." [10]

Frankel agreed with Reform on the existence of change in Judaism in the past and on the need for growth in the present. But the school he founded parted company on three fundamentals. *He opposed the elimination of the national elements of Jewish tradition as embodied preeminently in its ceremonials and legal system.* These rest, in turn, upon two basic postulates, *the authority of Jewish law* and *the peoplehood of Israel.*

Obviously Frankel and his successors, both in Germany and in the United States, have not solved all the problems inherent in their position. The crucial difficulty has lain in determining *the source and nature of the authority behind Jewish law,* since Conservative Judaism accepts the result of modern scientific scholarship regarding the past development of Judaism and believes that its growth in the present and future is both inevitable and necessary. Both Zechariah

Frankel in the nineteenth century and that great exemplar of Conservative Judaism in the twentieth, Solomon Schechter (1850–1915), sought to meet the problem by proposing that the basis of authority lies in *Kelal Yisrael* or Catholic Israel, which determines what elements of Judaism are vital, obsolescent, or obsolete.[11]

It was not difficult to demonstrate that this process had been at work throughout the history of rabbinic and medieval Judaism, giving the Jewish tradition its protean capacity for growth and adjustment, while retaining its sense of continuity with the past. On the other hand, it was not easy to indicate how the process is to operate in the present, seeing that Jewish tradition is being honored far more in the breach than in the observance by most Western Jews, who, thanks to Hitler, now constitute the majority of world Jewry. If we were to follow literally the verdict of the practice of the majority of contemporary Jews, it would mean the abrogation of such basic fundamentals as the Sabbath and festival observances, the regimen of daily prayers and dietary laws, and much else besides that is basic to traditional Judaism.

It is therefore clear that while the concept of Catholic Israel is both fruitful and true, being validated by centuries of Jewish experience, it cannot suffice today in its original form. Elsewhere I have sought to reinterpret Schechter's theory that authority is vested in *Kelal Yisrael*, in order to have it apply to our present situation.[12]

Undoubtedly ambiguities, unclarities, and differences of viewpoint still to be resolved remain within the movement. Nonetheless, the basic retention by Conservative Judaism of traditional practices, its flexibility with regard to necessary changes, its liberalism with regard to the body of doctrine and belief, and its tolerance of differences have united to make it the most rapidly growing movement in contemporary Judaism, with a strong impact upon its sister movements to the right and to the left.

The basic outlook of the three movements in their classic forms may now be set forth schematically as follows: *Reform declares that Judaism has changed throughout time and that Jewish law is no longer binding. Orthodoxy denies both propositions, insisting upon the binding character of Jewish law and negating the view that Judaism has evolved. Conservative Judaism agrees with Orthodoxy in maintaining the authority of Jewish law, and with Reform that Judaism has grown and evolved through time.*

If we may be permitted to revert to the analogy of the vase for the last time, we have seen that major efforts were made to salvage one or another indispensable element of the organic totality of Judaism and have it do duty for the whole. We have traced, albeit briefly, the attempts to build Jewish identity in terms of culture, be it the scientific study of the Jewish past, the revival of the Hebrew language, or the cultivation of Yiddish literature. We have traced the various movements that sought to preserve the strand of the Jewish religion out of the multiform tapestry of the Jewish tradition of the past.

Culture and religion are two basic elements in Judaism, but there is a third—ethnic loyalty.

The most colorful and dramatic effort to salvage one element out of the whole lay here in the field of nationalism, of which Zionism is the most important but not the only manifestation. In view of the obviously nonreligious character of the age and the remoteness of Jewish culture from the lives of most modern Jews, some Jewish thinkers were led to search for meaningful Jewish identity in Jewish nationalism or ethnic group allegiance. Both in Eastern Europe and in the West, Jewish leaders arose who found the common denominator of Jewish belonging in the goal of the restoration of the Jewish people to its ancestral home-land. Zionism, whose official program was expressed in the Basel platform in 1897, set forth as its goal "the securing of a legally secured, publicly recognized, homeland for the Jewish people in Palestine." This dynamic cause could and did appeal to men of every religious persuasion and of none, and it reflected the spirit of the age in propagating the idea of a secular nationalism which had made so much progress in nineteenth-century Europe. Various leaders and thinkers in the East, such as Leon Pinsker and Ahad Ha'am, and Theodor Herzl and Max Nordau in the West, were joined by many others to create the multiple spectrum of the Zionist movement, which ran the gamut from ultra-Orthodoxy to total disbelief, from upper-class capitalism to left-wing socialism. Within fifty years after its founding by Theodor Herzl, the Zionist movement won a great and shining victory in the establishment of the State of Israel—perhaps the only authentic miracle of the twentieth century.

This was not all. Zionism made highly significant contributions to Diaspora Jewry as well. It gave the modern Jew a sense of building and achievement utterly at variance with the usual picture of Jewish disintegration and of frantic efforts at preservation that met his gaze elsewhere on the Jewish scene. It promised to convert the *Luftmensch* of the ages, the petty trader and the starving artisan, who possessed no economic security anywhere, into a normal, healthy, productive human being.

The Zionist ideal served to revitalize every other movement in Jewish life. It was the dynamic power behind the revival of Hebrew both as a spoken tongue and as a modern literature. It transformed the content and character of Jewish education. It was central to the philosophy of Conservative Judaism and, as we shall see, became increasingly important in the later development of Reform. It fired the enthusiasm of large segments of the Orthodox community, in spite of the traditional injunction to wait patiently for the Messiah.

Yet essentially Zionism has been a movement with its fundamental goal centered on Palestine. It cannot of itself serve as a way of life for Jews in the Diaspora who, for whatever reasons, are unwilling or unable to settle in the State of Israel. In part, the recent history of the Zionist movement testifies to the tragic paradox that nothing fails like success. The Zionist movement is fighting for its life precisely because the State of Israel, the fulfillment of its dream, has preempted most of its functions, so that it has difficulty in finding a *raison d'être*. When it is authentic, secular Zionism has only one plank in its program for Diaspora Jewry, as David Ben-Gurion has always insisted: all Jews have the obligation to migrate as quickly as possible to the State of Israel, where alone Jewish life can be truly lived.

To be sure, such single-minded consistency is rarely met with. Sincere Zionists play a significant role in strengthening other positive movements in Jewish life and in deepening their Jewish content. In a word, the sense of Jewish national unity, like Jewish culture and Jewish religion, is a necessary but not a sufficient condition for the preservation of Judaism in the world.

It is now roughly a century since all these regenerative forces designed to preserve the Jewish identity by salvaging one or another aspect of the Jewish tradition came into being. The nineteenth century witnessed the birth of these various movements primarily in Germany. The twentieth century witnessed their dissemination throughout the Western world. The six decades of the present century may well be described as the most momentous in Jewish history. This period has seen the virtual extermination of European Jewry, the rise of a new, populous center of Jewish life on the American continent, and the establishment of the State of Israel as an independent and viable member of the family of nations. These three major events, virtually without parallel in Jewish history, have had a powerful effect upon the directions taken by every movement in Jewish life and particularly upon the schools of Reform, Orthodoxy, and Conservatism.

While the theoretical differences among the three movements are still valid, in practice the gap has been narrowing. To the unbiased observer it is clear that Orthodoxy, Conservatism, and Reform in America have, by and large, been drawing together and developing a larger degree of similarity than existed four decades ago. Paradoxically, the greater homogeneity of outlook and practice among the three groups has been accompanied by a strengthening of denominational loyalties and a sharpening of organizational rivalries, due in large measure to the development of elaborate central agencies in Reform, Conservatism, and Orthodoxy. For the foreseeable future these groups will retain their identity.

It should not be astonishing that the American scene has played a decisive role in developing a greater similarity among all three groups. The impact of American conditions and attitudes on the various denominations in Protestantism has been frequently studied and expounded. That the impact of the American way of life on Catholicism has been far more substantial than was once believed becomes clearer each day. It was not to be expected that exposure to the American environment, its opportunities, temptations, and problems, would affect Judaism any less than it has the Christian churches.

The second great factor was the emergence of the Zionist ideal. From the very inception of the movement at the Basel Congress several American rabbis of the Reform group participated in the Zionist cause. While Reform Judaism officially continued for decades to oppose Jewish nationalism, Zionism increasingly captured the loyalty both of the rabbinate and the laity. Today the vast majority of adherents of all three religious groups accept the peoplehood of Israel as a fundamental postulate of their religious world outlook, and recognize the land of Israel as their spiritual homeland.

This basic principle of Jewish peoplehood was underscored both negatively and positively during the past two decades. The Nazi holocaust, which destroyed six-sevenths of European Jewry, was a bloody reminder to Jews of all religious persuasions and of none, that they shared a common destiny and were members of a single people. The establishment of the State of Israel eighteen years ago, its heroic defense and its steady progress and development, have brought to virtually all Jews a new sense of pride and identification with the traditional homeland of the Jewish people. From it has emerged a greater concern with the teaching of the Hebrew language and a higher measure of appreciation of Jewish observances, even in Reform. In the other groups, which never surrendered the sense of Jewish peoplehood, the impact has been even more striking.

To understand the present condition of Judaism, it must be kept in mind that each group represents a coalition of forces. Orthodoxy contains many varieties, particularly on the extreme right. As one studies Jewish history, one is struck by the fact that after each great calamity a wave of extreme pietism swept over significant segments of the community. This was true after the Crusades, the Spanish persecutions of 1391, the Expulsion in 1492, and the Chmielnicki massacres in Poland in 1648. A similar phenomenon is in evidence today. Right-wing Orthodoxy has become active and articulate in the United States with the influx of surviving members of Polish Hasidism and German ultra-Orthodoxy. They have zealously attempted to establish the concept of isolationism, both vis-à-vis the majority of American Jews and the larger American community. In a few instances, as we shall see, they have created viable communities of their own.[13] Generally, they look askance at forms of cooperation, either in the practical or the theoretic sphere, with those who do not share their viewpoint.

While the pressure they exert upon the mainstream of American Orthodoxy is considerable, they are less significant in numbers and in influence than the more moderate elements grouped around Yeshiva University in New York and the Hebrew Theological College in Chicago. The rabbis trained in these seminaries and the laity to whom they minister are acutely conscious of the demands of modern life. In their congregational as well as personal lives they represent various degrees of accommodation between the tradition and the contemporary scene. Often they prefer such terms as "traditional" and "modern Orthodox" to describe their standpoint.[14] Several years ago, shortly after the establishment of the State of Israel, many members of this group hoped for the establishment of a Sanhedrin, a central religious tribunal in Israel, which would serve as the supreme arbiter in religious law. The idea of the Sanhedrin was propagated with great vigor and learning by the late Rabbi J. L. Maimon in Israel, but the manifold difficulties facing the project are now generally recognized to be insuperable. The largest sections of American Orthodoxy continue to insist in theory upon the immutability of the Torah, but through a process of conscious interpretation and unconscious adaptation are drawing closer to the center.

Reform Judaism contains within its ranks a small splinter group which represents the standpoint of early nineteenth-century Reform. This element insists upon remaining totally oblivious of the last century of Jewish experience and thought. The strongest article of faith of this group is its negation of Jewish peoplehood and its hostility to the State of Israel. Its members are affiliated with a small but highly vocal organization called the American Council for Judaism, which has been repudiated time and again by the vast majority of responsible Reform leadership. As we have noted, the peoplehood of Israel is basic to Jews of all persuasions, and the State of Israel a source of prideful identification to them all.

The Columbus Platform adopted in 1935 by the Reform Central Conference of American Rabbis drastically modified the earlier Pittsburgh Platform not only with regard to the concept of Jewish peoplehood, but in adopting a far more affirmative attitude toward Jewish traditional practices. In the three decades that have elapsed since the latter document was issued, Reform synagogues have introduced many practices of a traditional character and have often intensified their educational program. Some Reform leaders have been calling for a ritual code for Reform, and others have gone so far as to urge the establishment of Reform day schools for maximum Jewish education. This increasingly sympathetic attitude toward Jewish tradition has not, it should be understood, meant a return to the principle of the binding character and authority of Jewish law, but it has created a far closer sense of identification with *Kelal Yisrael*, the totality of Israel.

Conservative Judaism, like its sister movements, includes several trends within its ranks. At the left is a highly influential movement in contemporary Jewish life known as Reconstructionism. It was founded by one of the seminal thinkers of modern Jewry, Professor Mordecai M. Kaplan, and draws some of its adherents from Reform and from secular circles as well.

Reconstructionism is best conceived of on two levels, as a broad sociological theory of Jewish life and as a more limited theological reinterpretation of Jewish tradition. Its sociological approach to Jewish life is set forth in its credo— *Judaism is the evolving religious civilization of the Jewish people.* This affirmation is no new doctrine in Judaism. In its emphasis upon Jewish peoplehood, the all-embracing character of the Jewish heritage and its evolving nature, Reconstructionism is basically a restatement of a position congenial to many, if not most, modern Jews. In its narrower, theological aspect, Reconstructionism, as expounded in the writings of Professor Kaplan and several of his disciples and associates, may be described as Jewish religious naturalism.[15] It espouses a humanistic conception of God and has surrendered such traditional Jewish doctrines as that of the election of Israel, Revelation, and the binding character of Jewish ritual practices, which it regards as "folkways" and not as "law."

At the furthermost pole from Reconstructionism is the right wing in Conservative Judaism. This group seeks to avoid any clear-cut definition of the content of the movement, alleging that it wishes to avoid further divisiveness in the Jewish community. In practice and to a lesser degree in theory, it adopts a negative position toward any proposed modifications in Jewish practice. Because members of this group occupy positions of authority in the institutions of Conservative Judaism, the group has a substantial measure of influence and power today.

The majority group belongs to the center, which believes that Conservative Judaism, possessing its own distinctive viewpoint, should articulate it clearly and unequivocally. This does not exclude seeking points of contact and areas of cooperation with other schools of Jewish thought. Most Conservative congregations have adopted such practices as family pews and various lesser changes in ritual observance. Most of them use the *Sabbath and Festival Prayer*

Book published by the Rabbinical Assembly and the United Synagogue. This official prayer book has slightly rephrased the traditional prayers for the restoration of sacrifices in the Temple, so as to express a reminiscence of ancient glories rather than a goal for the future. It has also modified several other passages, such as one of the traditional blessings that implies an inferior status for women. Nor has the Conservative movement excluded congregations which use the organ at services, or have abridged the Torah reading, or have officially permitted travel to synagogue services on the Sabbath. On the basic regimen of Jewish traditional practices, there is substantial agreement among all Conservative congregations.

Not satisfied with a purely practical consensus, individual scholars and teachers in the movement have sought to formulate the philosophy of Conservative Judaism in terms of their needs, aspirations, and outlook.[16] In spite of variations in detail, they would, I believe, agree that the philosophy of the movement may be formulated in two propositions: *Growth is the law of life, and the Law is the life of Judaism.*

In sum, the rise of modern tendencies in Orthodoxy and the growing appreciation of tradition in Reform, coupled with the all-but-universal recognition of Jewish peoplehood, have given American Judaism within the short space of a half-century a far greater degree of homogeneity than seemed possible at the turn of the century. Today most devotees of Orthodox, Conservative, and Reform Judaism would agree that the noun is more important than the adjective. The various contemporary theological currents of naturalism, rationalism, mysticism, and existentialism cut across the groups and have adherents in all camps. In their devotion to the State of Israel and their pride in its achievements, all groups are united. They are also increasingly conscious that the future of Judaism requires an intensification of the quality and the quantity of Jewish education for children, adolescents, and adults.

There is, too, a determination to emphasize the religio-ethical content of Judaism and its relevance to the problems of modern man. The perennial issues of man's nature and destiny, the purpose of life, the meaning of suffering, death, and immortality, the basis and nature of the moral law—on questions such as these scholars in all groups have sought to present the Jewish world view. Some have elucidated the insights and attitudes of the Jewish tradition which bear upon group relations, racial, religious, and national, and upon such crucial world issues as poverty, war, and peace. Even in the sphere of Jewish law and ritual and their relevance and applicability to modern life, where the differences among Orthodoxy, Conservatism, and Reform are most fundamental, there is a measure of fruitful interaction among the three groups.

The problems involved in the conservation and renewal of the Jewish tradition are more, not less, difficult today than in the eighteenth or nineteenth century. For Judaism must confront all the challenges that threaten Jewish particularity in an increasingly impersonal and technological world. In addition, like all religion it must speak to the mind and heart of modern man in his agonizing search for meaning in life, in his quest for goals in an age when all standards of conduct seem eroded, and in his yearning for hope in a world poised on the brink of destruction. In other words, the Jewish religion faces grave problems today, both because it is Jewish and because it is religion.

Assimilation, which in its various forms was the initial response of Western Jewry to the opportunities and temptations of the Emancipation, continues to take a heavy toll from the Jewish community. It is the price that modern Jewry must pay for life as a minority in an open society, which is striving, however hesitatingly, to divest itself of the last vestiges of discrimination on racial or religious grounds. By its very nature, assimilation is not an organized group movement with an articulated rationale. It generally takes the form of a decision by an individual to minimize or sever completely the ties binding him to the Jewish community. The motivations for assimilation are nearly as numerous as the individuals involved, and the patterns run the gamut from outright conversion, through intermarriage, to spiritual and cultural alienation from the Jewish tradition, unaccompanied by a formal break with the Jewish group.

The Jewish population of the United States is generally estimated at about five and a half million. No statistics or even trustworthy estimates are available with regard to the incidence of assimilation in its principal categories.[17] Most sociologists would agree that the process is ubiquitous and powerful, so that it is quite likely that the American Jewish community will not grow in numbers. Indeed, it may even decline somewhat in the next few decades, depending on whether the natural increase will be able to compensate for conscious or unconscious defections.[18]

In the far-flung struggle for the survival of Judaism in the modern world, many a defeat has been sustained but the war is far from lost. The banner of Jewish identification has not yet been hauled down all along the battle line. There are potent weapons still to be found in the arsenal of Judaism—its religious and ethical insights, its heroic history, its unconquerable trust in man as the copartner of God in building the world. And Judaism still has its defenders who man different sectors of the front and are resolved that Jewish character, Jewish wisdom, and Jewish faith shall not perish from the earth.

CHAPTER THREE

JEWISH LEARNING
AND JEWISH EXISTENCE

IT CANNOT HAVE escaped the attentive reader that one area of the world played a major part in the emergence of the various pathways to Jewish self-identification in the nineteenth century. That area was Central Europe, which included Germany and Austria as well as substantial sections of Hungary, Czechoslovakia, and the Balkan regions, where the German language and literature were the symbols of modern culture. This preoccupation with the German culture-sphere is due neither to accident nor to prejudice. German-speaking Jewry has been the great laboratory of the Jewish spirit in modern times. It was in Central Europe that the Jewish tradition and the Jewish community first met the challenge of the modern world, with all its power, its peril, and its promise. Here, every conceivable solution was proposed and every approach tried. As all roads were explored, some led to dead ends, while others opened into fruitful vistas.

It is true that the Emancipation and the Enlightenment had their origin in France, but French Jews were too limited in numbers and too weakly rooted in Jewish life to react sharply to the challenges posed by the bright new world into which they were catapulted. At the other extreme, the vast Jewish community of the Russian Empire was never afforded the opportunity of confronting the Emancipation and the Enlightenment. A few individual members might achieve their personal emancipation and enlightenment by dint of poignant inner struggle. Only German-speaking Jewry, which encountered the currents of the new age, was also sufficiently numerous and rooted in Jewish life to be conscious of the problems posed by the new opportunities and the new temptations.

We have dealt at some length with the various efforts to rehabilitate Judaism in religious terms, which produced the movements called Reform, Orthodoxy, Conservatism, and Reconstructionism. We have noted, too, the dramatic impact of Zionism upon Jewish destiny in the creation of the State of Israel.

All these approaches to Jewish life were ideological, that is to say, they did not merely call for intellectual acceptance of a body of ideas but for commitment in action by their devotees. Moreover, they were all group movements, the success or failure of which could be largely gauged by the number of adherents they were able to win to their cause.

While each of these positions contributed positive values to Jewish life and influenced the others, they nevertheless suffered from one inherent defect—being fundamentally competitive, they proved divisive in the community. Differences *per se* are not necessarily evil, if an underlying basis for unity exists. Paradoxically it was the Science of Judaism, the first movement for the regeneration of the Jewish spirit, which preceded the various religious and nationalist solutions, that gave promise of supplying an intellectual foundation for Jewish allegiance that could include men of every conceivable viewpoint. Today, a century and a half after its birth, this science may still prove an effective instrument for Jewish unity and creativity in the face of the competing ideologies and the varied political, social, and economic conditions to be found in world Jewry.

This movement, *die Wissenschaft des Judentums*, the free critical study of Jewish history, literature, and institutions, may fairly be described as the most original contribution of German Jewry to the treasure house of the Jewish spirit. It is noteworthy that no satisfactory translation of this term has yet emerged. Neither "the Science of Judaism" nor "Jewish research" nor "modern Jewish scholarship" is capable of transmitting its full dimensions. *Judentum* includes both the content of the Jewish heritage and its bearers. In other words, it encompasses both "Judaism" and "the Jewish community." As for *Wissenschaft*, it represents far more than "science" in its limited English connotation. It includes the disciplined study and critical investigation of the entire range of Jewish life, past and present, as embodied in its languages, literature, law, institutions, and history. It is the scientific method applied to the realm of knowledge.

To be sure, the roots of the Science of Judaism are much older than nineteenth-century German Jewry. There are adumbrations of scientific method and of the critical spirit in the pages of the Talmud. Such medieval disciplines as Hebrew philology, Biblical exegesis, and religious philosophy possessed a substantial measure of scientific validity and critical insight.

The authentic forerunners of the Science of Judaism are to be found in Renaissance Italy, where the Jewish community and tradition first encountered the challenge and the stimulus of Western culture. The sixteenth-century scholar, Elijah Levita, whose researches into the Masoretic text of the Hebrew Bible still possess great value, and his far more original contemporary, Azariah dei Rossi, were the most significant figures in the Italian Jewish Renaissance but by no means the only ones. Nonetheless, it remains true that German Jewry was the source and vital center of the Science of Judaism. Even when the discipline was cultivated in Eastern Europe, it bore the stamp of German culture and philosophic thought. To this very day the greatest practitioners of the Science of Judaism have in large measure been German-born, German-speaking, and German-trained.

Now the Nazi holocaust has destroyed this great creative center of the Jewish spirit by the extermination of the six million sons and daughters of the Jewish people in Europe. Our generation has witnessed the end of the German Jewish center on the one hand, and on the other, the emergence of two new centers for Jewish life, one on the North American continent and the other in *Altneuland*, the State of Israel. Between the catastrophe and the rebirth there is a causal and not merely a chronological connection. A new era in Jewish history begins, marked by a revolutionary transformation of the past and by countless new challenges and opportunities. At this transition point it is eminently in order to consider the history of the Science of Judaism, analyzing its goals, its achievements, and its weaknesses in the past, and assaying its problems and potentialities in the future.

At the end of the eighteenth century, when the modern age imperiously knocked at the gates of the ghetto and demanded admittance, its inhabitants were by no means lacking in intellectual armor. Quite the contrary, the Jewish communities, still living under medieval conditions, possessed a millennial tradition of learning which was deep and intense, reaching back to the days of the Bible and the Talmud. Judaism could boast of an unbroken chain of academies extending from France and Germany, through Italy and Spain, back to Babylonia and Palestine. Some of these *Yeshivot* had lasted a thousand years, longer than the proud universities of Oxford and Paris. The Jewish people had produced a vast and variegated literature, of which the Bible and the Talmud were the fountainhead and from which issued countless tributary streams: commentaries and lexica, expositions and summaries, responsa and codes.

It is true that the stream had grown narrower in the later Middle Ages with the growing restrictions on Jewish life, but it had never dried up. In fact, the eighteenth century, which saw Western Jewry rocked to its foundations by the impact of the Emancipation and the Enlightenment, coincided with the careers of two of the most luminous spirits produced by traditional Judaism, the Gaon Elijah of Vilna, the greatest exemplar of rabbinic learning, and Israel Baal Shem Tov, the founder of Hasidism.

In spite of these signs of vitality, however, Torah, the traditional lore and learning of Judaism, proved virtually useless when it first encountered the challenge of the modern world in the last decades of the eighteenth century and the first decades of the nineteenth.

When confronted by the ideas, attitudes, and methods of modern science and philosophy, normative Judaism appeared defenseless and unprepared. For the Jewish tradition had been virtually isolated from the context of general culture for centuries, ever since the Golden Age in Spain and its brief afterglow in medieval Italy and Holland. In no modern language nor, for that matter, in Hebrew, could an interested reader find a history of the Jewish people, a satisfactory biography of great Jewish figures, a survey of Jewish literature, a study of Jewish law and institutions, an accurate edition of Jewish classics, or a modern interpretation of Jewish religious ideas and practices.

Nor could the traditional pursuit of Torah serve the second great need of Western Jewry—the achievement of political, social, and economic rights as full-fledged citizens. This goal, it was felt, depended on the rehabilitation of Judaism in the eyes of the world. In the brave new world being born, it was necessary to reveal the beauty of Shem if they were to be permitted to live in the tents of Japheth. But in achieving both these basic objectives of Western Jewry, apologetics and emancipation, the traditional study of the Torah seemed irrelevant and remote.

As we have noted, the effort to present the Jewish past as a creative and valuable element in human life and culture was first made by a group of German Jewish intellectuals who founded the ill-fated Society for the Science of Judaism in the second decade of the nineteenth century. The Society was short-lived, being deserted in a few years by virtually all its members, except for Leopold Zunz. Luitpold Wallach has pointed out that the collapse of the Society and the failure of its hopes were not inherent in the project.[1] He notes that the movement was championed by young men who, for psychological reasons, found little approval among their elders, and no Maecenases to back their scientific projects. This brash and revolutionary undertaking by young men was also felt to be an affront to the principle of seniority, which had been operative in Jewish life for centuries. Moreover, the limitations on Jewish rights in Germany, which virtually closed the door on academic careers for these young intellectuals, did not affect the economic opportunities of Jewish merchants and manufacturers. For the academician, there was no future in being a Jew; the businessman could manage to survive and even to prosper.

The sense of loneliness and isolation under the spell of which Zunz began his scholarly labors was not dissipated throughout his long and creative life. It must, however, be confessed that, in no slight measure, it was due to drawbacks in his own temperament. Even when the Science he had fathered had burgeoned into a many-faceted discipline, he felt himself alone. He could not point to a school of disciples who had been directly trained by him. Nonetheless, within a century after the publication of Zunz's pioneering study, *Etwas über die rabbinische Literatur*, which appeared in 1818, the Science of Judaism had become recognized as part of humanistic studies throughout the world. This was no mean achievement for a lonely pioneer and a relatively small group of coworkers and followers. To do justice to the novelty and character of this new branch of learning, we must come to grips with the essential characteristics of the traditional study of Torah, as well as of the new learning.

First and foremost, the students of Torah approached their enterprise in an attitude of total acceptance and wholehearted reverence. Respect for the ancients, which was always deeply ingrained in the Semitic mentality, had been carried to extreme lengths in the later Middle Ages. Its attitude to the past might well be summarized in the Talmudic utterance, which was indeed frequently quoted by medieval writers: "If earlier generations were as angels, we are as men; if they were men, we are as donkeys." [2]

Few Jewish scholars after the sixteenth century possessed any of the capacity for original and critical thinking which characterized such rabbis as Akiba or Meir in the Tannaitic era, or the Amoraim Rab or Resh Lakish or such medieval giants of the spirit as Saadia or Maimonides. The present, it was firmly believed, could only repeat the past, or at best add glosses in the margin.

Second, the Torah was regarded as uniform in character. It was not approached as an organic whole in which each section was related to the other as a child is related to a youth, or a youth to an adult. Being the Word of God, it was all of one piece, unaffected by time or space, and all equal in relevance and value. It was perfectly logical for the Talmud to conceive of King David and his warriors as being sages seated in the Sanhedrin. In rabbinic thought, a second-century Palestinian rabbi of the Mishnah would be expected to be aware of a question posed by a Babylonian scholar living four centuries after his time and to have an answer ready. Maimonides could properly insist that the genealogy of Esau and his descendants set forth in *Genesis* (chapter 36) was on the same level of inspiration as the Ten Commandments.

Third, the Torah was self-contained. To be sure, an outside world existed; there were foreign governments to contend with, pagan practices to deal with, and vast numbers of non-Jews with whom the Jew came into regular contact. There was also recognition of the cultural achievements of the non-Jewish world, but they were not regarded as having any effect either upon the content or the nature of Torah. "Wisdom among the nations is to be found, but not Torah." [3]

In a later day, scientific Jewish scholarship might discover abundant evidence that the Jewish people had not lived in isolation either in the biblical or the Talmudic eras, but on the contrary, had had direct and intimate contacts with the Oriental and Greco-Roman worlds. But for medieval Jewry, enclosed in a physical and spiritual ghetto, all these memories of an earlier, more open society had long disappeared. The Torah was now conceived of as exclusively "Jewish," with no admixture of foreign influence.

Finally, the Torah, as traditionally studied in Eastern and Central Europe before the Emancipation era, was virtually limited to the Talmud, its commentaries and codes. Not only was philosophy proscribed for the generality, but such medieval pursuits as biblical study and poetry were neglected and viewed with suspicion and scorn.

When the Science of Judaism appeared on the horizon, it seemed to be at the farthest possible remove from the traditional pursuit of Torah. Its basic hallmark was the critical approach toward the past and its achievements. It was not necessarily lacking in respect for the great men and books of the past, but its approach could well be summarized in the Hebrew proverb *kabbeduni vehasheduni,* "Honor me, but suspect me." It derived its critical canons from the study of classical philology and modern historiography. Its devotees were trained to penetrate behind the fragmentary and imperfect records of the past, in order to discover, in Hermann Ranke's words, *wie es eigentlich gewesen,* "how it actually was."

A second fundamental feature of the Science of Judaism was its sense of history, its emphasis on the principle of development, its stress upon growth and change as the universal concomitant of all human institutions. Long before Darwin had applied the doctrine of evolution to the biological realm, it was a commonplace in historical and philological research. The idea of change and development was central to Hegel's dialectic of history, which was destined to be put to such varied uses in Krochmal's philosophy of Jewish history and in Karl Marx's theory of economic determinism. Zunz included the phrase "historically developed" in the titles of two of his works.[4] Actually, Ranke's formulation of the goal of historical research in general, *wie es eigentlich gewesen,* could have been better formulated as *wie es eigentlich geworden,* "how it actually became."

Today "historicism" has fallen out of favor in many circles. In part, this is a reaction to the extremes of the historical method, which stressed one factor in growth—that of change—and lost sight of the other—that of continuity. In this respect the reaction is both welcome and overdue. Thinkers like Dilthey and Troeltsch, who launched the revolt against "historicism," pointed out that there was a substantial degree of oversimplification in the nineteenth-century conception of history. Development was conceived of as unilinear—a straight line going ever onward and upward. It required a century of research—and what proved more crucial, a century of tragic experience—to teach twentieth-century man that history is better conceived of as a spiral, with depressions as well as elevations, with retreats as well as advances. The idea of automatic and inevitable progress is dead and the possibility of any progress at all is widely doubted in an age which has witnessed two World Wars, the Nazi holocaust, and the long line of totalitarian victories over the democratic ideal.

The hostility to "historicism" derives not only from a deep-seated disenchantment with the present condition of modern man. It also reflects a feeling of hopelessness with regard to his future. In an age of violent and worldwide revolution, a radically different attitude toward change has developed in the Western world. A century ago the leaders of thought and action, both in Judaism and in Western society as a whole, found the sense of history a valuable instrument for validating the changes in life and thought felt to be necessary. Today there is a widespread desire in many sectors of Western society to halt change and to interpose a principle of fixity and permanence against the new and disturbing forces that have been let loose in the world and which threaten havoc to traditional institutions and values. Hence the effort is made to minimize or ignore the evidence for change in the past history of the race, when it cannot be totally denied.

This tendency is particularly marked in the areas of religion and theology, which have traditionally been concerned with the permanent and the unchanging aspects of existence. It is no wonder therefore that the Science of Judaism, which is committed to the historical approach, is airily dismissed in some quarters as a passing phenomenon irrelevant to the basic concerns of contemporary, "post-modern" man.

Yet, after due allowance is made for all exaggerations and errors, it remains true that the principle of change and development in history can be ignored only by doing violence to the truth, thus gravely injuring the survival and progress of society. Growth, the vital balance between continuity and change, still remains the universal law of life.

In addition, the practitioner of the Science of Judaism, in contradistinction to the traditional Torah student, has a strong consciousness of the interaction of the Jew and the world. Scientific research found it easy to cite instances of this process in the Talmud, which is popularly regarded as the most "authentic" achievement of the native Jewish genius. Modern scholarship has revealed the affinities between Hillel's Seven Principles of biblical interpretation and the canons of Homeric exegesis as practiced in the Alexandrian schools. The complex relationships between Talmudic and Roman law have been explored. The impact of the daily life of the Hellenistic world upon the folklore and the culture of the Jew has become increasingly clear. The hundreds of Greek and Latin words in the pages of the Talmud and the Midrash offer striking evidence that rabbinic Judaism had not been lived in isolation from the Greek and Roman world.

Everywhere the Science of Judaism sought to explore these intergroup relationships. It tried to learn what Judaism had borrowed and, in turn, had contributed to general civilization and when and how it had acted as an intermediary between various cultural entities. One of its most significant enterprises was the effort to discover what aspects of world culture Judaism had rejected, as well as what it had modified and utilized for its own purposes. Though the term was not known at the time, the Science of Judaism thus laid bare the path of "creative assimilation," by means of which the Jewish heritage was enabled both to preserve its identity and sense of continuity with the past, and yet maintain its relevance and contact with the world of which it was a part.

This function of the Science of Judaism has remained basic throughout its history. Modern Jewish scholarship has disclosed the complex and fruitful relationship of give-and-take between the Jewish tradition and world culture which is written large on virtually every product of the Jewish spirit, notably the Bible, the Talmud, and medieval literature. Nowhere was this interaction of Judaism and world culture traced more significantly than in the study of the great classics of Jewish religious philosophy.

Finally, the Science of Judaism broadened the boundaries of Torah far beyond that of the study of the *Halachah*. Here it was returning to the Golden Age of Spanish Jewry and going beyond it. The Bible was restored to a position of primacy. The study of Hebrew, Aramaic, and other Semitic languages became basic. Ancient history, comparative religion, comparative law and folklore were all laid under contribution. Archaeology revealed the material substratum of Jewish culture and brought to light vast treasure troves of literary documents which shed light on the past, including communities and personalities whose very existence was previously not suspected. The systematic presentation of Jewish law along historical lines proceeded apace.

Philosophers and scholars studied and interpreted Jewish religious philosophy through the centuries. They traced its development from its inception with Philo in Alexandrian Egypt through Isaac Israeli and Saadia to its later figures, Gabirol, Halevi, Maimonides, and Crescas as well as their lesser colleagues, until it reached its aftermath in Spinoza. Jewish biography, virtually nonexistent in ancient and medieval times, became an important discipline. The vast and sprawling confines of multilingual Jewish literature, which seemed to resemble a jungle, were now plotted out and systematically set forth, as was the history of Jewish religious institutions. The far-flung communities of the dispersed house of Israel had developed extensive and varied rituals. The study of the history and development of the Jewish liturgy, both in its basic framework in Talmudic times and its later medieval elaborations, was meticulously explored. The capstone in the arch of the Science of Judaism was the emergence of Jewish history as an authentic scientific discipline.

As the nineteenth century continued and this massive intellectual effort began to bear fruit, the conviction grew that it would answer the felt needs of the age. Modern research would contribute richly both to the interpretation and defense of Judaism for modern men, both within the Jewish community and without. By that token it would help to buttress the claims of modern Jews to political, social, and economic rights. On the other hand, the traditional study of Torah seemed totally irrelevant to these basic enterprises of the age. No wonder it seemed a foregone conclusion that wherever the light of modern civilization would penetrate, traditional Torah was doomed. In 1818, Zunz expressed the conviction that Hebrew books would be virtually unavailable in 1918.[5] There is basic truth in the probably apocryphal tale that when the Russian-Hebrew poet, Judah Leib Gordon, visited the great Jewish bibliographer, Moritz Steinschneider, in Berlin, and told him that he was a Hebrew poet, the aged savant asked him: "Young man, in what century did you live?"

Had the Science of Judaism possessed no practical implications, but had merely enriched the boundaries of man's knowledge and understanding of himself through its researches, it would deserve an honored place among the humanities.

As a matter of fact, however, *Jüdische Wissenschaft* laid claim to much more, insisting that it had exerted a powerful and beneficent influence in the life of modern Jewry. Ismar Elbogen summarized the achievements—or at least the claim to achievement—of modern Jewish scholarship in these words: "The Science of Judaism did valuable service in dispelling erroneous notions of the Jews and Judaism among non-Jews. It aided in bringing about the emancipation of the Jews; it made Jews proud of themselves and their people; it improved education, clarified religious views, and played its part in the secularization of Jewish life." [6] Elsewhere he maintained that the Science of Judaism had had three important, popular effects: it had broadened the content and range of Jewish education to include the Bible, Jewish history, the Hebrew language and literature; it had served to stimulate the creation of Jewish nationalism; and it had contributed to the revival of the Hebrew language.[7]

Of these three claims, the first is largely true. Undoubtedly the curriculum of the modern Jewish school, which includes a variety of Jewish subjects, owes much to the Science of Judaism. Elbogen's second contention is more doubtful. To be sure, Jewish nationalism was able to draw upon the sense of peoplehood, which is reflected, for example, in Graetz's *History of the Jews*. By and large, however, modern Jewish scholars were not notable in the leadership they gave the Zionist movement or other forms of Jewish nationalism. One recalls Herzl's unavailing efforts to win over the adherence of Moritz Güdemann of Vienna to the Zionist cause. Elbogen's third contention is also questionable. The revival of the Hebrew language owed little, if anything, to the Science of Judaism.

Though the Science of Judaism was largely predicated

upon the concept of a Jewish people in the past, its practitioners were not in the forefront of the Jewish national revival in the present. Moreover, the discipline was largely preoccupied with the Jewish historical experience in the Diaspora, since Palestine played a relatively minor role during the past nineteen centuries as against such centers as Babylonia, Spain, Poland, and Germany. For these reasons, the Science of Judaism in its classic European phase has been criticized by Israeli scholars. For they reflect the new self-confident and even strident nationalism of the State of Israel with its widespread tendency to bypass or downgrade the nineteen centuries of Jewish exile.

It is, however, inherent in virtually every undertaking that it falls short of the vision of its projectors. That the Science of Judaism achieved less than its protagonists hoped for is undeniable. Yet it cannot be denied that its accomplishments are of genuine and abiding value.

It has to its credit original research of the highest caliber in all the fields of Jewish history, literature, and institutions. At least equally significant is the degree to which its results have been brought into the mainstream of modern culture. Rabbinic and medieval texts have been issued in accurate, critical editions, annotated and often translated. Dictionaries and encyclopedias in many languages summarize in systematic form the conclusions of modern Jewish scholarship. Institutions of learning, whose faculties have been staffed by men of genius and talent, were founded throughout the Western world. The Jewish Theological Seminary of Breslau was the first and perhaps the greatest of these institutions, but Berlin, Vienna, Budapest, Paris, London, Warsaw, New York, Cincinnati, and Jerusalem all have boasted important centers of Jewish research. Periodicals dedicated to the Science of Judaism have appeared in virtually every modern tongue, including Hebrew. Monographs and books have been issued in a steady stream, enriching the boundaries of man's knowledge.

At the same time, it must be noted that modern Jewish scholarship suffered from several basic defects which were largely inherent in its background. Being a product of the nineteenth century, it favored the ultrarationalistic approach to Judaism. It therefore failed to evaluate properly the role of the emotional and mystical factors in Jewish experience. Even Heinrich Graetz's classic work, *Die Geschichte der Juden,* is not free from blind spots. It exhibits this bias to the full in dealing with the Kabbalah, with the various Messianic movements, and with Hasidism.

Moreover, since the Science of Judaism was concentrated largely in Germany, its devotees had little sympathy or understanding for East European Jewry. By and large, the millions of Jews in Poland, Russia, and Romania, blessed with unquenchable Jewish vitality, lay outside the ken of the German Jewish *Gelehrten.* Men's feelings and actions are often superior to their intellectual positions or casual utterances. It would therefore be a mistake to take too seriously Geiger's words, written to Joseph Derenbourg in a letter dated November 22, 1840: "... That Jews in Prussia may have the chance to become pharmacists or lawyers is much more important to me than the rescue of all the Jews in Asia and Africa, an undertaking with which I sympathize as a human being. You may think differently on this subject, but I ask you to believe me that this is my honest conviction, intimately interwoven with the entire structure of my intellectual view of things...." [8]

In addition to these drawbacks which inhered in the specific locale which gave it birth, modern Jewish research suffered from a third defect, the virtual neglect of the Bible by modern Jewish scholarship. It seemed as though Jewish scholars were determined to validate an old rabbinic comment. For the ancient Sages had explained that the Mishnah or Oral Law had remained unwritten because God had foreseen that the day would come when the Bible, or Written Law, would be taken over by non-Jews.[9]

There were various factors that contributed to the neglect of biblical studies by modern Jewish scholars. The nineteenth century saw the Higher Criticism of the Bible reach its highest point of development in the classic formulation of the Graf-Wellhausen school. There was a measure of exaggeration in Solomon Schechter's epigram, "The Higher Criticism is the higher anti-Semitism." But it would be fatuous to overlook the personal prejudice of many of the devotees of the Higher Criticism, which undoubtedly played its part in the constant effort to reduce the value, the antiquity, and the originality of the Hebrew Scriptures. Even when anti-Semitism was not the motive, there was the fundamental approach of traditional Christianity, which saw the Old Testament as the inferior forerunner of the New Testament.

For these reasons, it becomes easy to understand the neglect of biblical research by modern Jewish scholars. With only a few exceptions, even those of liberal views found it difficult to subject the Bible to this type of merciless analysis and atomization. A few Jewish scholars, like the more conservative Christian scholars, attempted to refute one or another aspect of the Higher Criticism, but they were voices crying in the wilderness. However, the structure of Higher Criticism was too imposing and too extensive to yield to such isolated efforts. Jewish scholars tended either to accept the results of the Higher Criticism or they avoided the subject altogether. Most of the creative work done by Jewish scholars in the field of the Bible was peripheral.

Even biblical exegesis, the interpretation of the text, in which the great medieval Jewish commentators had distinguished themselves, was but little cultivated by modern scholars. To be sure, practical necessity dictated the preparation of Bible translations into the various vernaculars spoken by modern Jews. By and large, however, they were reworkings of the standard Christian versions of the Old Testament, with a few dogmatic mistranslations omitted.

However, if full justice is to be done to the Science of Judaism, it should also be noted that all these drawbacks were in large measure finally overcome. The sins both of commission and of omission committed by *die Wissenschaft des Judentums* were corrected during its sunset days in Germany before World War II and in Israel, Great Britain, and the United States in the post-Nazi period. The study of the Bible has undergone a renascence in Israel and throughout the world. The results of Near East archaeology have helped to create a new attitude of respect toward the basic credibility of the Bible and a deeper understanding both of its relationship to the surrounding environment and its unique elements. Jewish scholarship in the field of Bible is today significant and fruitful.

It is noteworthy that Martin Buber and Franz Rosenzweig, to name only the best-known figures, rediscovered the extraordinary creative capacities of East European Jewry at first hand. They called attention to the deep fountains of idealism to be found in the congested areas of the Pale of Settlement in Eastern Europe, before and during the First World War. Buber brought back some of the rich spiritual treasures of Hasidism to enrich and deepen the spiritual life of Western man. Nor was it accidental that Buber and Rosenzweig collaborated on the production of a creative Jewish translation of the Scriptures into German for twentieth-century German-speaking Jewry.

Today contemporary Jewish scholarship includes research in such characteristic achievements of East European Jewry as the Yiddish press, literature, and drama, the progressive Jewish labor movement, and Zionism in all its phases and schools.

There is poetic justice in the fact that the mystical and Messianic strands in the Jewish tradition, scorned or ignored by rationalist scholars in the nineteenth century, have found their scholarly redeemer in a twentieth-century German Jewish scholar. It is Gershom Scholem who has restored them to their place within the variegated pattern of the Jewish tradition through his brilliant and fruitful researches. Yet, even after the achievements of the Science of Judaism are fairly evaluated and the weaknesses properly discounted, the conclusion is inescapable that the discipline has not fulfilled the high hopes reposed in it, not merely by its youthful progenitors in the *Verein für die Wissenschaft des Judentums*, but by its more mature and sober practitioners in later periods. Perhaps it should not have been expected that it would create a way of life for modern Jews or fill their Jewish existence with adequate cultural content. But it did succeed in providing the raw material from which various schools of Jewish thought—cultural, national, and religious—could draw the stones for building their own edifices for the human spirit. This, to be sure, is no mean achievement.

We are, however, not concerned with the past of the Science of Judaism. We are interested in its present status and its future potential. In this connection, it should be noted that *Jüdische Wissenschaft* has suffered a steady decline in vitality and creative energy during the century and a half of its history.

At least three main stages may be discerned in its career. First came the great pioneers, Zunz, Rappaport, Krochmal, Frankel, Geiger, who were fired by their vision of its potentialities for grappling with the crisis of Judaism in their time.

Then came the great synthesizers, who erected imposing

surveys of large areas of Jewish history and literature. The most famous and influential was undoubtedly Heinrich Graetz's *History of the Jews*, written in German and translated into many languages. Less influential, but nonetheless significant, was I. H. Weiss's five-volume Hebrew work *Dor Dor Vedorshav*, a critical and all-inclusive survey of the history of biblical and rabbinic law and tradition.

The third stage consisted of gifted scholars who utilized their refined technical skills to correct errors and fill in details in the work of their predecessors. As was perhaps inevitable, their concern with the trees often led them to lose sight of the forest. Analysis replaced synthesis and the growth of a technical jargon helped to establish a professional caste, remote from life and its concerns.

Today much, though fortunately not all, of the Science of Judaism consists of writings by professors writing for other professors. The goal of disinterested Jewish scholarship has been identified all too often with uninterested—and uninteresting—Jewish research; objectivity has degenerated into irrelevance to life.

Obviously, as a science progresses, a technical vocabulary necessarily develops. A specialized terminology is needed to help in the organization of the subject matter being studied and to expedite the communication of ideas. Technical terms serve as a shorthand code for scholars. Not too rarely, however, we encounter scholars who strain after a recondite vocabulary and style as if their purpose were to discourage having too many readers. It is undeniable that in many scholarly circles obscurity is prized as a sign of profundity, while lucidity is scorned as a mark of superficiality. The scholar who strives to present his subject matter in clear, attractive, and well-organized form, both in the academic lecture hall and on the printed page, often finds himself stigmatized as lacking in deep and authentic learning.

The situation goes beyond the matter of style—it penetrates to the very content of research. Obviously every genuine scholarly achievement must rest on the painstaking collection of data, which in themselves may be of little consequence. The great classical scholar, Wilamowitz-Moellendorff, gave this wise warning to his students: "Do not be disappointed that when you dig for pearls you may find worms. But do not make the mistake of imagining that the worms are pearls." More often than one likes to admit, however, the collection of data becomes an end in itself. The scholar studiously refrains from making any significant generalizations on the basis of the evidence even about the past. He recoils in even more pronounced distaste from drawing any conclusions from his studies that can help illumine and guide the present.

That these defects are to be found in other branches of research and are not limited to Jewish scholarship is scant comfort. The truth is lost sight of that the ultimate justification of all technical learning lies in the degree to which its results are brought into the mainstream of general culture, and thus are made to enrich the pattern of civilization and direct its course.

The two basic motivations of the Science of Judaism which were at work during its greatest and most fruitful period, apologetics and emancipation, are of no importance today. The activity continues, but the impetus is gone. It is true that humanistic studies generally cannot vie in attractiveness for our youth with the scientific and technological disciplines of our age. Undoubtedly, many factors enter into this state of affairs. Yet basically it is a matter of relevance—rightly or wrongly, the natural sciences are felt to be highly significant and therefore exciting, the social sciences seem somewhat less so, and humanistic studies tend to be dismissed as peripheral and largely decorative activities.

In his now famous lecture, *The Two Cultures*, C. P. Snow pleaded for breaking down the iron curtain between literature and science. He pointed out how ill-informed literary men generally were on scientific fundamentals. The converse is equally true—scientists are much too often ignorant or scornful, or both, of literature, philosophy, and religion.

It is already clear that this state of affairs has undermined the spiritual health of contemporary man and impoverished his cultural life, but it will not change until and unless the literature and thought of the past are generally recognized as relevant to the modern world. The scientific study of the Jewish past seems to be merely a branch of general humanistic studies, and a minor one to boot. No wonder it appeals to relatively few creative young Jews, even the most Jewishly educated and committed among them.

Does this betoken the early end, or at best the continued decline of modern Jewish scholarship? It has indeed been argued in some quarters that having been born with the emancipation of German Jewry, the Science of Judaism will die in the Hitler and the post-Hitler era. This answer is not only too simple; it is contradicted both by the facts and the needs of the day. I should like to propose an affirmative answer to the question as to whether a significant future is possible for the Science of Judaism. We may put it in terms of the classic Hegelian dialectic: *The traditional study of Torah is the thesis and the Science of Judaism the antithesis. What is now required is the synthesis of both on a new and higher level.*

The truth is that there prevails an ambivalent relationship between the traditional Torah and *die Wissenschaft des Judentums*, a relationship both of opposition and of affinity. Ostensibly the Science of Judaism arose as a conscious replacement, if not as an act of revolt against traditional Torah. Thus Zunz once stated that "the rabbis are taking the attitude that they had inaugurated this Science, whereas it originated, on the contrary, in the struggle against them." Nonetheless, however vigorously the Science fought against traditional learning, its greatest practitioners were all reared "on the knees of Torah" and were never able to extricate themselves from some of the fundamental values in the traditional concept of Torah.

To be sure, there were modern Jewish scholars who loudly proclaimed their total devotion to "scientific objectivity"—and their complete detachment from the contemporary scene. They did not suspect the truth Max Scheler taught that an emotional interest in research, far from impairing the value of the enterprise, may actually enhance it.[10] Yet in spite of formal protestations to the contrary, modern Jewish scholars continued to cherish the faith in the eternity of Israel and in the abiding value of its tradition. This held true not merely for Samson Raphael Hirsch, for whom the Torah was immutable, but also for Zechariah Frankel, who saw the tradition as perpetually vital and self-renewing, and for Abraham Geiger, who felt it necessary to purify the divine essence of Judaism from what he regarded as secondary and lower accretions. Virtually all scholars, even those who had wandered far from the traditional way of life in their personal practice, believed that in some sense "the Eternal of Israel does not deceive." Without this sense of the abiding values to be found in Jewish experience and deposited in Jewish literature, it would have been psychologically impossible for scholars to devote their lives, often undergoing privation and neglect, to elucidating the tradition and revealing its content.

Finally, the traditional pursuit of the study of Torah represented a remarkable balance between two ideals, which in a logical sense might seem to be mutually opposed. Through the centuries, Jewish teachers and moralists have extolled the ideal of *Torah lishemah*, "knowledge

for its own sake," the pursuit of learning without any ulterior motive, even one as rarefied as the reward of God.
However—and this is fundamental—the ideal of Torah as
an end in itself was never felt to be in contradiction to the
ideal of *Torat hayyim*, "the Torah as a gateway to life."
Whatever the logician might argue, Jewish life held fast to
both ideals. Understanding the world and man's place in it,
fairly and unafraid, went hand in hand with the continual
effort to make this body of knowledge relevant to life.
Thus when the question was posed before the rabbis in the
Academy at Lydda as to which was more important, study
or action, the conclusion reached was thoroughly characteristic for Judaism: *Gadol Talmud Torah shehatalmud
mebi lide ma'aseh*, "Study is greater, because study leads to
right action." [11]

   This ideal of learning as the royal road to living was embodied in the careers of the greatest Jewish scholars in
every age: Saadia Gaon, Moses Maimonides, Joseph Karo,
Elijah of Vilna, Rabbi Abraham Isaac Kook, and countless
lesser figures. The student of Torah always felt that it was
relevant to life because no matter how minute the issue before him, or how recondite the subject of the study, it represented a fragment of the revelation of the will of God.
Answering a difficulty in a super-commentary on the Talmud or solving a difficult passage in Maimonides' *Code*
might seem far removed from the Revelation on Sinai, but
though the line might be long, the connection was unmistakable.

   These two ideals of *Torah lishemah* and *Torat hayyim*
may be restated in secular terms. The first is the lofty goal
of objectivity, the love of truth without fear or favor. The
second represents the principle of relevance to life, serving
the cause of human welfare through the love of truth, the
advancement of righteousness, and the creation of beauty.
The scientist in the laboratory, the scholar in the library,

the student of Torah in the *Beth Hamidrash*, all bear witness to the union of these ideals. To be responsive to life
without surrendering the love of truth—this is the mark of
learning at its highest. Where either element is suffered to
decline or to disappear, scholarship is doomed to increasing
sterility, as soon as the momentum of earlier and of more
creative periods is exhausted.

This is clearly illustrated in the history of general culture. The Golden Age of classical studies in Western Europe coincided with the period of the Renaissance when
the rediscovery of Greek literature served as a liberating influence from the shackles of the Dark Ages and the intellectual limitations of scholasticism. When the process was
completed, classical studies reverted to the status of an
esoteric pursuit, engaged in by erudite scholars, whose contributions were rarely world-shaking.

Another illustration is afforded by the history of biblical
studies. Western Europe knew two bright periods in biblical scholarship. The first came during the sixteenth and
seventeenth centuries when the study of the Hebrew language acted as the fulcrum for the Reformation, which
gave to the Book, rather than to the Church, the position of
primacy in the spiritual life of man. The second came in the
nineteenth and twentieth centuries, when biblical studies
served as the instrument for restructuring the pattern of religious belief, which had been gravely shaken by modern
science and philosophy.

What is true of the Jewish study of Torah and of the
scientific pursuit of general knowledge applies to the history of the Science of Judaism, which is derived from both.
Modern Jewish scholarship was most fruitful when it was
most closely wedded to the demands of life. Zunz's first
masterpiece, *Die gottesdienstlichen Vorträge der Juden*
("The Preachments of the Jews"), published in 1832, was
projected in order to demonstrate that the sermon had al-

ways been a thoroughly Jewish institution and should therefore not be banned as an innovation in the modern synagogue. This work, which has been called, with some exaggeration, "the most important Jewish work of the nineteenth century," was a basic exposition of the growth and development of the Midrash, the Haggadah, and the prayer book. It marked the first effort to create order and meaning in the vast and hitherto unexplored recesses of Jewish literature.

Five years later, in 1837, Zunz published his *Namen der Juden*, which challenged a Prussian decree forbidding Jewish parents to give so-called "Christian" names to their children. Zunz demonstrated that Jews had always freely used names borrowed from the general environment and the Government retracted most of the restrictive edict.

In 1840 Zechariah Frankel published his *Die Eidesleistung der Juden* ("The Oaths of Jews"), which was evoked by his desire to abolish, or at least to mitigate, the disgraceful Jews' Oath. His severely practical purpose did not prevent his work from being a careful study of the Jewish law on testimony and court procedure.

In 1857 Abraham Geiger published his *Urschrift und Übersetzungen der Bibel* ("The Original Text and Translation of the Bible"), which sought to buttress his conception of Reform Judaism by tracing the development of the Jewish interpretation of the Bible in the rabbinic period. Conversely, David Hoffmann defended the thesis that Orthodox Judaism possessed integral unity, by revealing the various strata of law that entered into the overall structure of the *Halachah*.

In certain quarters today the tendency has developed to look down upon the achievements of *die Wissenschaft des Judentums* and to ignore its implications, on the ground that the discipline as a whole draws its impetus from "ulterior" motives—the desire to facilitate Jewish emancipation by winning respect for Judaism and civil and political rights for Jews. Those who adopt this lofty stance reveal the all-too-human tendency to bite the hand that feeds us. Few of those who decry the Emancipation and modernism have rushed to turn in their citizenship papers or to surrender the material and cultural advantages of the modern era.

This consideration aside, the truth is that in being responsive to life modern Jewish research was essentially in the spirit of traditional Jewish learning, indeed, of all vital scholarship. In its Golden Age, the Science of Judaism possessed a strong interest in the contemporary scene, coupled with a rigorous dedication to the search for truth. Whenever the first factor unduly affected the second in the work of a given scholar, other scholars were generally available —and eager—to make the necessary correction!

The truth—or its closest possible approximation— resulted from the interaction of the researches and the controversies of scholars. For total objectivity was not a goal in itself, nor was it within the realm of attainment. Like infinity, Truth remains a flying goal, perpetually eluding the searcher, who nevertheless does catch a glimpse of the heavenly creature.

If modern Jewish scholarship is to recapture its pristine enthusiasm and once again feel the exhilaration of "a watcher of the skies, when a new planet swims into his ken," it can do so only if it absorbs these two basic values of Torah, an attitude of basic acceptance of the value of the Jewish heritage and a faith in the Jewish future. Above all, it must join an objective love of truth to a genuine concern with life and its problems.

The old nineteenth-century goals of *Jüdische Wissenschaft* are no longer operative today. But there are basic and far-reaching functions which modern Jewish scholarship, and it alone, can perform in this post-Emancipation era. The first and ongoing function which it shares with all natural and human sciences is to provide the basis for a viable world view for modern man. It is to the Science of Judaism that we must look for the raw material out of which a living conception of the Jewish tradition can be fashioned. We sometimes imagine that it is a peculiar sign of our age that men feel a sense of alienation from the roots of their being. It was a long time ago that Joseph von Eichendorff declared, "We long to go home, but we do not know where to go." The modern Jew, like all earlier generations, must rediscover and reaffirm for himself the goals of human life and rededicate himself to the ideals of wisdom and beauty, justice and freedom, which alone make peace possible and life worth living.

These objectives were enunciated with incomparable sincerity and depth in the great classical traditions of Hellas and of Israel, and they were carried forward in their medieval and modern embodiments of philosophy and of religion. But they cannot be taken over ready-made from earlier eras. What is valid in these insights and attitudes must be set forth and interpreted anew, and applied to our society, with its infinitely greater needs and capacities. A philosophy of Judaism dealing with perennial issues must, nevertheless, be relevant to the age or it is meaningless. It must, therefore, draw upon all the insights and face all the challenges emanating from the general culture of the day. At the same time, a Jewish theology will be authentically Jewish only if it is based on a genuine knowledge of the manifold sources of the Jewish tradition. This creative and indispensable task has been undertaken from widely varying standpoints by such representative figures of German Jewry as Hermann Cohen, Franz Rosenzweig, Leo Baeck, and Martin Buber, as well as by such other thinkers as Rabbi Abraham Isaac Kook in Israel, Mordecai M. Kaplan and Abraham Heschel in America.

For this process to be intellectually valid, it must rest upon the foundation of solid and unimpeachable scholarship. Upon this foundation, all the various schools of Jewish religious and philosophic thought denominated as Orthodoxy, Conservatism, Reform, Reconstructionism, and Humanism, as well as the variations within each school, will be able to rear their specific world views. At the same time, they will be able to retain the sense of continuity with the past and a feeling of fellowship with all their people, because of the conviction that they are rooted in a common tradition and share in a single brotherhood. This task of revealing and interpreting the insights and values of the tradition must be performed anew in every generation. By that token, it remains a timeless enterprise for the human spirit.

There are several other functions for Jewish scholarship which are timely rather than timeless: The contemporary Jew needs to rethink his relationship to the free society in this post-Nazi era, when communism emerges as a major challenge to the democratic West. This requires an understanding of the historic interaction of the Jew and the world in all the different eras and societies of the past and present. For this purpose, scientific Jewish learning is an indispensable tool.

A few years ago David Ben-Gurion threw the Jewish world into a turmoil by asking, "Who and what is a Jew?" The question must be answered, not on a basis of passion or partisanship, but through as objective a study as possible of the realities of the Jewish position throughout the world. This question of the nature of Jewish identity, to which we shall return in the next chapter, demands an answer—not only for the sake of the individual Jew, who seeks to establish his relation to the general community. It is also a prerequisite, as we shall see, for finding a solution to the complex question of the relationship of Israeli and Diaspora Jewry.

That is not all. Whether we applaud or lament the fact, it is clear that barring a catastrophe, that would incidentally gravely threaten the State of Israel as well, most of world Jewry will continue to live outside the confines of the State. It therefore follows that they will continue to be possessed of different attitudes and to be confronted by radically different problems. Here, Jewish scholarship on a worldwide basis has another vital function to perform. Being a branch of culture, learning naturally and legitimately reflects the society which gives rise to it. If this be true, we may anticipate that Israeli scholarship will probably tend to emphasize the distinctively Jewish elements in our past and present. Diaspora scholarship, on the other hand, has the equally significant task of helping to trace the historic interaction of the Jewish people and of its neighbors throughout history. In that creative tension between particularism and universalism, which runs as a thread through the entire pattern of Jewish history, Israeli scholarship will tend to highlight the first, and Diaspora learning the second.

In all these respects, modern Jewish research can perform an indispensable function in creating a fruitful and creative mutuality between Israel and the Diaspora, where each partner would both give and receive.

The conclusion is clear. *Contemporary Jewish scholarship will discover a true* raison d'être *if it does not take refuge in an ivory tower remote from life, but occupies itself with the basic concerns of the twentieth-century Jew. It must help him meet the perils which threaten the survival of the humane ideals of Western civilization, which owe so much to the genius of Israel. It must strengthen the unity of the Jewish people the world over. It must help guarantee the survival of Judaism, by endowing the Jewish heritage with new vitality and relevance to life.*

The synthesis here proposed is not limited to one direction. If it is true that a revitalized Science of Judaism will need to absorb some basic values from Torah, it is equally true that Torah will need to absorb some basic values from the Science of Judaism. Today the ghetto walls have fallen everywhere. There will undoubtedly remain tiny enclaves of voluntary ghettos, colorful curiosities from the past. But any large-scale teaching of Torah to great numbers of youth and adults either in Israel or in the Diaspora will be unable to shut out the modern world. It will need to embody elements of the critical method and spirit, reckon with the sense of history and take into account the interrelationship of the Jew and the world. I am not suggesting that the traditional study of Torah and the modern Science of Judaism will merge into a single discipline. They do need, however, to draw closer together and learn from one another for their mutual benefit and enrichment.

All groups in the Jewish people, from the ultra-Orthodox to the extreme freethinkers, share a common heritage in a three-thousand-year-old Torah which they each interpret by their own lights. But they also share a younger legacy, only a century and a half old, which is also of genuine value, the Science of Judaism, which all must cultivate and the results of which they can all utilize as the basis of their individual world views.

If our civilization survives at all, it will be as a free and open society in which isolation will be impossible. A vital, modern Jewish scholarship is uniquely equipped to help break down the barriers between Judaism and humanity, both in the spirit of the Jew and in the life of the world. For with due apologies to the Latin writer, Terence, the Jew of today and tomorrow must emblazon upon his escutcheon the motto, *Judaeus sum et nihil humani neque Judaici a me alienum esse puto*—"I am a Jew and nothing human or Jewish is alien to me."

CHAPTER FOUR

THE NATURE
OF JEWISH IDENTITY

IN DISCUSSING the character of Jewish life before the Emancipation we saw that both the natural and the compulsory community shared one basic characteristic—they nurtured and sustained the organic character of the Jewish tradition. This trait marked Jewish life throughout the period of independence and autonomy in Palestine and during the centuries of ghetto life in the Middle Ages, which lasted well into the twentieth century for the bulk of modern Jews who lived in Eastern Europe. Because of the organic character of Jewish life as they experienced it, ancient and medieval Jews were not troubled by the issue which may well be described as the hallmark of the modern Jew: What is a Jew? What is the nature of the Jewish group? In what sense do I belong to this community?

The great philosophic classics of the Middle Ages and the vast legal literature, which included the all-embracing law codes as well as thousands upon thousands of Responsa on specific questions, never felt called upon to discuss the nature of Jewish identity. The tenth-century philosopher Saadia had declared, "We are a people only by virtue of

the Torah." The medieval mystics had formulated the
aphorism, "God, Torah, and Israel are one," thus underscoring the unity and interrelatedness of religion, culture,
and peoplehood. These formulations sufficed the needs of
Jews until the Emancipation.

The question, which did not exist for the consciousness
of ancient and medieval Jewry, became a burning issue for
the modern Jew. It is safe to say that no aspect of the Jewish problem has been talked and written about so exten-
sively as the nature of the Jewish group and the character
of Jewish allegiance. One can sympathize with the widespread desire to drop the subject as unexciting and incon-
clusive and turn to newer themes. Yet, if it is driven out
through the door it returns through the window. It cannot
be avoided in any serious discussion of the position of Judaism in the modern world. It came to the fore, as we have
seen, when the Western world offered and Jews accepted
the boon of Emancipation. The spirit of the transaction,
for it was a *quid pro quo*, an exchange and not a gift, was
indicated in Clermont-Tonnerre's ringing declaration, "To
the Jews as Jews nothing; to the Jews as men everything!"

To validate, so it was thought, the right of Jews to citizenship and equality in the modern state, the effort was undertaken to reduce Judaism to the dimension of a religious
sect paralleling that of the various Christian denominations.
Thus Judaism was now defined as a "religion."

As time went on and it became clear that the Jewish religion was not shared equally by all modern Jews, and that
many were indeed indifferent or even hostile to it, another
formula was needed. The view was advanced by Zionists
and other nationalist groups that Jews were a "nation,"
differing from other people only in being temporarily
homeless until they could return to their ancestral country.
Throughout the nineteenth century a passionate debate
was carried on as to whether Jews were a "religion" or a

"nation." Finally, the well-known Hebrew poet, Judah Leib Gordon, expressed his distaste for the entire discussion in the refrain of a satiric poem, the assonance and pungency of which cannot be transmitted in translation, *Lo 'am 'anahnu velo 'edah 'ela 'eder,* "We are neither a nation nor a sect, but a flock of sheep!"

Not only were there large numbers of Jews who were not religious in any meaningful sense, but many others did not necessarily share the aspirations for a return to Zion. Yet they regarded themselves and—what was equally significant—were regarded by others as Jews, sharing an indefinable yet undeniable bond which linked them to other Jews and differentiated them from non-Jews. What category of belonging could describe their position?

The nineteenth century had created a conveniently cloudy term, "race," which seemed to possess an aura of scientific validity. Philologists had noted that there are two great families of languages, the vast, widely scattered Indo-European or Aryan group, which had many subgroups, and the considerably more limited group of Semitic languages. It was an easy but fatal step for pseudoscientific thinkers like Gobineau and Chamberlain to transfer these terms from languages to ethnic groups and to speak of Aryan and Semitic peoples. It was always clear to knowledgeable people that the concept of race was a farrago of nonsense. Indo-European languages were spoken by dark-skinned Hindus in India, as well as by a vast variety of whites varying from the Greeks to the Swedes, from the Italians to the Russians. Even in the Semitic group, which was far more concentrated geographically, Ethiopic was spoken by Negroes, Arabic by swarthy inhabitants of the desert, and Hebrew by a people which had absorbed countless ethnic strains during its millennial history of wanderings on three continents.

Nonetheless the term "race" persisted in general usage

for two principal reasons. It seemed to be a convenient term to describe Jews, since it suggested one basic element lacking in the terms "religion" and "nation"—the element of kinship and common descent. In addition, it had the virtue of being free from any link, be it to a religious outlook or a nationalist ideology. It focused attention upon past descent, not upon present commitment.

Only time was to offer a bloody demonstration of the truth that intellectual error is the prelude to moral obloquy. The doctrine of race became the cornerstone of Nazi ideology, in the name of which millions of human beings were brutally done to death. Today it is clear that it would be best if the term "race" were expunged from the modern vocabulary. It is highly questionable whether it should be applied even to the various branches of the human family on the basis of their pigmentation, white, black, brown, red, and yellow. Even here it introduces divisions which are in part imaginary and in part exaggerated, and sets up a wall which is belied by the constant intermingling of stocks, so that the term "pure race" is meaningless and fraught with peril.

Be this as it may, the bloody and meaningless term "race" has no significance when applied to Jews. The term "religion," to be sure, underscores the central element in the Jewish heritage. Yet it is by no means coextensive with it. There are Jews who are deeply Jewish without being religious, and there is much in Judaism that transcends creed, ritual, and ethics, the three constituents of religion. It is also obvious that "nationality" or "nation," commonly understood to refer to political allegiance, cannot apply to modern Jews who live throughout the world and are citizens of the various countries in which they live. They therefore share distinct political loyalties, besides differing in their social and economic viewpoints and interests.

Nonetheless, both terms continue to be used, with disastrous consequences for the understanding of the realities of the Jewish position in the modern world. A small but highly articulate group of Jews, fearful for their status as citizens of their native land, shrilly proclaim from the housetops that they have nothing in common with Jews elsewhere except "a religion," which they struggle to free from contamination with national or cultural elements. Thus the members of the American Council for Judaism, which represents this standpoint, are in mortal terror of the possibility that their position as American citizens may be challenged by the obvious pride and interest most Jews show in the State of Israel. As a result, they have not hesitated to fraternize with Arab monarchs and dictators who have repeatedly proclaimed their unswerving intention to annihilate Israel.

On the other hand, the State of Israel would seem, at first blush, to demonstrate the appropriateness of the term "nationality" for the Jewish group. For here Jews exhibit all the marks of a nation, such as a territory, a language, a culture, and an independent government. Yet if we penetrate more deeply into the situation it becomes clear that even here the term is inappropriate. For a Jew in Israel is an Israeli by nationality, exactly like an Arab or a Druze in Israel. Apply the term "nationality" to the Jewish group and a complex of questions remains unanswered, indeed unanswerable. What is the role of the State of Israel in the life of Diaspora Jews who do not live within its borders nor give it political allegiance? What is the link between Israeli Jews and the Jews of the Diaspora? What is the bond uniting the various groups of Diaspora Jewry, as for example, the Jews of the United States and those of Argentina or Italy? What relationship will subsist between Israeli Jews and Diaspora Jewry, not merely today but tomorrow, as brothers become cousins of first, second, third, and fourth degrees?

In the past it was assumed that these questions affected only Jews in the Diaspora. They were dismissed as examples of the anomalous character of Jewish life in exile and of the abnormalities which would ultimately bring about the disappearance of Diaspora Jewry. In the Jewish State, on the other hand, it was felt that the Jewish group would take on all the attributes of normal life as it took its place among the nations of the world, and the problem of Jewish identity would disappear. Less than two decades have elapsed since the State of Israel was established. It has already become clear that the establishment and progress of the new State is one of the few authentic miracles of the twentieth century, which has brought healing and hope and the assurance of a future to the Jewish people.

Nevertheless the State of Israel has not solved the issue of the nature of the Jewish group. Indeed, this problem confronting the modern Jew is still very much alive in Israel. As time goes by, all the citizens of the new State, Jewish, Christian, Islamic, and Druze, will share an ever larger fund of common experiences as inhabitants of the same country. On the other hand, the strong sense of unity and fellowship which most Israeli Jews feel with Diaspora Jewry is at present in large measure religious, and in a lesser degree cultural, besides being buttressed by a sense of family kinship. The last factor will be less and less significant with the passing of the present generation. The weakening of the sense of religious and cultural unity between the Israeli-born sabras and world Jewry, which is widely recognized, has been a source of mounting concern for Israeli leadership. Courses in "Jewish consciousness" have been introduced in Israeli government schools in order to cultivate a knowledge of Jewish tradition and an appreciation of the entire Jewish past, including the two thousand years of heroism and creativity in the Exile, and to stimulate a sense of community with world Jewry.

To be sure, the kind of unflinching consistency that spawned "religionists" of the type of the American Council for Judaism in the United States has also produced the school of "nationalists" in the State of Israel who call themselves "Canaanites." This small but articulate group proclaims that it has nothing in common with Diaspora Jewry but feels itself much more closely linked to the Middle East. Nor is this standpoint limited to official members of the group. Recently, the successful musical play, *Fiddler on the Roof*, was produced in Israel. By a curious paradox the Israeli actor playing the star role of Tevye, the milkman, who epitomizes the traditional East European Jew, told a reporter of the *New York Times* that he "had more in common with an Arab than with the Jews living in Galut."

Both the American Council for Judaism here and the Canaanites and their sympathizers in Israel recall the rabbinic legend about the inhabitants of the city of Sodom. They practiced a special brand of hospitality, by providing beds for wayfarers. When a hapless traveler came their way, he would be placed upon the bed and, if his frame proved too long, they would hack off his limbs so that he might fit its dimensions. In making the rich pattern of Judaism conform to the Procrustean bed of their petty theory, be it of Judaism as a simon-pure "religion," or as a normal "nationality," both the American Council for Judaism and the Canaanites testify to the truth of Emerson's observation that "a foolish consistency is the hobgoblin of little minds, adored by little statesmen and philosophers and divines."

That the nature of Jewish identity is not merely an exercise in semantics but on the contrary is a vital—and troublesome—issue for Israeli Jewry as well as for the world Jewish community, was dramatically demonstrated in the Brother Daniel case, decided in 1962 by the Supreme Court of the State of Israel. The case may well take its place with other judicial decisions that have become landmarks in doctrine and in law, such as the rulings by the U.S. Supreme Court in the Marbury and the Dartmouth College cases in the nineteenth century, the Everson and McCullogh cases, and the anti-segregation decision during the twentieth.

The basic facts may be set forth briefly: The case revolved around the application of a Carmelite monk, Brother Daniel, who was born of Jewish parents in Poland. During his youth he had been active in Zionist work and had heroically rescued hundreds of Jews from the Gestapo. While hiding in a Catholic convent he was converted to Christianity. In 1954 he joined the Carmelite Order of monks, hoping to be allowed to go to the land of Israel, and in 1958 the Church authorities finally granted him this permission.

Upon his arrival in Israel, Brother Daniel sought to register *as a Jew of the Christian faith*. When the case reached the Supreme Court all the judges were eloquent in their praise of Brother Daniel's heroic behavior in saving Jews from the Nazi butchers. Nonetheless, four of the five judges, Justices Silberg, Landau, Berinson, and Many, voted to deny his petition. Only Justice Cohn disagreed and voted to grant Brother Daniel's suit.

It should be emphasized that in this 4 to 1 decision of the Supreme Court denying his status as a Jew, there was no negation of the priest's right to continue to reside in the State of Israel or to apply for naturalization as an Israeli citizen with equal rights. This is, in fact, what Brother Daniel proceeded to do after the decision was rendered.

The issues in the case, however, far transcend the dimensions of the individual suit involved. As is the usual practice of courts, the Israeli judges sought to decide the issue on the basis of "what was in the mind of the legislators who enacted the Law of Return." Within this framework there was only one possible answer: for the legislators, as for virtually all Jews everywhere, the Jew who converts to another religion is no longer a Jew.

As one reads the judicial opinions rendered in the case, a striking paradox emerges. While the majority decision was the only one possible, it was clearly out of harmony with the judges' underlying presuppositions. On the other hand, the minority decision, which virtually all Jews would find unacceptable, was the only one consistent with the premises. Justice Cohn, the lone dissenter, put his finger on the gravamen of the case. He wrote: "If in the Diaspora we have been either a tolerated or persecuted minority, in our own State *we have become a nation like all other nations*, standing on our own feet. This revolution demands a change in values and in attitude, a revision in our *Galut* thinking." (Italics added.) It is clear that basically the other judges accepted Justice Cohn's contention but then found Justice Cohn's logical conclusion impossible to accept.

Actually, Justice Cohn's position evoked far more support than the 4 to 1 decision would indicate. Thus, when the Minister of Interior originally rejected Brother Daniel's application, he declared: "Times have changed and the wheel has come round full circle. Should a man who regards Israel as his homeland, who is passionately imbued with the desire to live here, but who is a Christian by religion, be denied entrance through the portals of the country for that reason only?" Similarly, Justice Berinson wrote in his decision: "As I have already said, if I were permitted to decide the question of whether the petitioner is a Jew or not according to my own personal sentiments, I would unhesitatingly reply in the affirmative." So even among the authorities who denied the application, there was a substantial body of opinion which held the law to operate unjustly.

The confusion goes even further. In the three decisions written to sustain the majority opinion (Justice Many con-

curred, but wrote no statement), there were several statements that were highly questionable or totally mistaken.
Thus Justice Berinson wrote:

It is strange that a Jew who is irreligious, and even actively
antireligious, yet remains a Jew, whereas the petitioner, who
became converted to another religion, but has remained de-
votedly attached to his people, is not regarded as a Jew. If only
he had declared himself a Buddhist—a faith which does not
require any conversion—and had become a Buddhist monk, he
would, apparently, have still been recognized as a Jew.

As a matter of fact, the learned judge was in error. Medieval *Responsa* are frequently concerned with cases of Jews
becoming Mohammedans, whether freely or under com-
pulsion. Nowhere are such individuals treated as anything
but converts. There is not the slightest reason to assume
that Buddhism would be regarded differently.

Even less justifiable was Justice Landau's attempted explanation of the underlying religious law. He was obviously operating with the familiar Hebrew saying which has
attained the currency of a proverb: "A Jew, even if he sins,
remains a Jew." His explanation was as follows: "It must be
remembered that Jewish religious law does not recognize
the possibility of a Jew's removing himself from the faith
even if he fervently wishes to do so. This stand on the part
of Jewish religious law does not arise from an attitude of
forgiveness and tolerance towards the apostate but from a
complete and contemptuous disregard of any desire on the
part of a Jew to turn to Christianity." This attempt to psy-
chologize is gravely mistaken. Thus it may only be pointed
out that this Talmudic statement emanates from a minor
Palestinian sage of the third century, when conversion to
Christianity was far from a significant threat to Judaism.

We may go further. The principle, "a Jew, even if
he sins, remains a Jew," is not a legal dictum but a religio-

ethical principle. As a matter of fact, it is a rephrasing of a homiletic comment attached to a biblical verse in the book of *Joshua.* We are told that when the Israelites sustained a defeat at the hands of the inhabitants of the city of Ai, and Joshua prayed for deliverance, the Lord said, *hata Yisrael* —"Israel has sinned." On this passage Rabbi Abba bar Zavda comments, "Although they sinned, they remain Israel." This statement was reformulated and generalized in post-Talmudic times to read *Yisrael aph al pi shehata Yisrael hu*—"An Israelite, even if he sins, remains an Israelite." As a religio-ethical doctrine of transcendent worth, the statement exerted an influence on Jewish law, but it did not determine it completely.

Actually, the status of a Jewish convert to another religion is complex in Jewish religious law.[1] In certain areas he is treated legally as a Jew. In other respects the convert is regarded as a non-Jew. Between these two clear-cut areas is a twilight zone where his status is ambivalent, where he partakes of the status of a Jew and of a Gentile.

Moreover, there are differences in attitude among the rabbinic authorities who span a period of over two thousand years. These differences reflect in part the divergences of personality and attitude of the rabbis. In perhaps larger measure they are due to the varied experience of the Jewish people under every conceivable variety of social, economic, and political order. Thus Rabbi Johanan declares that the biblical commandment which ordains the obligation of the Jew to return "the lost property of thy brother" applies to the convert as well, but his colleagues disagreed.

The welter of conflicting standpoints with regard to the status of the Jewish convert is another striking consequence of the failure to understand the nature of the Jewish group. As we have already noted in the Brother Daniel decisions of Israel's Supreme Court, only Justice Cohn clearly stated his conviction that Jews are a nation *kekhol hagoyim*—

"like all the nations." This doctrine, which is generally implicitly and more rarely explicitly stated, lies at the basis of most interpretations of Jewish nationalism. We cannot lose sight of the fact that Zionism has achieved the miracle of a reborn Israel. Nonetheless, it cannot be too strongly stressed that the doctrine of "a nation like all the nations" is profoundly at variance with the entire tenor of Jewish tradition.

The Jewish tradition has always fought the idea that Israel is a people like all others. On the contrary, the Torah stresses the uniqueness of Israel virtually from the moment of its birth at Mount Sinai. The book of *Exodus* declares: "Ye shall be unto Me a peculiar treasure among all the nations. Ye shall be unto Me a kingdom of priests and a holy nation." In *Numbers* we find Balaam's panegyric on Israel: "Behold, it is a people dwelling alone, not to be reckoned among the nations." *Deuteronomy* stresses this theme with matchless eloquence and power: "For thou art a holy people unto the Lord thy God: the Lord thy God hath chosen thee to be His own treasure, out of all peoples that are upon the face of the earth." David's expression of the same idea has entered the prayer book as a part of the authentic tradition: "Who is like unto Thy people Israel, one people unique upon the earth?" [2]

The Bible rarely, if ever, employs abstract conceptual categories of the kind that we associate with Greek speculative thought. Yet it is noteworthy that the word *le'um*—nation or nationality—is never applied to the Jewish people, though it occurs over thirty times in the Bible. Similarly, the word *goy*, which is even more frequent, is virtually never used to refer to the Jewish people and ultimately developed the connotation "non-Jew, Gentile." It is not accidental that in order to designate the Jews the Bible uses only the word *'am*, meaning "a people."

In our day, Martin Buber has trenchantly described this

uniqueness of the Jewish people: "Israel is not one member of the species 'nation.' It is the only example of the species 'Israel.' "

For the Bible and for all succeeding Jewish tradition, the essence of the uniqueness of Israel lay in its election—Israel has been chosen by God to be the witness of the Lord, the bearer of His word, as stated in *Leviticus:* "I shall be your God and ye shall be My people." The election of Israel is an article of faith that has often been denied, regretted, and even scorned, as in the famous quatrain: "How odd/of God/To choose/the Jews."

But the uniqueness of the Jewish people, quite aside from any belief in the election of Israel, is a basic fact of history. It cannot be ignored without doing violence to the past and misunderstanding the present.

This held true even in ancient times, when superficially the position of the Jewish people resembled that of its neighbors in possessing a land, a government, and a religion limited to itself alone. In this, the earliest period of Jewish experience, virtually all nations had group-religions expressive of their ethnic character, whether they were Babylonians, Egyptians, Syrians, Greeks, or Romans. Even then, however, Judaism was an ethnic religion "with a difference," set apart fundamentally from that of its contemporaries. From its inception, biblical religion possessed a strong universalistic outlook which transcended national boundaries. This trait is reflected in the early traditions of the origin of the human race depicted in *Genesis*, in the emphasis upon one God and His moral law embodied in the Decalogue, and in the persistent demand made even by the earliest prophets for righteousness from all men and nations, including their own people.

The history of Judaism reveals the uniqueness of its character. As Yehezkel Kaufmann has pointed out, biblical Judaism, the heritage of a tiny, weak nation clinging pre-

cariously to the shores of the eastern Mediterranean,
proved the only ethnic religion of the ancient world that
succeeded in winning the allegiance of millions of men who
were not ethnically Jews.

In the Middle Ages, the uniqueness of the Jewish people
became even more obvious. Here was a people able to survive and grow creatively during two thousand years of
exile, discrimination, and persecution, without land, government, or even central authority. No wonder the uniqueness of the Jewish people proved a source of misunderstanding, suspicion, and hatred. In his *Autoemancipation*,
Leo Pinsker accordingly suggested the need to "normal-
ize" Jewish life by return to the ancestral soil. Zionism
unfurled the banner of "the people of Israel to the land of
Israel" and achieved the major miracle of our age.

Undoubtedly, the extreme abnormality of medieval
ghetto existence has disappeared in the bright light of
Israel's independent life. But the realities of Jewish life *both
in Israel and in the Diaspora* belie the chimerical notion that
Jews are today "a nation like all the nations." The Jewish
people today is not a *goy* or a *le'um;* it is an *'am.* Israelis
constitute a *le'um* or "nationality"; Jews, an *'am,* or "people."

The Hebrew word *'am* derives from a Semitic root probably connoting "togetherness." Jews the world over today
differ in social outlook, political citizenship, economic
status, and religious attitude. Yet the overwhelming majority are conscious of the fact that they are members of one
people, sharing a common history and a sense of kinship inherited from the past, a common tradition and way of life
in the present, and a common destiny and hope for themselves and for the world in the future.

If we insist upon a modern sociological term, the Jews
may be described as a *religio-cultural-ethnic group.*

The link which binds them together is not political but

religio-cultural in essence, and the Jews' most sacred concept is the Torah, which is both their law and their lore, their culture and their code of practice, the basis of their way of life and their world view. This is true even for those Jews for whom it is the center from which they have diverged. What is crucial in this unique amalgam of kinship, culture, and faith is faith. That is why a Jew who insists that he belongs to another nation is still a Jew, while a Jew who adheres to another religion is no longer a Jew.

In sum, there are two fundamental truths concerning Jewish existence—*the uniqueness of the Jewish people and the centrality of the Jewish religion within the constellation of elements entering into Jewish belonging.* They are both illustrated by one other basic aspect of Jewish affiliation—the singular bond subsisting between Jews the world over and the Land of Israel.

No other group stands in a similar relationship to a country in which it is not domiciled. Consider the bond between Diaspora Jews and the State of Israel. On the one hand, the bugbear of "dual allegiance," which does not have the slightest basis in reality, may be dismissed as the invention of little minds. American Jews have no need to protest their wholehearted loyalty and allegiance to the United States. It is clear to all, except to those who refuse to see, that they have no political allegiance to the State of Israel, nor does the government of the young republic expect it of them.

On the other hand, American Jews do not look upon the State of Israel as the "old country," from which they have emigrated in order to avoid poverty, exploitation, discrimination, or political tyranny. It is not part of the receding past for them, as are Germany and Italy, Ireland and Russia for the millions of first-generation, second-generation, and third-generation Americans who originated in those lands. They have no childhood memories of Israel as *die alte heim* ("the old home").

Yet American Jews do not want to forget Jerusalem, or to weaken their ties to Israel. On the contrary, they wish to strengthen them in themselves and their children. There is a strong sense of proud identification with Israel which, it is hoped, will not weaken with time, but rather grow stronger. The bond is not one of personal origin or political loyalty: it is spiritual in essence—a link with the historic past of the Jewish people concentrated in the concept of the Holy Land, where the patriarchs, prophets, psalmists, and sages walked and created. This spiritual-cultural bond between world Jewry and the Land of Israel is unique. It is without analogy among any other people.

The recognition of the unique character of Jewish people, and this insight alone, holds the key to an understanding of the realities of the Jewish position throughout the world. These involve the three distinct but related areas of concern: The Diaspora Jew must grapple with the problem of his relationship to his fellow citizens in the land of his sojourn and citizenship, on the one hand, and to Israeli Jews on the other. And there is the question confronting Israeli Jews as to their relationship with Diaspora Jewry on the one hand and with their non-Jewish fellow citizens in the State of Israel, on the other. Somewhat more remote, but equally fundamental, is the abiding issue of the role of the State of Israel within the family of nations—whether Israel is to be merely another tiny focal point of nationalism in the Middle East or whether it has a world function, which derives from the imperatives of its extraordinary religious and ethical tradition.

If the principle of Israel *kekhol hagoyim* be adopted, we may reach a logical conclusion which most Jews, within Israel and outside, would find totally unpalatable. This possibility is described by the English Zionist, Joseph Heller, in his excellent book, *The Zionist Idea:* "Since religion does not belong to the characteristic features of nationality, it is at least theoretically conceivable that under different circumstances a distinct religious faith might no longer be an indispensable mark of the Jewish community." Such a state of affairs would be possible, however, only if the Jewish people were to commit spiritual suicide or, more mercifully, if it were to die and be resurrected as an Israeli nation.

That the possibility which Heller foresaw in theory was an impossibility in fact, was highlighted by the decision in the Brother Daniel case. Here was an accurate reflection of the sentiments of the vast majority of the Jewish people, both within the State of Israel and outside its borders.

It is only against the background of the true nature of the Jewish group as an *'am*, a religio-cultural-ethnic group, that we can hope to understand the attitude toward the Jew who converts to another faith that is manifest in traditional rabbinic law and in contemporary Jewish life.

When a Jew converts to another religion he cannot, by that act, undo his biological kinship with his Jewish ancestors and brothers. His physical origin is an irreversible fact, as untold numbers of converts and descendants of converts discovered to their cost when the Nazi persecutions began. This physical link binding Jews in an unbroken line to their ancestors, Abraham, Isaac, and Jacob, underlies the profound religio-ethical doctrine, "A Jew, even if he has sinned, remains a Jew."

This general principle is reenforced in Jewish law by two other considerations.

First is the undeniable fact that many, if not most, converts from Judaism in the past were driven to apostasy either by the threat of physical persecution or by the subtler, but equally potent power of the material advantages inherent in belonging to the dominant faith. However unheroic and self-seeking such converts might be, the hope remained that those who had deserted their ancestral faith might some day be won back to Judaism. This hope finds expression in those aspects of traditional Jewish law, referred to above, which continue to treat the convert as a Jew.

This "liberal" tendency naturally came to the fore when a convert actually reverted to Judaism. Always there were narrow-minded members of the community who wished to ostracize or at least penalize the repentant sinner. Maimonides, in his famous *Epistle to Yemen,* penned an eloquent plea to his Jewish brothers to remain steadfast in their loyalty to Judaism, while in his *Responsa* he urged forgiveness for those weaker members who had strayed from the fold but had returned. Rabbenu Gershom, "the Luminary of the Exile," ruled that a *Kohen* who returns to Judaism may continue to offer the Priestly Benediction in the congregation.

The second motive for treating the convert as legally Jewish relates to the high emphasis upon the sanctity of the marriage bond which was always basic to Judaism. The entire structure would be seriously weakened if the bond between husband and wife were to be declared null and void because a Jew had converted to another faith. To treat this sacred covenant lightly without due process of law might also add an additional roadblock to prevent the convert's return to Judaism. Moreover, since many cases of conversion in the past were compulsory, it would have been heartless to dissolve the marriage.

At the same time, in other areas the convert was treated as no longer a Jew. Jews who persisted in their attachment to Judaism in the face of all the blandishments and the threats leveled against them quite naturally reacted negatively to those who had taken the easier way. This psychological factor aside, Jewish law could not ignore the fact that the individual in question had turned his back on his tradition, severed his association with his people, and cut his link with Jewish destiny. Hence, Jewish law tended in many other areas to treat the convert as he wished to be treated—as a non-Jew.

In sum, the convert is unable to undo his physical kinship with the Jewish past. He has, however, surrendered the Jewish way of life in the present and his identification with Jewish destiny in the future. The ambivalence of Jewish religious law with regard to the convert is a reflection of the ambiguity of his position—he is apart from the Jewish people and yet still a part of it, alienated but not yet a total alien, separated but not completely severed. By his conversion, he cannot free himself of his *obligations* as a Jew. He has, however, forfeited his *privileges* as a Jew.

In modern times, the motivations of the past for conversion undoubtedly continue to operate. But a new factor has entered the situation. Today there are instances—and Brother Daniel is an example—of completely voluntary and sincere converts to Christianity or to other faiths. It is therefore entirely fair, and incidentally in conformity with the spirit of traditional Jewish law, to recognize that in the case of a convert of this type, the non-Jewish aspects of his present position should be granted primacy over the vestiges of his Jewish origin.

The State of Israel, to be sure, is a secular state, extending to citizens of various faiths and of none the equal protection of its laws. But the Law of Return of 1950 is obviously not an ordinance granting the right for *Israelis* to return to the land of Israel. That would be so self-evident as to be absurd. The Law of Return extends a special privilege to *Jews who are not Israelis*. It embodies a perhaps unconscious but totally justified recognition that each Jew, like the Jewish people as a whole, stands in a unique relationship to the State of Israel.

How can we explain the apparent paradox, which troubled Justice Berinson, that a Jewish atheist qualifies as a

Jew, whereas a Jewish convert to Christianity does not?
The truth is far deeper than is implied in the epigram that
atheism is also a form of theism. It resides in the recognition
that the point of departure for a Jewish nonbeliever lies in
Judaism. A Jewish agnostic or atheist shares his people's
history, its way of life and its sense of destiny, even if in
fragmentary and distorted form. The Jewish festivals are
his, and his day of rest in the State of Israel will be Satur-
day, not Sunday like the Christians or Friday like the
Mohammedans. It is true that he has surrendered what Jewish tradition regards as a basic and fundamental element
about God and the universe, its core of belief. Yet he has
not severed his link with the house of Israel. Moreover,
there is aways the hope that his children may return to a
fuller identification with the Jewish tradition, for he has
not completely cut the umbilical cord. We may well apply
to him the words written centuries ago by Maimon, the father of Maimonides: "I prefer to have a Jew who clings to
Judaism with his whole hand rather than a single finger.
But it is better that he hold on with a single finger than let
go altogether."

Quite otherwise is the situation of a convert to another
religion. He has identified himself with another historic
community, sharing not only its beliefs but its way of life
and its aspirations for the future. It is not merely that he
denies Jewish beliefs but that he affirms non-Jewish doctrines. It is not merely that he does not observe the Sabbath
and the festivals or hold sacred the *sancta* of Jewish observance, but that he observes alien festivals and Sabbaths
and venerates other *sancta*. He is therefore, and rightly so,
no longer a Jew and cannot claim the privileges of the Law
of Return which is applicable to Jews. He can be an Israeli,
for this secular status is open to men of every faith.

The Law of Return is no arbitrary caprice, no unthink-
ing legislative enactment; it is the direct consequence of

nearly four thousand years of history which has established this *'am*, this people, as unique upon the earth, standing in a special relationship to a tiny corner of earth which is forever holy.

A correct understanding of the unique character of the Jewish group also supplies the key for comprehending the attitude of Judaism toward the acceptance of proselytes into the Jewish fold. While both daughter-religions of Judaism, Christianity and Islam, are actively engaged in sending missionaries throughout the world to convert nonbelievers to their respective faiths, there is no such organized missionary activity among Jews. To be sure, Judaism has always made provision for non-Jews who sincerely wish to enter the Jewish community as proselytes. In modern times there has been a steady influx of men and women into Judaism, which is larger in extent than is generally supposed, though no figures are available. But at present and for hundreds of years past, the Jewish religion has not sought to persuade the world to accept its message. It is therefore widely believed, both by Jews and by non-Jews, that Judaism is characterized by a lack of interest in conversion, if not by downright opposition to it.

The truth of the matter is, however, quite otherwise.[3] The record of history makes it abundantly clear that in the greatest periods of Jewish life, notably in the creative ages in which the Bible and Talmud came into being, the Jews engaged in an active effort to propagate their faith among all men. In Jewish tradition, Ruth the Moabite girl who became the ancestress of King David, and Naaman, the Syrian general who was stricken with leprosy and learnt to revere the God of Israel, are the prototypes of the "righteous proselytes" who came to "nestle beneath the wings of the Divine Presence." In the period of the Second Temple, Queen Helene of Adiabene, a kingdom in Syria, was converted to Judaism, together with her whole household, and was one of the great benefactresses of her coreligionists in Judea. In the century after the destruction of the Temple by the Romans, a Roman nobleman, Aquila, who may have been a kinsman of Emperor Nero, was converted to Judaism and became a disciple of Rabbi Akiba. Aquila was the author of a remarkable translation of the Bible into Greek for the use of Greek-speaking Jews, after the older Septuagint had been preempted by the nascent Christian Church.

These and other famous converts aside, there were hundreds of thousands of intelligent Gentiles—Greeks, Romans, Syrians, and Egyptians—who no longer believed in the pagan faiths in which they had been reared. Thousands of them were profoundly attracted by the Jewish conception of One God, the lofty moral code of Judaism, and the beauty of its way of life. Many committed themselves to Judaism completely and were welcomed and absorbed into the Jewish community. Rabbinic sources call these converts "righteous proselytes." Others adopted most aspects of Judaism, without undergoing the full rites of conversion, though often circumcising their children at birth. This mass movement into Judaism reached its peak during the 400 years between 200 B.C.E. and 200 C.E., the centuries immediately before and after the rise of Christianity. This influx into Judaism was actively stimulated by Jews living in Palestine as well as in the Diaspora, as is clear from the complaint in the New Testament that the Pharisees, the accepted leaders of Rabbinic Judaism, "compass land and sea to make one proselyte" (*Matthew* 23:13).

After the destruction of the Temple by the Romans in the year 70, as Jews were scattered far and wide, some Jewish travelers and traders went to the distant corners of the earth, carrying their faith with them. Such exotic Jewish communities as the Yellow Jews of Kai-fung-foo in China, who became extinct only during the last century, the

Falashas or black Jews of Abyssinia, and the brown Jews of India represent pure racial types and are much more probably the result of Jewish proselyting activity than the products of intermarriage between Jewish settlers and the native population, though such unions undoubtedly took place.

It was not until Christianity became the dominant religion of the Western world that this Jewish missionary activity came to a halt. The medieval Church made it a crime for a Christian to accept Judaism, punishable even by death for the convert, as well as for his Jewish mentor. As a result, the average Jewish community in the Middle Ages found it more politic to discourage converts.

What is remarkable is that in spite of the perils involved in conversion, there were cases throughout the Middle Ages of men and women who found their way to Judaism and were accepted into the Jewish people, many of them dying as martyrs for their new faith. These included the father-confessor of Louis the Ninth of France; a warrior in the Crusades; a convert who became a distinguished Talmudic commentator; the wife of the mayor of Cracow; the Polish count Valentin Potocki, as well as countless humbler folk who traversed the same highway to what Judah Halevi called "the despised faith."

The most famous conversion to Judaism in the Middle Ages took place in Russia. It involved the entire royal court and a substantial part of the population of the kingdom of Chazaria, which occupied the extensive territory between the Volga and the Don rivers. For hundreds of years Chazaria was both an outpost of Judaism and—as we shall see below—the only state in Europe granting full religious tolerance for Christians and Mohammedans.

The list of accessions to Judaism can be carried on to the present day. The fact remains, however, that active organized missionary activity ceased in Judaism, primarily because of the pressures of the dominant faith, and secondarily, because of an atrophy of the talents required for the enterprise.

These sternly practical considerations were reenforced by a unique theory going back to the Talmud, and even earlier, to the Apocrypha—the doctrine of the Noachide Laws.

We shall have occasion later to explore the content of the Noachide Laws and their implications for the theory of religious liberty. Here it suffices to point out that traditional Judaism yields to no other religion in its conviction that it represents the true faith, so far as it is given to man to comprehend God and His purposes. But it never developed a Jewish counterpart to the Christian doctrine: *nulla salus extra Ecclesiam*, "no salvation outside the Church." While traditional Christianity taught that only those who accept the faith in the Saviour would be saved, Judaism never maintained that men and women outside the Jewish fold were doomed to damnation. On the contrary, Judaism declares that every human being is capable of attaining salvation. He who observes the cardinal religious and ethical principles embodied in the Seven Laws of the Sons of Noah has his "share in the world to come," without the necessity of converting to Judaism and accepting its specific system of beliefs and its extensive regimen of observances.

Today there is a widespread quest for a new faith among many sensitive men and women who were reared in traditional religion. This search may derive in part from a recognition that for all its great achievements and high aspirations, twenty centuries of Christianity have not succeeded in humanizing man. The sincerity and idealism of modern Christian teachers are beyond question. But perhaps men require a new emphasis, if not a different conception of man's nature and duty and of his relationship to the universe. Among those who are spiritually homeless in their nominal faith, some at least may feel that Judaism can supply this need. As we have noted, Judaism has always made provision for sincere converts seeking to enter its portals.

Now there is a division of opinion among Jews as to whether an active campaign to win accessions from the general community ought to be undertaken. It is scarcely likely that it would take the form of overt missionary or evangelical procedures. Even the advocates of the idea generally have in mind the creation of centers of information on Judaism that would be available to all inquirers, Jewish and non-Jewish alike.

Jewish tradition has insisted, as a prior condition for conversion, upon the importance of sincerity on the part of the would-be proselyte and his freedom from ulterior motives. In two fundamental respects Judaism poses difficulties for a would-be convert that he would not encounter in Christianity. In Judaism the accent is not merely upon a new set of beliefs, but upon a new pattern of practice that requires a complete transformation of one's way of life affecting every activity. Moreover, Judaism is an ethnic faith in which peoplehood is organically bound up with religion. When a proselyte becomes a Jew, he is not merely adopting a new religion but is also accepting membership in a new people. Because he shares the life of the Jewish people, the Jewish proselyte, like a "native son," prays to "the God of our fathers, Abraham, Isaac, and Jacob." The proselyte to Judaism has therefore taken on a much more difficult task than a convert to Christianity.

These inner spiritual hurdles do not exhaust the problems of the neophyte in Judaism. By his act he has voluntarily taken on all the external burdens of Jewish life. Discrimination and persecution, which have been the lot of the Jew through the ages, may have their ebb and flow, and our day may mark their low point, but anti-Semitism is by no means dead. The Talmud was very conscious of these disabilities when it declared: "The would-be proselyte in our day must be warned, 'Do you not know that Israel is aggrieved and persecuted, hounded and exposed to trouble?' " (*Yebamot* 47a).

When, however, the proselyte persists in his desire to enter the Jewish community, accepting the responsibilities of adherence to Judaism and the liabilities associated with the Jewish group, he becomes *Yisrael lekhol dabhar*, "An Israelite in every sense." Henceforth he is spiritually a descendant of Abraham, the first proselyte, bound in kinship to the Jewish people, besides sharing the religio-cultural tradition of Judaism as his heritage.

In sum, the status both of the proselyte to Judaism and of the convert from it are instances of the many problems in Jewish life that can be properly solved only if we recognize the unique character of the Jewish group.

The biblical description of Israelites as an *'am segullah* is rendered in the Authorized Version as "a peculiar people." In a sense not intended by the translators, the phrase highlights the truth that Jews cannot be subsumed under the categories applied to other aggregations of men.

This concept of the uniqueness of the Jewish people must be a cardinal doctrine for all Jews, believer and nonbeliever alike, who are not content with making obeisance to the Jewish past but strive to safeguard its present and build its future. The secular Jew can validate his faith in the uniqueness of Israel, as being the result of the specific Jewish historical experience, which has no analogy among other groups. Given an experience without precedent, the Jewish people developed a group character without parallel.

For the believing Jew, the uniqueness of Israel is at least equally real, but it is not completely explicable in naturalistic terms. For him, the special character and destiny of Israel points to the Divine election of Israel. History demonstrates, but does not explain, how and why this tiny people was singled out for a unique role in the life of mankind, to be the bearer of Torah, the living and suffering witness of God, serving at once as the symbol, the measuring rod, and the exemplar of man's humanity. In the face of the miracle and mystery of Israel's existence, and the glory and the tragedy of its survival, Jews need to remind themselves that they were promised not that the truth would be easy—but that as the seal of God, it would make them indestructible.

CHAPTER FIVE

JUDAISM
AND FREEDOM OF CONSCIENCE

UNDERLYING the far-flung struggle for the preservation of Judaism is the conviction that it possesses values and insights of great significance for mankind. A striking instance is the Jewish contribution to freedom of conscience. A detailed examination of this doctrine as it emerged in Judaism is justified not only because of its inherent interest but because of its direct bearing upon the prospects for Jewish survival in the modern world. For it is clear that the preservation of the tradition depends upon two factors. The first is internal—the recognition by Jews of the significance and value of their heritage and their consequent willingness to commit themselves to its cultivation and enhancement. The other factor is external—the creation by the majority group of a climate which makes it possible for Judaism to exist by right and not by sufferance as a respected and meaningful element in the spectrum of a pluralistic society.

Wherever the minority encounters the monolith of intolerance, whether it be the bigotry of an all-powerful church or the fanaticism of an all-powerful state, the survival of the tradition becomes a desperate struggle, often waged in secret against overwhelming odds. Even for the dominant groups in society, freedom of conscience is a *sine qua non* for religious health and vitality. For a religious minority, such as the adherents of Judaism, freedom of conscience is the very breath of life.

There is therefore a substantial measure of poetic justice in the historical fact, generally unknown or ignored, that biblical and rabbinic Judaism are the seedbed for a religious theory of freedom of conscience. To a far greater degree than the two other monotheistic faiths of the Western world, traditional Judaism evolved a doctrine of men's right to religious freedom. Nor did it remain on the level of abstraction. It was applied concretely to Christianity and Mohammedanism. Indeed, one of the most important religio-ethical values in the Jewish tradition lies precisely here—the demonstration that it is possible to unite fervent loyalty to one's own world view and way of life with a genuine recognition of the rights of others to differ.

The significance of this uniquely Jewish approach to other faiths is by no means merely historical. It may well help to buttress the position of religion in the free society of today and in the world community of tomorrow. For if religion is to survive in our times, it must learn how to combine depth of commitment with breadth of outlook—a consummation rarely achieved even today either by groups or by individuals.

Before we proceed to document the significant contribution of Judaism in this area, there is one important truth that needs to be recalled, particularly because of the strong tendency to ignore or deny it. Religion has made many great contributions to civilization, but freedom of religion is not among them. The ideal of religious liberty is essentially a gift we owe to the secularists. To be sure, there were individual, great-souled believers and a few religiously motivated societies which had recognized the ideal even earlier, but these were the exception, not the rule.

Perhaps the earliest instance in history is the Tartar kingdom of the Chazars in Central Russia, which lasted from the sixth to the tenth century. The rulers and upper classes were converted to Judaism in the eighth century, and they accorded full religious liberty to Christians and Moslems as well.[1] The Dutch kingdom established by William the Silent in the sixteenth century adopted the principle of toleration, though there were limitations to the doctrine in practice. Roger Williams, in establishing the colony of Providence Plantations, or Rhode Island, in the New World, made full freedom of conscience the basis of the commonwealth. The Catholic Lord Baltimore extended the right of worship to Protestants. But these were isolated and exceptional cases.

By and large the principle of freedom of conscience became widely held and increasingly operative only with the Age of Reason. We have already traced the major challenge to religion posed by the Enlightenment, which weighed the teaching and the practice of the Christian Church and found them both wanting. As a result, all of Western Europe in the eighteenth century reechoed to the cry of Voltaire, which was also his judgment on the Church: *Écrasez l'infâme,* "Crush the infamous one!"

Nor was the attitude of the eighteenth-century thinkers more favorable toward Judaism, as the relevant articles in the French *Encyclopédie* demonstrate. Quite the contrary. Here the hostility of the philosophers to accepted religious ideas was augmented by ignorance of Judaism, of which they knew nothing beyond the Bible. Moreover, Voltaire and his colleagues succeeded in retaining anti-Semitic attitudes even after they had surrendered any belief in the New Testament drama of salvation, which had originally engendered these anti-Jewish prejudices. This remarkable feat of dissociation has been repeated time and again by modern, "enlightened" people. As Israel Zangwill put it in a mordant epigram, "Many a Christian who is certain that Jesus never existed is sure that the Jews killed him."

Thus the ideal of freedom of religion came into being with the rise of secularism in the modern era. With the weakening of religious attachment among large segments of the population, came the conviction that "one religion is as good as another," in many cases a euphemistic restatement of the unspoken sentiment that one religion is as bad as another! But whatever its motivations, secularism is to be credited with making freedom of religion not only a working principle but also an ideal for modern man. In this sense, if we may adopt a phrase of Horace M. Kallen, secularism may be described as the will of God.[2]

We cannot fail to be grateful for this gift of the spirit. Yet when we examine the ideal of religious liberty on secular foundations, it becomes clear that it suffers from several grave limitations. Its first obvious weakness is that, given its secular origin, the principle of religious liberty would work best where religious loyalty is weakest or nonexistent. If the soil from which freedom of conscience grows is religious indifference, and if all religions are regarded as equal in value or in lack of value, it is obvious that the effectiveness of the principle will be gravely compromised for those who regard religion as of supreme significance in human life. This applies especially to those who regard their own religious tradition as possessing a unique measure of truth. Yet the history of mankind has shown that the doctrine of freedom of conscience is most essential in instances where religious loyalty is fervent and the danger of hostility to those outside the group correspondingly greater. Thus a secularly motivated doctrine of religious freedom can serve least where it is needed most.

Moreover, liberty of conscience in a secular framework

can create, at best, only a truce and not a state of peace among the religious groups. This truce is dependent upon the presence of a secular policeman, be it the state or a society in which religious loyalties are weak. On the other hand, if the members of a given social order hold their religious commitments fervently, neither law-enforcement agencies nor official opinion nor even a Constitution is likely to sustain religious liberty in practice for long. If, as Supreme Court Justice William O. Douglas declared, "We are a religious people whose institutions presuppose a Supreme Being," freedom of religion will be imperiled when Americans take their pretensions to religiosity seriously, and the doctrine remains rooted only in a secular outlook. Moreover, in a society where one religious group predominates in numbers and in power, liberty of conscience will be in grave jeopardy, if its foundations are purely secular.

Finally, even if religious believers accept the practice of religious liberty but do not relate it to their religious world view, it will have no binding power upon their consciences. They may extend freedom of religion to those who differ with them, but it will be, at worst, a grudging surrender to *force majeure,* and at best a counsel of prudence limited in scope and temporary in application. Unless a nexus is established between the religious tradition to which the believer gives his allegiance and the doctrine of religious liberty, he will still be in danger, even if he takes no overt act in that direction, of violating the Divine commandment, "You shall not hate your brother in your heart" (*Lev.* 19:17). Thus, the integrity of the ethical code by which he lives will be gravely compromised.

In sum, a secular doctrine of religious liberty suffers from all the liabilities to which secular morality is subject.[3] It can deal only with gross malfeasance and not with the subtler offenses of attitude and spirit—what the Talmud calls "matters entrusted to the heart." Nor can it supply the dynamic for an enduring allegiance to the ideal, even when it is within the power of a given group to impose its will on others.

For all these reasons, it is necessary for each religious tradition which takes seriously its obligation to live and function in a pluralistic society to go back to its own resources in order to discover what it can contribute to a religiously oriented theory of religious liberty.

At the outset, we need to recall that the concept of religious liberty possesses three distinct yet related aspects. Like so many ethical values, its roots lie in the instinct of self-preservation. In other words, *the first and oldest aspect of religious liberty is the right which a group claims for itself to practice its faith without interference from others.* The extension of this right to other individuals and groups is a great leap forward—both in time and insight, which requires centuries to achieve and at times remains unattained to the present day. Indeed, even in our time instances are not lacking of groups in virtually every denomination who define the right to religious liberty as the right to deny religious liberty to those who differ with them.[4]

In this respect religious liberty is no different from any basic right, like freedom of speech or assembly, which is first fought for and achieved by a group on its own behalf. Only later—and often halfheartedly—*freedom of conscience is extended to other groups who differ in belief and practice.* Finally, the third and most difficult stage in religious liberty emerges—and it is far from universal—when a religious group, dedicated *to its belief and tradition, is willing to grant freedom of thought and action to dissidents within its own ranks.*

The Jewish people has played a significant role in the emergence of religious liberty in its first aspect. With regard to the other two aspects, we believe that Judaism, rooted in the Jewish historical experience, has some significant insights to offer all men. Finally, no other large religious group has as great a stake in the present and future vitality of the doctrine as the Jewish community.

It is true that virtually every religious group finds itself a minority in one or another corner of the globe and unfortunately can point to infractions of its right to worship and propagate its faith. This is true of Protestants in Spain and Latin America, of Catholics in communist lands, and of Christians generally in Africa and the Middle East. On the other hand, as we have seen, Jews have the distinction of being a minority almost everywhere and always.

It is therefore eminently proper that the people for whom religious liberty is so fundamental be the first to take up arms in defense of this right. The earliest recorded war for religious liberty is the struggle of the Maccabees against the Syrian Greek King Antiochus Epiphanes, which broke out in 168 B.C.E. The Maccabean struggle was initiated not for the sake of political liberty, territorial aggrandizement, national honor, or booty. It represented the armed resistance of a group of Palestinian Jewry who were resolved to protect their religious faith and way of life in a world where a determined effort was being made to impose the uniform pattern of Hellenistic culture and Greek religion on the entire Middle East.

Had the Maccabees not fought, or had they fought and lost, the Hebrew Scriptures would have been destroyed, Judaism would have perished, Christianity would not have been born and the ideals of the Judeo-Christian heritage, basic to Western civilization, would have perished. There was therefore ample justification for the practice of the early Church, both in the East and West, which celebrated a festival on August 1, called "the Birthday of the Maccabees," testifying to the debt which Christianity, as well as

Judaism, owes to these early intrepid defenders of freedom of conscience.[5]

Thus the long struggle was launched for the first and oldest aspect of the concept of religious liberty. From that day to this, there have been communions which have conceived of religious liberty almost exclusively in terms of their right to observe their own beliefs and practices. For such a group the degree of religious liberty in a given society is measured by the extent to which it, and often it alone, is free to propagate its faith. Religious liberty is defined as "freedom for religion" and "religion" is equated with the convictions of the particular group.

This limited conception of religious liberty has a long and respectable history behind it. It is noteworthy that the only instances of forcible conversion to Judaism were carried out by descendants of the very same Maccabees who had fought for religious liberty. The Maccabean prince, John Hyrcanus (135-104 B.C.E.), forced the Idumeans, hereditary enemies of the Jews, to accept Judaism. His son, Aristobulus, Judaized part of Galilee in the northern district of Palestine.[6] These steps were dictated less by religious zeal than by practical considerations, a universal characteristic of mass conversions to our own day.

For centuries the doctrine that "error has no rights," unmitigated either by intellectual subtlety or by practical considerations, continued to hold sway. Heresy, that is to say, dissident views within dominant religious organisms, could be suppressed either individually or collectively, by peaceful persuasion or physical force. For heresy was viewed as illegitimate and sinful and hence worthy of the heaviest penalties. With the rise of Protestantism, which emphasized "private judgment" and the reading of the Bible as the unmediated Word of God, a multiplicity of sects emerged. What was equally significant, their legitimacy was, at least in theory, not open to question by the state. Religious liberty now became a practical necessity for the body politic as well as a burning issue for minority sects. Basically, it is to these minority groups that the world owes a debt for broadening the concept of religious liberty.

Yet by and large the ideal to which the various sects gave their loyalty was religious liberty for themselves. When the Puritans left England and later emigrated from Holland to Massachusetts, they were actuated by a passionate desire for freedom of conscience, but in this sense only. Protestant dissenters, Catholics, Jews, and nonbelievers could expect scant hospitality in the Bay Colony, and when any appeared within its borders, they were given short shrift. Various disabilities for non-Protestants survived in some New England states as late as the nineteenth century. Only slowly and painfully has religious liberty, which began as a practical policy designed to establish articles of peace among opposing sects, emerged as an ideal to which men have given their loyalty, quite independently of ulterior considerations.

Freedom of religion in an open society must necessarily presuppose two elements which were less obvious in the stratified societies of earlier days. *It must include religious equality*, for there can be no true religious liberty if the formal freedom of worship is coupled with legal, psychological, or financial liabilities. To be sure, the minority group cannot reasonably expect the same level of importance *in society* as the majority. But it has the right to demand that there be no restrictions or liabilities placed upon it *by the state*. In other words, full religious liberty means that the state will recognize the equality of all believers and nonbelievers, even though in society the relative strength of various groups will necessarily impose disadvantages upon the poorer or the less numerous sects.

To cite a hypothetical case, a Protestant worshiping in a

modest dissenters' chapel, or a Jew offering his devotions in a simple prayer room, could not reasonably object to the presence of a resplendent Catholic church in the community. But they would have legitimate grounds for objecting to a legal ordinance forbidding the building of a large Methodist church or an elaborate Jewish synagogue in the area.

There is one additional element essential to full religious freedom—*Religious liberty is not being truly safeguarded if it is purchased at the cost of religious vitality*. Frequently, the position of those who seek to maintain the traditional American concept of the separation of church and state is misunderstood, because it is attributed solely to the desire to avoid religious disabilities for minority groups. It is true that the position of religious believers who oppose utilizing the power and resources of the state to buttress the claims of religion may parallel that of secularists. But there is another, and at least equally deep, motivation for religiously committed men who regret the erosion of the principle of separation. They are sincerely concerned for the preservation of religious vitality. Here, majority groups have as direct an interest as the minority.

We have thus far dealt with the first aspect of the ideal of religious liberty—the right which every religious group claims for itself to practice its faith freely, without restriction or interference from others. With regard to the two other aspects of the ideal of religious liberty, more theoretic in character, we believe that the specific Jewish historic experience has significance for other religious groups, as well as for the preservation of a free society itself.

As we have noted, there is, theoretically at least, no problem with regard to freedom of conscience for those who maintain that all religions are equally good—or bad. But this is true only in theory. The history of twentieth-century totalitarianism has demonstrated that religious intolerance is far from impossible under communism and fascism. Religious bigots can learn many a lesson in practicing their craft from the antireligious bigots of our age. The contemporary savage persecution of religion by atheistic regimes makes the classic instances of religious intolerance of the past seem almost idyllic by comparison.

Nonetheless, it is true that the problem of evolving a theory of religious tolerance and putting it into practice is not easy for those believers who are convinced that they are the sole or chief repositories of religious truth and that those who differ from them are mistaken. In this connection the attitude of Jewish tradition is particularly interesting. It arose within a religion which believes profoundly that it is the authentic revelation of God and that all other faiths possess, by that token, a greater or lesser admixture of error. Since such a standpoint is widespread among communicants of most creeds, it should be useful to examine the theory and practice of Judaism both with regard to dissidents within its own community and toward non-Jews seeking to maintain their own creeds.

In order to comprehend the Jewish attitude toward religious differences within the community, it must be kept in mind that Judaism was always marked by a vast variety of religious experience, which is given articulate expression in the pages of the Hebrew Scriptures. The Hebrew Bible contains within its broad and hospitable limits the products of the varied and often contradictory activities of priest and lawgiver, prophet and sage, psalmist and poet. It reflects the temperaments of the mystic and the rationalist, the simple believer and the profound seeker after ultimate truth. The reason inheres in the fact that the Hebrew Bible is not a collection of like-minded tracts but, in the words of a great modern exegete, is "a national literature upon a religious foundation." [7]

This characteristic of the Bible set its stamp upon all suc-

ceeding epochs in the history of Judaism. It is not accidental that the most creative era in its history after the biblical
era, the period of the Second Temple, was the most "sect-
ridden." Even our fragmentary sources disclose the existence of the Pharisees, the Sadducees, the Essenes, and the
Zealots, to use Josephus' classic tabulation of the "Four
Philosophies." We know too from the Talmud, the Dead
Sea Scrolls, and other sources that each of these parties was
divided into various groups, which were often strongly opposed to one another. The Samaritans were also a significant group of dissidents, highly articulate in their divergence from a Jerusalem-centered Judaism. It was in this
atmosphere that the early Jewish sect of Christians first appeared, adding to the charged atmosphere of vitality and
variety in Palestinian Judaism. There were also countless
additional patterns of religious nonconformity in the various Diaspora communities.

To be sure, all these groups of Judaism shared many fundamentals in their outlook, but there were important divergences, both within each sect and among them.[8] The
Talmud records that among the Pharisees the differences
between the schools of Hillel and Shammai were deep-
seated and broke into physical violence at one point.[9]
Nonetheless, the Talmud declares, the Shammaites and the
Hillelites did not hesitate to intermarry and "He who observes according to the decision of Beth Hillel, like him
who follows the school of Shammai, is regarded as fulfilling
the Law," because "both these and the others are the words
of the Living God."[10] No such encomiums were pronounced on the Sadducees, who contradicted the fundamentals of normative Judaism. Those holding Sadducean
views were stigmatized as "having no share in the world to
come."[11] In this world, however, it is noteworthy, neither
they nor any others of these sects were ever officially excommunicated by the dominant Pharisees.

In the Middle Ages a variety of factors combined to contract this latitude of religious outlook. First, the constantly worsening conditions of exile and alien status required, it was felt, a greater degree of group homogeneity. Second, the basis for most of the earlier dissident viewpoints disappeared with the destruction of the Temple and the Exile. Thus the standpoint of the supernationalist Zealots was now totally meaningless, while that of the Sadducees, who centered their religious life in the Temple at Jerusalem, was completely irrelevant to the life of an exiled people.

Third, the widespread emphasis on religious conformity imposed by the medieval world on its aberrant sects also proved a model and example. Father Joseph Lecler points out in his massive two-volume work, *Toleration and the Reformation*, that St. Thomas Aquinas was relatively tolerant "toward pagans and completely intolerant toward heretics." St. Thomas explicitly stated that "to accept the faith is a matter of free will, but to hold it, once it has been accepted, is a matter of necessity."

No such precise and logical theory was ever elaborated in Judaism. The Jewish community lacked the power to compel uniformity of thought, even in the relatively rare instances when the leadership was tempted to embark upon such an enterprise. Nonetheless, some efforts *were* made to restrict religious liberty in the Middle Ages. The history of these undertakings is significant for the intrinsic nature of the Jewish tradition.

Somewhat paradoxically, the attempt to impose a measure of uniformity on religious belief was due to the emergence of medieval Jewish philosophy, which was nurtured in Aristotelianism, and to lesser degree in Platonism. Maimonides, the greatest Jewish thinker of the Middle Ages, confidently proposed a set of *Thirteen Principles*, which he hoped would serve as a creed for Judaism. Though his statement attained wide popularity, and was printed in the traditional prayer book as an appendix, lesser men did not hesitate to quarrel with both the content and the number of articles of belief in his *Creed*, and it never became an official confession of faith.

An even more striking illustration of the enduring vitality of the right to religious diversity in Judaism may be cited. Uncompromisingly rationalistic as he was, Maimonides declared that to ascribe any physical form to God was tantamount to heresy and deprived one of a share in the world to come. Nowhere is the genius of Judaism better revealed than here. On the same printed page of Maimonides' *Code* where this statement is encountered, it is challenged by the comment of his critic and commentator, Rabbi Abraham ben David of Posquières, who writes: "Better and greater men (than Maimonides) have ascribed a physical form to God, basing themselves on their understanding of Scriptural passages and even more so on some legends and utterances, which give wrong ideas." [12] The critic's standpoint is clear. Rabbi Abraham ben David agrees with Maimonides in denying a physical form to God, but he affirms the right of the individual Jew to maintain backward ideas in Judaism without being read out of the fold on that account! The right to be wrong is the essence of liberty.

Nevertheless it is clear that the spirit of medieval Judaism was far less hospitable to religious diversity than was rabbinic Judaism in the centuries immediately before and after the destruction of the Temple. Thus, while none of the earlier sects was ever excommunicated, the medieval Karaites who rejected the authority of the Talmud in favor of the letter of Scripture were excommunicated by various individual scholars. At the same time, other scholars refused to invoke the ban against them and ultimately a more lenient attitude prevailed.[13]

Excommunication against religious diversity was invoked

again in the eighteenth century. This time the target was Hasidism, a pietistic folk movement which arose in Eastern Europe. Ultimately, the sect abated its hostility toward rabbinical Judaism. Today the Hasidim and their rabbinical "opponents," together with a mediating group, all live relatively peaceably within the household of Orthodox Judaism.

In the nineteenth century, when the Reform movement first began to appear in Central Europe, some Orthodox rabbis in Central and Eastern Europe sought to stem the tide by invoking the ban against the innovators. It had proved largely ineffective in the field of ideas even in the Middle Ages; now, it was completely useless. It served only to drive deeper the wedge between the traditionalists and the nontraditionalists, and was tacitly abandoned.

In sum, religious liberty within the Jewish community exists *de facto*. It is recognized *de jure* by all groups in Reform and Conservative Judaism and by substantial elements in Orthodoxy as well.

It need hardly be added that divergences among the groups—and within them—are often sharp, and the personal antagonisms among some of the advocates of different positions are all too frequently even sharper. The upsurge of "religiosity" which followed in some quarters in the wake of the irruption of Nazi savagery and the mass bestiality of World War II had a powerful impact upon Jews as well as upon Christians. The tendency toward extreme pietism reappears after major catastrophes with so much regularity that it may be called a "law" in Jewish history.[14] It has strengthened the tendency to withdrawal and insulation against the world among many survivors of the Hitler holocaust and exacerbated their antagonism to all those outside their particular group. This spirit is very much in evidence today, but it is a mood of the day, if not of the moment, and it will pass. If history is any guide, these attitudes of isolation and hostility will be softened with time, as a fund of gentler experience accumulates. In any case, the harrowing events of the last three decades cannot abrogate the tradition of three millennia.

An observation is in order with regard to the status of religion and the state in Israel. The Israeli Cabinet includes a Minister of Religions (in the plural), who is charged with the supervision and the maintenance of the "holy places" of all the three great religions and with the support of their institutional and educational requirements. It is paradoxical but true that at present there is full freedom of religion in Israel for everyone—except for Jews! Catholic and Protestant Christianity, Islam and Bahai, all enjoy the fullest freedom of expression, including the opportunity for zealous missionary activity among Jews, which has aroused not a little antagonism. In addition to the Minister of Religions, Israel has three Chief Rabbis, who are of unimpeachable Orthodoxy, except for those Orthodox groups who deny their authority!

With the Chief Rabbinate as its symbol, Orthodoxy is the only officially recognized Jewish religious group in Israel today. Yet here too the innate tradition of dissent finds uninhibited expression. Thus, when the new and magnificent headquarters of the Chief Rabbinate was erected in Jerusalem, many of the leading Orthodox scholars announced that it was religiously prohibited to cross the threshold of the building! Side by side with these tensions within Israeli Orthodoxy are various other groups—Reform, Conservative, and Reconstructionist—representing a wide spectrum of modernism. In spite of harassment and opposition, they have already established a foothold in the country and ultimately will demand and receive full recognition.

No long-term conclusions may therefore be drawn from the present union of religion and state in Israel. It is partial and subjected to increasing strain and stress. Whether the ultimate pattern of religion-state relationships will approximate the American structure is problematic, though the American experience is frequently invoked as an ideal. The ultimate disestablishment of religion in any sectarian form is, however, inevitable.

The conclusion is unassailable that the nature of Judaism, buttressed by its historic experience, makes the freedom of religious dissent a recognized reality for virtually all members of the community *de facto,* even by those who would not recognize it *de jure.*

Of more general interest than the attitude of Judaism toward religious divergence in its own midst is the concept of religious liberty for other creeds, elaborated by the Jewish tradition.

This attitude derives, in large measure, from another unique characteristic of the Jewish tradition, which is frequently misunderstood not only by those outside the Jewish community but by many who are within it. This trait, deeply rooted in normative Judaism, is the balance between particularism and universalism.[15] The Jewish conception of freedom of religion is the resultant of two forces that superficially appear as contradictory—the retention of the specific national Jewish content in the tradition on the one hand, and on the other, an equally genuine concern for the establishment among all men of the faith in One God and obedience to His religious and ethical commands.

It is frequently argued that with the appearance of Judaism intolerance became a coefficient of religion. It is undoubtedly true that in a polytheistic world view, tolerance of other gods is implicit, since there is always room for one more figure in the pantheon, and the history of religious syncretism bears out this truth. On the other hand, the emergence of belief in One God necessarily demands the denial of the reality of all other deities. The "jealous God" of the Old Testament who forbids "any other gods before

Me" therefore frequently became the source of religious intolerance. So runs the theory.[16]

Now it is true that Judaism was strongly exclusivist in its attitude toward paganism. It insisted upon the uncompromising unity of God and refused to admit even a semblance of reality to other gods. Nonetheless, biblical Judaism reckoned with the existence of paganism from two points of view. Though logicians might have recoiled in horror from the prospect, the fact is that Hebrew monotheism, the authentic and conscious faith in the existence of One God, did accord a kind of legitimacy to polytheism—for non-Jews. In part this may have derived from a recognition of the actual existence of flourishing heathen cults. In far larger degree, we believe, it was a consequence of the particularist emphasis in Judaism which, being dedicated to preserving the specific group character of the Hebrew faith, was led to grant a similar charter of legitimacy to the specific *ethos* of other nations, which always included their religion.

Whatever the explanation, the fact is clear. No book in the Bible, not even *Isaiah* or *Job*, is more explicitly monotheistic than *Deuteronomy*: "Know therefore this day, and consider it in thine heart, that the Lord He is God in heaven above, and upon the earth beneath; there is none else" (4:39). Yet the same book, which warns Israel against polytheism, speaks of "the sun, the moon and the stars . . . *which the Lord thy God has assigned to all the nations under the sky*" (4:19, comp. 29:25). Thus the paradox emerges that the particularist element in Judaism proved the embryo of a theory of religious tolerance.

The second factor that helped to accord a measure of value to non-Jewish religion is one more congenial to sophisticated religious thinkers. A broad-minded exponent of monotheism would be capable of recognizing, even in the pagan cults against which Judaism fought, an imperfect, unconscious aspiration toward the one living God. Perhaps the most striking expression of this insight is to be found in the postexilic Prophet Malachi: "For from the rising of the sun to its setting, My name is great among the nations; and in every place incense is burnt and pure offerings, for great is My name among the nations, says the Lord of hosts" (1:11).

Nor is this the only instance in our biblical sources of broad-gauged universalism. The human sympathy of the author of *Jonah,* who exhibits the pagan sailors in a far more favorable light than he does the fugitive Hebrew prophet, the warm compassion of the book of *Ruth,* and the breadth of view of *Job,* which pictures the patriarch not as a Hebrew observer of the Torah but as a non-Jew whose noble creed and practice are described in his great "confession of integrity" (chap. 31), all testify to the fact that it was possible for Jews to maintain the unity and universality of God, while reckoning with the values inherent in the imperfect approximations to be found in the pagan cults.

Thus the two apparently contradictory elements of the biblical world view, the emphasis upon a particularist ethos and the faith in a universal God, both served as the matrix of a highly significant theory of religious tolerance in post-biblical Judaism. It is noteworthy that this concept was contemporaneous with a steady and unremitting effort to counteract the blandishments of paganism and win all men for Jewish monotheism through the use of persuasion. On the one hand, the biblical *Deutero-Isaiah,* the apocryphal *Sibylline Oracles,* the philosopher Philo of Alexandria, indeed the entire apologetic literature of Hellenistic Judaism sought to win the allegiance of men for the one living God of Israel. On the other hand, we encounter evidence in the pre-Christian period, perhaps as early as the third century B.C.E., of one of the most distinctive concepts of monotheistic religion, the doctrine of the Noachide Laws. The Apocryphal *Book of Jubilees,* written before the beginning of the Christian Era, attributes to Noah, who was not a Hebrew, a code of conduct binding upon all men:

In the twenty-eighth jubilee, Noah began to enjoin upon his son's sons the ordinances and commandments and all the judgments that he knew and he exhorted his sons to observe righteousness and to cover the shame of their flesh and to bless their Creator and honor father and mother and love their neighbor and guard their souls from fornication and uncleanness and all iniquity. (*Jubilees* 7:22)

This injunction is elaborated in the Talmud under the rubric of the Laws of the Sons of Noah.[17] According to this rabbinic view, all human beings, by virtue of their humanity, are commanded to observe at least seven fundamental religious and moral principles. These commandments include the prohibition of idolatry, sexual immorality, murder, and theft; the avoidance of blasphemy and of cruelty to animals by eating the limb of a living creature; and the establishment of a government based on law and order. When these principles, upon which all civilized society depends, are observed, Judaism regards the non-Jew as worthy of salvation, no less than the Jew who observes the entire rubric of Jewish law. Hence there is no imperative need for the non-Jew to accept the Jewish faith in order to be "saved."

These Laws of the Sons of Noah, it may be noted, seem to be referred to in the *New Testament* as well: "But that we write unto them, that they abstain from pollutions of idols and from fornication, and from things strangled, and from blood. . . . That ye abstain from meats offered to idols, and from blood and from things strangled and from fornication: from which if ye keep yourselves, ye shall do well. Fare ye well!" (*Acts* 15:20, 29).

This doctrine of the Noachide Laws is extremely interesting from several points of view. It represents in essence a theory of universal religion which is binding upon all men. Characteristically Jewish is its emphasis upon good actions rather than upon right belief as the mark of the good life. Ethical living rather than creedal adherence is the decisive criterion for salvation. Its spirit is epitomized in the great rabbinic utterance: "I call Heaven and earth to witness, that whether one be Gentile or Jew, man or woman, slave or free man, the divine spirit rests on each in accordance with his deeds." [18] In its all-encompassing sweep, this passage recalls the famous words of Paul, "There is neither Jew nor Greek, neither bond nor free, there is neither male nor female, for ye are all one in Christ Jesus." [19] Significantly, the equal worth of all men in the rabbinic formulation does not derive from common doctrinal belief nor does it depend upon it. It requires only loyalty to a code of ethical conduct.

Many contemporary religious thinkers are now seeking a theory which will combine complete loyalty to a specific tradition while accepting wholeheartedly the postulates of a democratic society, which is committed to pluralism as a reality and to religious liberty as a good. The issue is one which profoundly agitates the free world because of its practical importance in government and politics.

There is more than academic interest, therefore, in this rabbinic adumbration of a theory of religious tolerance resting upon a concept of "natural law." This doctrine of the Noachide Laws, be it noted, was not the product of religious indifference. It arose among devotees of a traditional religion who not only loved their faith but believed that it alone was the product of authentic Revelation. Yet they found room for faiths other than their own in the world, as of right and not merely by sufferance.

The principle of the Noachide Laws had originated in a pagan world. It obviously proved even more valuable when two monotheistic religions, Christianity and Islam, replaced paganism. Both "daughter-faiths" sought energetically to displace the mother and deny her authenticity. The mother-faith sought to repulse these onslaughts as effectively as possible by calling attention to what she regarded as their errors. But she did not, on that account, ignore the elements of truth which her younger and more aggressive offspring possessed.

The attitude of Judaism in the Middle Ages toward these two religions necessarily differed with the personality of each particular authority, his environment, and his own personal experience. The proximity of the Christian and the Jewish communities in Europe, and the consequent economic and social relationships upon which Jewish survival depended, compelled the early medieval rabbinic authorities to reckon with reality. In practice, if not in theory, they could not maintain the attitude that Christians were pagans and that all the restrictions upon intercourse with idolators enjoined in the Talmud could be summarily applied to them.

Originally, the medieval authorities modified the earlier Talmudic ordinances regarding pagans on a piecemeal, *ad hoc* basis, changing only such specific practices as affected the livelihood of Jews.[20] Ultimately, a more far-reaching and comprehensive revision of attitude toward Christianity and Christians emerged. It is striking that this positive result was the consequence of one of the most negative aspects of medieval Jewish-Christian relations—the public religious disputations forced upon Jews.[21] These debates compelled Jews to think through the general principles governing their attitude toward non-Jews. It became clear that there were significant differences between the pagans of antiquity, to whom the Talmud refers as "idolators," and the Christians who were their contemporaries in the Middle Ages.[22]

Thus the tragic disputation convened in Paris in 1240 between the convert Nicholas Donin and four Jewish representatives led to the public burning of twenty-four carloads of Hebrew books. The chief Jewish spokesman was Jehiel ben Joseph of Paris, who was assisted by Moses of Coucy. It is a tribute to the greatness of Moses' spirit that in spite of this grim exhibition of fanaticism, he developed a new insight into the character of the dominant faith, which was undoubtedly stimulated by his participation in the debate. Time and again he called upon his brethren to maintain scrupulous ethical standards in dealings with Christians, basing himself on broad religious and moral considerations.[23] Not expediency but regard for the honor of Israel and the avoidance of *Hillul Hashem*, "the desecration of the Holy Name," became the fundamental motivations.[24]

The practical need for a *modus vivendi* between Jews and Christians could not be denied, since they lived in closest proximity with one another throughout Europe. Simultaneously, the outlines of a theory of religious tolerance were being laid by Jewish thinkers living in Mohammedan as well as in Christian countries. The teaching of the second-century Talmudic sage, Rabbi Joshua, "There are righteous among the Gentiles who have a share in the world to come," [25] was slightly but significantly broadened by Maimonides into the generalization, "The righteous among the Gentiles have a share in the world to come." [26] Thus the principle that salvation was open even to those outside the Jewish fold remained normative and served as the basic principle underlying the Noachide Laws. The medieval poet and philosopher, Judah Halevi, wrote, "These peoples [i.e., Christianity and Islam] represent a preparation and preface to the Messiah for whom we wait, who is the fruit of the tree which they will ultimately recognize as the roots which they now despise." [27]

Rabbi Menahem Meiri, who lived in thirteenth-century France when several expulsions of Jews from that country took place, wrote, "Those among the heathen of the ancient days who observe the seven Noachide precepts, i.e., refrain from idol worship, desecration of God's name, robbery, incest, cruelty to animals, and have courts of justice, enjoy the same rights as Jews; how much the more so in our days, when the nations are distinguished by their religion and respect for law! We must, however, treat equally even those who have no systems of law, in order to sanctify the Name of God." [28] He distinctly declares that "in our days idolatry has ceased in most places," and describes both Muslims and Christians as "nations disciplined by the ways of their religions." [29]

Moreover, even the trinitarian concept of Christianity, which Judaism emphatically repudiated as impugning the Unity of God, was not generally regarded as sufficient to deny to Christianity the character of a monotheistic faith. The twelfth-century Talmudic commentator, Rabbi Isaac the Tosafist, set forth a legal basis for the view that belief in the Trinity was legitimate for Christians in his statement: "The children of Noah are not prohibited from *shittuf*, i.e., associating the belief in God with that in other beings." [30] This utterance achieved such wide scope and authority that it was frequently attributed by later scholars to the Talmud itself.

Maimonides, with his penchant for systematic canons of thought, was strongly critical both of Christianity and of Islam. Living all his life in Islamic countries, with few direct contacts with Christians, he tended to react negatively to the trinitarianism of Christianity and to its Messianic claims for Jesus as the Saviour. On the other hand, the uncompromising emphasis upon the unity of God in Mohammedanism, with which he was in constant contact, gave him a greater degree of tolerance for Islam, though he castigated the sensuality of the Prophet Mohammed. Even the adoration of the Ka'abah, the black stone of Mecca, was regarded by Maimonides as a vestige of polytheism which had been reinterpreted in Islam, a remarkable anticipation of modern scholarly attitudes.

In a passage in his great code, *Mishneh Torah*, which appears mutilated in the printed texts because of the censor, Maimonides rejects the claim that Jesus was the Messiah, on the ground that he failed to fulfill the Messianic function as envisioned in Scripture and tradition. He then proceeds:

"The thought of the Creator of the world is beyond the power of man to grasp, for their ways are not His ways and their thoughts are not His thoughts. All the words of Jesus the Nazarene and of Mohammed, who arose after him, came into being only in order to make straight the road for the King Messiah, who would perfect the world to serve God together, as it is said, 'Then I shall turn all the peoples into a clear speech, that they may all call upon the Lord and serve Him shoulder to shoulder.'

"How is that to be? The world has already been filled with the words of the Messiah, and the words of the Torah and the commandments. And these words have spread to the furthermost islands among many people uncircumcised of heart or of flesh, who now discuss the Commandments of the Torah. Some declare that these commandments were true, but are now no longer obligatory and have fallen into decline, while others declare that there are secret meanings within them, not according to their obvious intent, and that the Messiah had come and disclosed their secret connotations.

"But when the true King Messiah will arise, he will succeed and be raised to glory and then they will all return and recognize they had inherited falsehood, and that their Prophets and ancestors had misled them." [31]

Elsewhere Maimonides declares that Christians are idolators because of their trinitarian beliefs.[32] In this regard, he goes further than the warrant of his rabbinic sources. Nor was his attitude shared by most of his contemporaries. His great predecessor Saadia (882–942), the first great figure in medieval Jewish philosophy, who also lived under Islam, declared that the Christians' belief in the Trinity is not an expression of idolatry but the personification of their faith in life, power, and knowledge.[33] Thus it is clear that in his negative view Maimonides not only ignored the Talmudic passage quoted above but was at sharpest variance with Jewish scholars like Rashi and Meiri, who lived in Christian countries, knew Christians at first hand, and recognized their deeply rooted belief in the One God.

Later rabbinic authorities like Moses Rivkes, Hayyim Yair Bacharach (1638–1702), and Rabbi Jacob Emden (1697–1776) explicitly recognized a common tradition linking Judaism and Christianity, when they pointed out that Christians believed in God, the Exodus, Revelation, the truth of the Bible, and *creatio ex nihilo*.[34]

In the eighteenth century Moses Mendelssohn wrote a famous reply to the Protestant minister, Johann Casper Lavater. In it, he expounded the traditional Jewish doctrine, speaking in the accents of eighteenth-century Enlightenment:

"Moses has commanded us the Law; it is an inheritance of the congregation of Jacob. All other nations we believe to be enjoined to keep the law of nature. Those conducting their lives in accordance with this religion of nature and of reason are called 'virtuous men from among other nations,' and these are entitled to eternal bliss (*sind Kinder der ewigen Seligkeit*)."

There was an obvious apologetic intent and a consequent exaggeration in his next statement:

"The religion of my fathers, therefore, does not desire to be spread. We are not to send missions to Greenland or to the Indies in order to preach our faith to these distant nations. The latter nation, in particular, observing as it does the law of nature better than we do here, according to reports received, is in the view of our religious doctrines an enviable nation."

It is true that an active missionary campaign has not been carried on in Judaism ever since the pre-Christian centuries, when Hellenistic Judaism won untold pagans for "reverence for God" and thus helped lay the foundation for the rapid spread of Christianity. In the Middle Ages the external facts of history united with the inner nature of Judaism to preclude large-scale efforts to win non-Jews to Judaism.

As we have noted, some voices are being raised in the Jewish community in favor of an active campaign to bring the message of Judaism to the non-Jewish world, though without employing conventional missionary techniques.

For several years, an active group called the Jewish Information Society with headquarters in Chicago has sought to disseminate the teachings of Judaism to all and sundry. Efforts by individuals have also not been lacking. In 1965 the Union of American Hebrew Congregations, the parent body of Reform Judaism, formally endorsed the idea of an active campaign to propagate Judaism in the general community. Both in Reform circles and elsewhere, among religious leaders and the laity, the issue is being warmly debated. But both the proponents and the opponents of the idea are at one in recognizing the legitimacy of non-Jewish faiths and the availability of salvation to all who observe the basic spiritual and ethical principles embodied in the Noachide Laws. Jewish teachers of all schools of thought wholeheartedly affirm the right of all men to the fullest liberty in religious practice and belief.

The attitude of Judaism toward the three aspects of religious liberty may therefore be summarized as follows:

1. Judaism insists on total freedom of religious belief and practice for itself, which includes full equality before the law, with no pressure, overt or subtle, being used to persuade Jews to attenuate vital religious commitment, which is to be freely given or not at all.

The millennial experience of Jewish disability and exile in the ancient and the medieval world has strengthened the Jewish attachment to freedom of conscience. In addition, the modern world has demonstrated that the material and intellectual position and progress of Jews, both individually and collectively, is most effectively advanced in an atmosphere of religious liberty.

2. Judaism accepts the existence of differences within the Jewish community and accords to dissidents the right to their own viewpoint and practice, at least *de facto.*

The deeply ingrained individualism of the Jewish character, its penchant for questioning, and its insistence upon rational conviction, have made dissent a universal feature of the Jewish spiritual physiognomy. As a result, all groups have achieved freedom of expression and practice. Though efforts to limit or suppress this liberty of conscience among Jews have not been totally lacking and undoubtedly will recur in the future, they are invariably accompanied by a bad conscience on the part of the Jewish apostles of intolerance. They thus reveal their weak roots in the tradition that they are ostensibly defending and betray their predestined failure to achieve their ends.

3. Judaism recognizes the existence of other religions among men *de jure* and their inherent right to be observed. To be sure, there inheres a measure of naïveté, as there is of oversimplification, in Albert Einstein's utterance, "I thank God that I belong to a people which has been too weak to do much harm in the world." But more than mere incapacity inheres in the Jewish attitude toward religious liberty. The balance between the universal aspirations of

Judaism and its strong attachment to the preservation of its group character impelled it to create a theory that made room in God's plan—and in the world—for men of other convictions and practices. This insight has remained basic to the Jewish outlook.

The great monotheistic faiths, Christianity and Islam, which are so intimately linked to Judaism in their origins, content, and historical experience, occupy a special place in the hierarchy of religious truth. Many modern Jewish religious thinkers, following in the footsteps of their medieval predecessors, go further and see in the rise and progress of Christianity and Islam the sign of the Divine plan for the salvation of mankind. But the right of men to profess and practice their faith, whatever it may be, is universally recognized.

All three elements in Jewish experience, tradition, temperament, and history have united to make religious freedom, both for the Jewish community and the larger family of mankind, an enduring ideal and not merely a temporarily prudential arrangement. Undoubtedly Jews have fallen short of the lofty standards of their tradition in this as in other respects. Yet by and large Jews have remained loyal to the ideal of freedom of conscience, not only for themselves but for all men.

CHAPTER SIX

JUDAISM

IN THE CHRISTIAN WORLD VIEW

THE EVENTS of the past decades, both in Germany and in the United States, have demonstrated that the cultivation of "good will" is not enough in an age of crisis. To be sure, a friendly personal attitude toward men of different religious and racial backgrounds is highly praiseworthy. But it is not likely to survive the buffetings of adverse circumstance or the strains of group tensions, if it is purely emotional. What is required is an intellectual and moral base for good will, rooted in the conscious recognition of the right of all men to be different. A virile spirit of brotherhood and mutual regard between Christians and Jews must rest upon an understanding by each of the content and spirit of the religio-ethical traditions of the other. Moreover, the conventional "interfaith" stress upon "the things that unite us," genuine though they be, bypasses all the elements of divergence which are the breeding grounds of ill will and prejudice and supply the rationale for discrimination and persecution.

As we have seen, Judaism offers a striking illustration of the possibility of coupling a fervent attachment to one's own tradition with a recognition of the rights of other men to divergent patterns of belief and action. In an age striving for ecumenicism, the Jewish attitude toward Christianity, discussed in the last chapter, should therefore interest Christians who are striving to foster mutual respect both within the various branches of the Church and vis-à-vis the non-Christian world.

It must be confessed, however, that the importance of the Jewish attitude toward Christianity is primarily theoretical. Since Jews constitute a minority group everywhere in the world except in the State of Israel—and even there they are conscious of being a tiny island in an Arab sea—they do not possess either the power or the influence to be determining factors in the destiny of twentieth-century man. By and large, Jews are far more likely to be on the receiving end than on the dispensing end of ill will and prejudice. To set up a totally impossible hypothesis, even if Jews were filled with a violent antipathy toward Christianity and its devotees, they would be able to do little or nothing to give practical expression to their hostility or to affect the lot of the dominant majority. This observation does not, of course, imply that Jews are free from the moral and intellectual obligation to understand the content of Christianity and its basic concerns.

On the other hand, the Christian has an obligation to strive after an understanding of Jews and Judaism not only for moral and intellectual reasons, but on compelling practical grounds—because it is a matter of life or death for the Jewish people. There is a categorical imperative for Christians to seek to penetrate to the genuine spirit and content of Judaism and to the innermost attitudes and emotions of their Jewish fellow citizens, precisely because the majority has the power to work its will upon the minority.

The time is long overdue for eschewing the body of prejudices, whether theological or atheistic, which constantly reappear in new guise and are heralded as "a fresh look" or "a new approach" to "the Jewish problem." Nor is much help to be gleaned from the romantic philo-Semitism of men of good will that bears little relationship to the realities of Jewish life. In sum, neither Shakespeare's Shylock nor Sir Walter Scott's Rebecca, neither George Eliot's Daniel Deronda nor Charles Dickens' Fagin, how-ever touched up or modernized, can serve as an authentic portrait of the Jew. As Berton Braley wrote in his sonnet "To a Photographer":

> This is not I—this fatuous thing you show,
> Retouched and smoothed and prettified to please;
> Put back the wrinkles and the lines I know;
> I have spent blood and brain achieving these.
> Out of the pain, the struggle and the wrack,
> These are the scars of battle—put them back!

It is not easy for Christians to achieve a genuine under-standing of Judaism and the bearers of the tradition. The task will call upon all the resources of integrity and intelli-gence of the Christian community, and will need to be car-ried on in every domain of the private and public sector. The process should begin with the youth in the schools and must be intensified in the universities and the seminaries where the religious teachers of tomorrow are being trained. For it is a truism that the philosophy of education cher-ished by any society represents its conception of the ideal future. What the school seeks to realize is men's vision of tomorrow, sufficiently close to the present to be within the realm of realization, and sufficiently better than the present to fire the hearts and minds of men.

In asking what role Judaism should occupy in contempo-rary education, both general and religious, we are in effect asking what attitude shall the people of the Western world adopt toward the Jewish heritage and its living

exemplars in the twentieth century. The answer cannot
be given in the simple black-and-white terms popular in
the past. Judaism impinges upon the life and thought of the
modern world in at least four related yet distinct areas,
each of which needs to be delimited and taken into account:

A. *For its own sake, Christianity must maintain and
deepen its understanding and attachment to the Hebrew
Scriptures.* This should include not merely a familiarity
with the text and content of the Old Testament but a
knowledge of the three-thousand-year-old tradition of biblical interpretation in Judaism as well. This is desirable for
the laymen; for teachers of religion it is indispensable.
Today it is clear that Marcionism in any form, which
denies the sanctity and authority of the Old Testament,
leads to a fatal distortion of the Christian message and that
a Christianity cut loose from its roots in the Hebrew Scriptures has neither strength nor staying power. When the
early Church stigmatized Marcionism as a heresy in the second century, it revealed its essential healthy-mindedness. In
our day the bloody neo-Marcionism of Aryan Christianity
in Nazi Germany has demonstrated that the attempt to divorce the Christian world view from the Hebrew Scriptures is a heresy that is finally expiated in blood.

Moreover, what is needed is the full Old Testament, not
an expurgated or abridged selection. Scholars like Professor
W. S. Davies have pointed out that modern scholarship
understands that the biblical heritage of Christianity is not
restricted to the prophets of Israel but must include the
Law, which tended to be downgraded in Christian circles.
In Professor Davies' words, "The agony of our time has
made it easier for us to do justice to the legal tradition in
Judaism." [1]

We may go a step further. The Hebrew canon recognizes three sections in the Hebrew Scriptures. By the side

of the Torah and the Prophets, the Bible contains the Hagiographa, which enshrines the products of biblical wisdom. How much religious depth would Christianity lose without the *Psalms* and how much narrower would its intellectual horizons be without the books of *Proverbs, Job,* and *Ecclesiastes!* It is the totality of the Hebrew Scriptures which cries out for understanding and use by the teachers and expounders of Christianity.

Now the Jewish people who created the Bible have continued to study the Scriptures and to cultivate the Hebrew language in an unbroken tradition for three millennia. The fruits of this far-flung activity are particularly important today when a far greater degree of respect for the authenticity of the traditional Masoretic text of the Bible has come into being among modern scholars. Correspondingly, they will find abiding scientific value in the work of Jewish grammarians and exegetes, both medieval and modern.

In addition, there is a quest today for new insight into the deeper implications of the biblical text for modern man. This is evident in the pages of Kierkegaard, Rosenzweig, Tillich, Buber, Niebuhr, Heschel, and many other thinkers. This enterprise has much to gain from contact with the religio-ethical interpretation of the Bible to be found in the vast expanses of the Talmud and Midrashic literature.

Modern Christian scholars who rediscover the treasures of Jewish biblical scholarship will be reviving an honorable Christian tradition. It goes back to such Church Fathers as Origen, who in his stupendous *Hexapla* collated all the extant Greek versions of the Hebrew Bible with the Hebrew text, and Jerome, whose Vulgate was a massive effort to discover the *Hebraica veritas* for the good of the Church. Both scholars frequently consulted Jewish teachers and cited views of rabbinic exegesis. This tradition of scholarly collaboration continued, though with interruptions, through the Middle Ages. It is embodied in the work of great biblical and rabbinic scholars, both in Protestantism and Catholicism, such as Egidio, Reuchlin, Munster, the Buxtorfs, Lightfoot, and many more.

Luther leaned heavily upon the Latin commentaries of Nicholas de Lyra, which were largely an epitome of the medieval Jewish commentator, Rashi (1040–1105). As a result, Luther's classic translation of the Bible into German has been described, with some exaggeration, as a German version of Rashi. On the other hand, the English Authorized Version of 1611 drew primarily upon Rabbi David Kimhi. These commentators, and the other great Jewish medieval scholars such as Abraham ibn Ezra, Abulwalid ibn Ganah, and many more, still possess rich treasures that are often overlooked—to our loss.

Moreover, Jewish biblical interpretation has continued uninterrupted to the present day. When this rich quarry is ignored, as Catholic exegesis was wont to be ignored until recently in Protestant circles and as American scholarship still tends to be overlooked overseas, the level of our common understanding of Holy Writ is gravely impoverished. Fortunately, the ecumenical spirit is making itself increasingly felt in various cooperative scholarly undertakings.

B. *A knowledge of Judaism is essential to Christians for an understanding of the background of Jesus, the Apostles, Paul, and the early Church.* There should be no need to labor the point that it was not biblical religion which nurtured the human career of Jesus but rabbinical Judaism. We may delimit his environment still further as being basically Pharisaic Judaism. Jesus shared the same Pharisaic attitudes and beliefs which were accepted among virtually all Jews in his day, with the exception of the Sadducees. All the other sects, the Essenes, the Zealots, and the Apocalyptists, represented extreme formulations of one or another element of Pharisaic teaching.

Such basic elements of faith as the resurrection of the

dead, the Messiah and the Kingdom of God, the primacy of the two commandments to love God and one's neighbor, without which Christianity is inconceivable, were all Pharisaic doctrines. The massive commentary on the New Testament by Strack-Billerbeck, as well as the writings of Abrahams, Schechter, Montefiore, Moore, Herford, Morton Smith, and countless other scholars, have indicated hundreds of points of contact between the earliest Christian circles of Jesus, his disciples and followers, and rabbinic Judaism. When Paul, whose Diaspora background was radically different from that of the Palestinian Jesus, described himself as "a Pharisee, son of a Pharisee" (*Acts* 23:6), he was underscoring the truth that it was rabbinic Judaism —modified, to be sure, in different circles and varying countries—which was the universal spiritual climate of world Jewry and the soil from which Christianity sprang.

Here the discovery of the Dead Sea Scrolls and the elucidation of their contents have wrought a veritable revolution in our understanding of the sources of Christianity. In the past it was generally believed that by and large the faith and ethical teaching of Christianity were Jewish in origin, while the theology and ritual of the Church represented the influence of Hellenism and Oriental religion. This attitude was supported by the fact that parallels between Jewish rabbinic sources and the New Testament were most plentiful for the *Synoptic Gospels* and much rarer for the *Gospel of John* and the *Pauline Epistles*.

Today much of the content of early Christian thought and practice that was previously thought to have its source in extra-Jewish circles, whether in Hellenistic thought or in the mystery religions, is now seen to emanate from the life and outlook of the Dead Sea Sectarians. It is true that the Dead Sea Scrolls show many affinities of content and expression with the *Fourth Gospel* and the *Epistles*. Such elements as the boundless faith in the Righteous Teacher, the ideals of celibacy and of property held in common, the emphasis upon purity, the conflict between "the children of light" and "the children of darkness," the Messianic interpretation of Scriptural passages, the communion meal of the faithful, which is a prototype of the Messianic banquet at "the end of days"—all these features of the early Christian Church are represented in our documents.

It has now become clear that much of the assumed Gentile influence on early Christianity is not Gentile at all. The Christian debt to Judaism becomes immeasurably enlarged, for it now includes both the mainstream of normative Judaism and the lesser currents of Jewish sectarianism.[2]

The evidence for this relationship is so extensive that Dupont-Sommer has observed that it is a delicate question "to determine wherein and to what degree Christianity represents an original manifestation of the human spirit, a task to which theologians will feel impelled to address themselves."

It should not be necessary to point out that in describing Christianity as the offspring of Judaism we are not denying or minimizing its own individuality. In order to explore the nature of this complex relationship to Judaism and reveal the unique character of the Christian vision, one requires a knowledge of Judaism from within, as well as of Christian life and thought. Here the New Testament alone cannot serve as an all-sufficient source. The *Gospels* and the *Epistles* are the expression of an embattled Church fighting for its life, with all the passions, blind spots, and exaggerations that are the inevitable concomitants of conflict. The student and teacher of Christianity requires some firsthand knowledge of the great literary documents of normative Judaism: the Mishnah, the Talmud, and the Midrash, which are indispensable for a full understanding of the origins and development of Christianity. Fortunately these original sources, as well as a reliable scholarly literature dealing with them, are today available in English and other modern languages.

The first two aspects of Judaism we have thus far discussed are essentially concerned with the past, though their implications for the present are far-reaching. The two other aspects of Judaism that cannot be ignored are basically contemporary, though rooted in the past.

C. The Christian world must strive to divest itself of the vestiges of theological animus, often decked out in "scientific" garb. *Jews and Judaism must be recognized as living elements of the modern world and not as a "fossilized relic of Syriac society," to cite Toynbee's famous and unfortunate phrase.* Toynbee's utterance was a secularized version of a widespread religious theory. According to this view, Jews are members of a petrified community, which for two thousand years since the advent of Christianity has shriveled up and lost all its positive attributes except that of being a stiff-necked people.

In spite of the hoary antiquity of this doctrine born of religious controversy centuries ago, it may be suggested that its retention is not essential to Christian loyalty and vitality. There is sufficient creative capacity within Christian theology to evolve a conception of the role of the Jewish people in the Christian world that will be both truer and kinder. This revision of outlook needs to begin with Christian scholars and teachers, but it must reach the "grass roots" in the pew and the classroom and ultimately affect "the man in the street." For modern Judaism is not the vestigial remains of Old Testament religion, though obviously rooted in it. To describe Judaism in terms of the Old Testament is as misleading as would be a picture of contemporary American life derived solely from the Constitution. It is, to be sure, the basic law of the land, but it is far from coextensive with our present legal and social system. Modern Judaism is the product of a long and rich development of biblical thought. It possesses a normative tradition embodied in the Mishnah and the Talmud, as well as in the *Responsa* and the Codes of the post-Talmudic period, which continue to enrich its content to the present day.

Nor is this all. By the side of the dominant strands in normative Judaism are the aberrant tendencies, sectarian and heretical, that were never without influence and cannot be ignored. These include the apocryphal and pseudepigraphical literature, recently enriched—and complicated —by the sensational discovery of the Dead Sea Scrolls. The Middle Ages, building upon their biblical and talmudic antecedents, created the strands of philosophy, mysticism, legalism, and messianism, all of which contributed to the character of modern Judaism. The various schools, conventionally subsumed under the headings of Orthodoxy, Conservatism, and Reform that we discussed above, do not begin to exhaust the variety of religious experience and attitude to be found in the Jewish community.

In brief, modern Judaism in all its forms is not biblical Judaism, not even Talmudic Judaism, nor even medieval Judaism, but the resultant of all three, modified, enriched, and challenged by two thousand years of Western civilization.

Some Christian thinkers who have penetrated to the spirit of the Jewish tradition have discovered within it resources that can enrich the content of the Christian world view and help us meet some of the massive problems confronting the free society of the West and the international community of tomorrow. In such areas as sex, personal morality, and the family, nationalism and the international community, the relationship of religious loyalty and freedom of conscience, the authentic Jewish tradition has insights and attitudes of value not only to its devotees but to all men, and particularly to its partners in the Judeo-Christian tradition.[3]

For these insights to become manifest we need a true dialogue, which is a conversation among equals. In the Middle Ages, Christians talked to Jews or, more accurately, at them, but never with them.

While public religious debates are now a thing of the past, the objective has survived into the present, albeit in slightly modified form. The effort to demonstrate the superiority of Christianity remains central to the missionary enterprise. For Orthodox Christians, it takes the form of presenting the so-called "proof texts" of the Old Testament which, it is alleged, find their fulfillment in the New. The evidence is, of course, convincing only to those who have already accepted the belief in the central role of the Savior in the drama of human salvation. Acceptance of the religious truth of the Christian dispensation is, in the last analysis, an act of faith, not subject to argument and logical demonstration.

It is here that liberal Christians, paradoxically enough, are sometimes faced by a greater problem than their more Fundamentalist brethren. Those who tend to accept a less literal interpretation of the traditional Christian creed are impelled to rest their case for the value of Christianity not on its dogmatic content but on its alleged ethical superiority over Judaism.

The well-worn and threadbare contrast still continues to be drawn between the Old Testament "God of justice" and "the God of love" of the New Testament. Every competent scholar, Christian and Jewish alike, knows that the Old Testament conceived of God in terms of love as well as of justice, just as Jesus' God manifested himself in justice as well as in love, for justice without love is cruelty, and love without justice is caprice.

Nevertheless the practice still goes on in the pulpit and in popular publications, of contrasting the primitivism, tribalism, and legalism of the Old Testament with the spirituality, universalism, and freedom of the New, to the manifest disadvantage of the former.

This contrast between the Testaments is achieved by placing the lower elements of the Old Testament by the side of the higher aspects of the New. The process, however, is as misleading as would be the results of the opposite procedure. Thus, one of the most sympathetic and appreciative students of the New Testament, Claude G. Montefiore, writes in an eloquent passage in his *Synoptic Gospels* (II, 326):

Such passages as Matt. XXV:41 should make theologians excessively careful of drawing beloved contrasts between Old Testament and New. We find even the liberal theologian Dr. Fosdick saying: "From Sinai to Calvary—was ever a record of progressive revelation more plain or more convincing? The development begins with Jehovah disclosed in a thunder storm on a desert mountain, and it ends with Christ saying: 'God is a Spirit: and they that worship Him must worship in spirit and in truth'; it begins with a war-god leading his partisans to victory, and it ends with men saying 'God is love; and he that abideth in love abideth in God, and God abideth in him'; it begins with a provincial Deity, loving his tribe and hating his enemies, and it ends with the God of the whole earth worshipped by a 'great multitude, which no man could number, out of every nation and of all tribes and peoples and tongues'; it begins with a God who commands the slaying of the Amalekites, 'both man and woman, infant and suckling,' and it ends with a Father whose will it is that 'not one of these little ones should perish'; it begins with God's people standing afar off from His lightnings and praying that He might not speak to them lest they die, and it ends with men going into their chambers, and, having shut the door, praying to their Father who is in secret" (*Christianity and Progress*, p. 209).

Very good. No doubt such a series can be arranged. Let me now arrange a similar series. "From Old Testament to New Testament—was ever a record of retrogression more plain or more convincing? It begins with, 'Have I any pleasure at all in the death of him that dieth,' and it ends with, 'Begone from me, ye doers of wickedness.' It begins with 'The Lord is slow to anger and plenteous in mercy'; it ends with, 'Fear him who is able to destroy both body and soul in Gehenna.' It begins with, 'I dwell with him that is of a contrite spirit to revive it'; it ends with 'Narrow is the way which leads to life, and few there be who find it.' It begins with, "I will not contend for ever; I will not be always wroth'; it ends with 'Depart, ye cursed, into the everlasting fire.' It begins with, 'Should not I have pity upon Nineveh, the great city?' It ends with, 'It will be more endurable for Sodom on the day of judgment than for that city.' It begins with, 'The Lord is good to all, and near to all who call upon him'; it ends with, 'Whosoever speaks against the Holy Spirit, there is no forgiveness for him whether in this world or the next.' It begins with, 'The Lord will wipe away tears from off all faces; he will destroy death for ever'; it ends with, 'They will throw them into the furnace of fire; there is the weeping and the gnashing of teeth.' " And the one series would be as misleading as the other.

Another widespread practice which should be surrendered is that of referring to the Old Testament verses quoted in the New as original New Testament passages. The Golden Rule continues to be cited from the New Testament, when the fact is that, like any Jewish teacher, Jesus was citing the Hebrew Scriptures (*Matt.* 22:38; *Luke* 10:27) as did Paul (*Romans* 13:9). To adduce one more instance, in an excellently written tract intended for general distribution, the author contrasts the God who "orders Agag hewn to pieces before the altar" with the God "who taught through St. Paul, 'If your enemy is hungry, feed him' (*Romans* 12:20)." [4] If Paul were citing chapter and verse in his labors, would he have failed to point out that he was simply quoting *Proverbs* 25:21 verbatim?

In sum, it would seem to one who stands outside the Christian communion, but is conscious of its nobility and beauty and its power to lead men to greatness, that the modern spokesman for Christianity, if he is to be worthy of his high calling, should have an understanding of Judaism on three principal levels: *the biblical period*, which created the Old Testament from which he draws spiritual sustenance; *normative or rabbinic Judaism*, which is the background of Jesus, the Apostles, Paul, and the early Church; and *modern Judaism*, which still has its truths to speak to men and which serves as the spiritual home of several millions of his Jewish neighbors and fellow citizens. This understanding the preacher and teacher should transmit to the people.

D. *This last observation suggests the fourth area where there is a burning need for greater understanding on the part of both the clergy and laity—the character and outlook of contemporary Jewry.* Today priests, ministers, and rabbis are being brought into contact during their college and seminary training with such disciplines as politics, economics, sociology, psychology, as well as the natural sciences. It is increasingly recognized that unless the insights of religion are related to these fields they will remain suspended in mid-air and, having no grip upon the human conscience, will exert no practical effect upon human conduct. The parish minister and the priest, the church administrator and the religious educator, will serve the needs of a pluralistic society of equals more truly if their background will include a comprehension of the lives and institutions, the groups and divisions, the problems and the goals of their Jewish neighbors. The present volume, it may be added, is a modest attempt to contribute to this enterprise.

In one sense, this call for an apparently secular approach to contemporary Jewry is of greater practical moment than the more traditional theological approach we have previously urged. Modern Jews are profoundly aware and deeply appreciative of the vast reservoir of good will to be found among their Christian friends and neighbors. They know them as generally humane and compassionate, fair-minded and tolerant in their individual relationships; and allowing for the weaknesses of human nature, Jews attempt to reciprocate in kind.

However, to speak frankly, it must be confessed that most Jews do not see the same virtues in evidence in the Christian community viewed as a collective entity. However paradoxical it may seem, it is almost as though men's actions were better than their professions! There is far too much evidence in the history and etiology of anti-Semitism that seems to support the view that Christian men and women display good will because they are human and exhibit prejudice because they are Christian.

The two major events of modern Jewish history, the Nazi holocaust and the establishment of the State of Israel, underscore the reasons for this feeling. Jews recognize that there is genuine contrition in many Christian religious circles for the horrible extermination of six million Jewish men, women, and children, who were noncombatants and were cruelly done to death by Nazism. Jews are also realistic enough to realize that the horrors of the crematoria and the gas chambers cannot loom as large for Christians as for Jews. Though their emotions are deeply involved, Jews are increasingly recognizing that they must try to forgive what they cannot forget and try to forget what they cannot forgive. But the wounds are deep and the scar tissue takes time to form.

Jews are also deeply appreciative of the warm sympathy of many distinguished religious leaders. Thus Professor Amos N. Wilder speaks of "the deep reappraisal into which all Christians *must have been shocked* by the mass persecutions of the recent period." [5] [Italics ours] But Jews wonder how widely the rank and file of Christians share the sense of contrition which he and other sensitive leaders, Catholic and Protestant alike, have expressed. In a poll conducted by the University of California, close to half the Americans polled agreed with the statement that "Jews should stop complaining about what happened to them in Nazi Germany."

The Nazi persecution is one phenomenon where Jews sense a less than adequate response from their Christian neighbors. One fervently hopes that this kind of beastliness belongs to the past and will never raise its head again. The State of Israel, which is part of the pulsating present, is another major event where the Christian attitude is often disappointing to Jews. It cannot be too strongly emphasized that virtually all Jews who feel any sense of attachment to their heritage are profoundly dedicated to the State of Israel as their spiritual center and a major refuge for their oppressed brethren. If "home" may be defined as "the place they must let you in when you knock," the land of Israel is the homeland of world Jewry in no political sense but in spiritual terms.

We have sought above to delineate the truly unique nature of the Jewish group which is best described by the biblical term '*am*, "people." This insight is the key to the understanding of the special relationship of Jews to the land of Israel. Everywhere in the free world Jews are deeply committed to the lands of their sojourning and are thoroughly integrated into the political, economic, and cultural life of their native or adopted fatherlands. Nevertheless they harbor a love for that little corner of the earth's surface where their people had its origin, where their tradition was born, where their brothers are masters of their own destiny, and where their cultural and spiritual heritage can grow without let or hindrance. There are untold numbers of non-Jews, both within the Church and without, who have recognized this unique character of Jewish peoplehood and have therefore been able to understand the special relationship of modern Jews to the State of Israel.

Since the State of Israel is not only an objective reality but an essential element in the world view of most Jews, any true understanding of contemporary Jewry must seek to include the State of Israel, the only genuine democracy in the Middle East. What is desired—and desirable—is not that the Christian Church become a partisan of the State of Israel, or that it undertake to defend its every act and attitude. Jews themselves, both in Israel and throughout the world, have not hesitated to criticize many aspects of Israeli life, and the writer is no exception. But what Jews would like to see is a growing recognition by Christians of the legitimacy of Jewish rights in Palestine which, incidentally, does not and need not imply any denial of the legitimate rights of the Arabs. The State of Israel must be seen against the background of the Jewish tragedy in the twentieth century—the Nazi holocaust in the recent past, and the barring of the gates against the admission of Jews in many lands of the democratic West and their persecution in the communist East. Far too many well-intentioned members of the Christian community have yet to recognize that even now the State of Israel represents literally the only asylum of life and hope for untold numbers of oppressed Jews the world over.

Is it too extreme to suggest that the free world did not emerge with flying moral colors from the Nazi holocaust and that much more might have been done to minimize the Nazi murders and to save the victims? Now the State of Israel, whose existence is gravely threatened from many quarters, is another litmus paper testing the moral fiber of the Western world.

In the Bossey Consultation of the World Council of Churches in September 1956 it was stated with respect to the State of Israel: "We cannot say a plain 'Yes.' Nor can we say a plain 'No,' because the church does not stand for a vague cosmopolitanism." [6] One is well aware of the complex considerations that entered into this carefully balanced statement. But in view of the burden of guilt which lies upon the Western world, one had a right to hope that expediency would not triumph quite so completely. What should have been forthcoming was not a blanket endorsement of the State of Israel, but an unequivocal statement emphasizing the historic right of the Jewish people to a homeland for its body and its soul.

So, too, expediency and political motives were distressingly in evidence in the struggle that intervened between the first and the final draft of the schema on the Jews issued by the Second Vatican Council. It was freely confessed that there was substantial pressure from Arab states and Catholic prelates in Muslim lands, directed against the earlier version which explicitly absolved Jews, both past and present, of the crime of "deicide." Powerful forces objected to righting this massive historic wrong, a false charge which has been expiated in oceans of Jewish blood. The conservatives opposed any rectification of this age-old evil on two grounds. They invoked several New Testament passages that seem to lend color to the charge of deicide. Regrettable as this stand was, it was at least comprehensible. What was difficult to understand was the argument that a theological reformulation of Catholic teaching on the subject would be regarded as political support for the State of Israel! The final draft, weakened, though still welcome, was the result of a compromise between the contending groups in Rome. The test of its value and significance will lie in the degree to which the spirit of John XXIII and the schemata of the Vatican Council will be translated into the daily life of the Christian believer, as Cardinal Cushing has forthrightly observed.

It should not be difficult for believing Christians who cherish the Bible to reject the falsehood that the Jews who return to Israel are lackeys of capitalist imperialism, as communist propaganda asserts, or the agents of Western colonialism, as the Arab dictators and monarchs proclaim. The Jewish settlers in the State of Israel are members of an ancient people who, as in the days of Ezra and Nehemiah, are striving to restore their national life in its ancestral home. Though driven from Palestine by force of arms, they have continued to pray and aspire for their restoration for nineteen hundred years of exile, and have never abdicated their historic claim to the Promised Land, enunciated in the pages of the Bible.

This last consideration should carry weight with Christians who revere the Scripture as the word of God. Dr. Chaim Weizmann was once asked at a British Royal Commission hearing what the basis of the Jewish title to Palestine was. He answered, "Gentlemen, you are under the impression that the mandate is our Bible. The truth is that the Bible is our mandate."

Undoubtedly the existence and progress of the State of Israel confronts many believing Christians with theological issues. But these difficulties should be treated as problems and not as obstacles to the expression of the moral will. The creative capacity of Christian thinkers can surely prove more than equal to the task of validating the new experience by the light of an age-old religious truth. The *aggiornamento*, "updating," now going on in the Roman Catholic Church is impressive testimony to this vitality in Christendom. A living theology should be able to come to terms with the realities of life.

There is one more tension area which must concern all who are sincerely interested in furthering the dialogue of Christianity and Judaism. This is the long-standing practice of Christian missionary activity among Jews. The traditional Christian doctrine was expressed by the International Committee on the Christian Approach to the Jews at its conference in 1931: "Judaism is as much without Christ as Mohammedanism and Hinduism, Buddhism and Confucianism. Either all people need Christ or none."

Jews have always been hurt by the assumption of superiority which underlies the widespread efforts being made to convert them to Christianity. Today this assumption is resented by all other non-Christians as well, Mohammedans, Hindus, Buddhists, and Confucianists. Each of these traditions is able to demonstrate, to the satisfaction of its own communicants at least, that it possesses adequate resources for the spiritual and ethical life of its devotees. Indeed, many of the spokesmen of non-Christian religions, surveying the history of the Western world in which slavery, war, massacre, and exploitation of the weak have been constants during these past twenty centuries, are prepared to argue for the moral superiority of their own specific religious tradition.

Be this as it may, it is clear that the missionary goal when directed to Jews vitiates the effort to establish genuine good will. It will be recalled that in one of the earlier drafts of the proposed schema on the Jews at the Second Vatican Council, the Christian duty of practicing kindness to Jews was closely linked to the Christian hope for the conversion of the Jews. It aroused a storm of protest not only within the Jewish community but among many leaders of the Roman Catholic Church and untold Catholic laymen, who did not abate a jot or tittle of their loyalty to their church but who understood and honored the sincerity of Jews' loyalty to Judaism. Fortunately this ill-considered addendum was muted in the final draft and the call for fairness and friendship to the Jewish people was not linked to ulterior considerations.

Modern Jews understand that through the centuries

Christians have expressed their love for their fellow men by striving to bring them within the pale of Christian belief. On the other hand, Christians should understand that Jews are no less sincere in their love for their fellow men. However, Judaism believes that "salvation" is not exclusively "of the Jews" (*pace* the New Testament!). Because of the rabbinic teaching that "the righteous of all nations have their share in the world to come," Judaism accords to all men the right to preserve their own religious tradition and group individuality.

Can Christianity be asked to abandon its hope of converting Jews to the Gospel? A few Christian thinkers, like Reinhold Niebuhr, have not hesitated to answer this question in the affirmative, though most Christian teachers would probably not agree. Increasingly, there is a growing emphasis in Christian circles not upon missionary activity directed toward the Jews but, in Professor Wilder's words, upon a witness to Christian truth which "will take the form either of silent deeds of justice and goodness or of dialogue without ulterior motives." [7]

Christians are not called upon to abandon their hope for a world converted to the Gospels, any more than traditional Judaism has given up the Prophetic faith that the day will come when "the Lord shall be one and His name one." If the election of Israel, which is basic to the Christian claim, has any meaning, it must be that men must leave to God the achievement of His purpose through and with His people at "the end of days." Men must learn to express their hopes in a spirit of humility, always conscious that His thoughts are not our thoughts and His ways are not our ways.

There are welcome signs of the dawning of a new day even in this sensitive area. At a Jewish-Catholic Colloquy held in 1965 at Saint Vincent's Archabbey at Latrobe, Pennsylvania, a group of Catholic and Jewish thinkers explored for three days the relationship of their traditions and their communities. According to one published report on the Colloquy, "repeated questions on the need to convert Jews were answered either that conversion is the work of God and is accomplished only by example, not by force; that the conversion of the Jews is a matter of the entire people turning to the Christ, not of individuals; hence it is for the end of days and God's good time, not as a matter of the Church's immediate practical efforts. The spirit of Pope John could not have been more steadfastly and sincerely manifested." [8]

To urge a modification of the Christian attitude and practice on missionary activity is not as radical a proposal as may at first sight appear. The history both of Christianity and of Judaism, and indeed of every living tradition, offers countless instances of doctrines as well as practices that were important at one period and then have receded into the background, sometimes to be revived in a subsequent age. In the history of Christian dogmatics, St. Paul's doctrine of justification by faith was of basic importance in his theology. Centuries later, it became the central theological issue in the Reformation, separating Catholics from Protestants. Nevertheless Professor John Macquarrie, who points out today that "justification" is a metaphor taken out of the law courts, does not hesitate to say that it "has probably been given an altogether exaggerated importance in the subsequent history of Christian doctrine." [9] To cite another instance, in the great churches of Christianity the Second Advent has never been abandoned, but it is not central and immediate in the present hour. Similarly, in Judaism such widely held traditional beliefs as the reality of angels and of Satan and the efficacy of kabbalistic rites have tacitly been abandoned by virtually all Jews. Many more instances of doctrines whose importance has been reduced could be cited.

It should therefore be possible for Christians to recognize that genuine conversion can come only through the grace of God and in His own time, and that the life of dialogue, which means talking together and living together, should not be vitiated by the hope of utilizing these contacts for missionary activities.

The Nazi holocaust, the State of Israel, and the Christian missionary tradition constitute three areas of profound concern to Jews who wish to love and respect their brothers and hope to be respected and loved by them. The Christian community of today and tomorrow needs to be led to a sympathetic understanding of Jewish attitudes and feelings on these crucial subjects.

According to Hasidic tradition, the great saint, Rabbi Levi Yitzchak of Berdichev, was wont to say that he had learned the meaning of love from a drunken peasant. One day he had occasion to come into an inn, in the corner of which two peasants were sitting over their liquor, far gone in their cups. They were at the sentimental stage, throwing their arms around one another and telling each other how much they loved each other. Suddenly, one turned to his companion and said, "Ivan, what hurts me now?" Ivan answered, "Peter, how should I know what hurts you?" Whereupon Peter said, "If you do not know what hurts me, how can you say you love me?" This, said the Rabbi, is the truest definition of love.

It is self-evident that the fostering of true understanding will redound to the well-being both of Jews and of Christians. Jews will be the beneficiaries of a healthier climate in which to live and function and raise their children. By overcoming the age-old heritage of prejudice, Christians will be demonstrating that the sins of the past need not remain the burden of the present or survive as the curse of the future.

The advantages that will accrue to Jews and Christians

from mutual respect based upon genuine understanding are incalculable. In addition, the Judeo-Christian tradition will be greatly enriched and benefited by the cross-fertilization that will result from a genuine dialogue between the two faiths. For each religion possesses profound insights of the greatest value, that are, however, not free from inherent weaknesses. Hence each tradition can serve as a salutary corrective to the other because of its varied content and emphasis.

What is the nature of the Judeo-Christian tradition? Indeed, does it really exist? To these questions we must now direct our attention.

CHAPTER SEVEN

THE JUDEO-CHRISTIAN
TRADITION—ILLUSION
OR REALITY

IN SEEKING to evaluate the problems of the survival of Judaism in a non-Christian world and its prospects for the future, we have been confronted by a basic paradox. On the one hand, the Hebraic tradition is the heritage of a numerically insignificant group of limited power. On the other hand, this body of religious and ethical ideas, primarily but not exclusively contained in the Bible, constitutes one of the basic sources of modern civilization.

In point of fact, the Bible itself has long transcended all limitations of origin and has become the common property of nearly a billion fellow human beings. The narratives of the Hebrew Bible have become part of the national history of men of every race and color, and the biblical heroes have entered the history of half the nations of the world. To be sure, the Hebrew patriarchs, prophets, psalmists, and sages have entered into the consciousness of Western man not directly through the impact of Judaism, but through the medium of its daughter-religion, Christianity.

It is this fact that has created a problem of extraordinary subtlety and complexity for those who seek to preserve the individuality of the Jewish tradition on the one hand, while keeping open avenues of communication and mutual influence with the dominant culture on the other. We have described the goal of modern Jewry as integration without assimilation, acculturation without absorption. But it would seem that this goal requires two distinct skills—the capacity to erect fences as well as to build bridges.

Nevertheless these arts are not contradictory to each other. As each human being is both different from his fellows and yet linked to them in untold ways, so Judaism and Christianity both possess their own individuality and yet are intimately linked to each other by twenty centuries of history. To deny the relationship is possible only by willfully ignoring the evidence. On the other hand, merely to affirm it in simplistic terms is an equally great disservice to the cause of truth. The reality and the nature of the Judeo-Christian tradition must be explored in depth if it is to be truly significant.

The problem cannot be simplified by regarding Judaism as the religion of the Old Testament, and Christianity as the religion of the New, with links to the Old. The relationship between the two faiths is both closer and more complicated than this common but mistaken allocation would suggest.

In describing Christianity as a "daughter-religion" of Judaism, we are underscoring an important historic fact to which we have already called attention. Christianity did not derive directly from the Old Testament but from rabbinic Judaism, which was already flourishing in the days of Jesus, the Apostles, and Paul. Thus the faith represented in the primitive church rested upon the thought and practice of post-biblical Judaism. Such elements in Christianity as the concept of God as Father, the faith in the advent of the Redeemer, the method of interpreting biblical texts in the *Gospels* and in the *Epistles* of Paul, the belief in the resurrection of the dead, as well as the system of ritual observances in the *Gospels* which include the Sabbath, the festivals, diet, and family relations—all these are not simply Old Testament religion but the way of life of rabbinic Judaism. The Hebrew Bible had, of course, been completed centuries before the birth of Christianity.

The concept of a mother-daughter relationship between Judaism and Christianity is significant in other respects as well. It recognizes that each possesses a distinct individuality. A child is never the facsimile of its parent, if only because another progenitor is involved in the process. In addition to normative Judaism or Pharisaism, there were other important influences which helped fashion the character of Christianity. These included elements from Oriental religion, Greek philosophy, the mystery cults, as well as non-Pharisaic minority sects in Judaism, as the Qumran Scrolls have dramatically revealed in our day. Moreover, the mother continues to live and grow older—one hopes wiser, too—even after the birth of her daughter! Thus, both Christianity and Judaism have followed their own separate paths subsequent to their separation. They have developed their distinct individualities, in spite of the close genetic relationship that continues to exist between them.

Finally, there is another implication in the metaphor of mother-daughter which needs to be spelled out. The attitude of Judaism and Christianity toward each other was by no means always one of parental love on the one hand and filial piety on the other, as we have seen. On the contrary, for the greater portion of their history the relationship generally followed the pattern described by modern psychology, which has emphasized that conflict, latent or overt, is normal in the attitude of parents and children. One fervently wishes that the analogy did not apply so well!

Christianity arose as a tiny sect within the Jewish community. Through the dynamic influence of Paul and his successors, it rapidly attained to independence. After competing successfully with paganism for the allegiance of the Greco-Roman world, the Christian Church soon achieved supremacy over the mother-faith both in numbers and in power. For most of the nineteen centuries that Judaism and Christianity have lived in proximity, their mutual attitude can only be described as basically one of antagonism, differing only in the degree of its virulence and in the modes of its expression.

When John Singer Sargent painted his series of murals for the Boston Public Library he created a furore that was not purely artistic. In one painting he depicted a resplendent maiden standing proud and erect, looking off into the distance in the proud consciousness of victory. She represented *Ecclesia Victrix* or the Church Triumphant. On the ground there huddled another figure, that of *Synagoga Victa* or the Synagogue Conquered. The mural was an accurate representation of the prevailing attitudes during the first seventeen centuries of common experience shared by Judaism and Christianity in the Western world.

To be sure, there were adumbrations of another attitude even during the Middle Ages among a few great-souled thinkers and saints who were able to rise above the narrow darkness of the hour and to see the lineaments of a new dawn. Here and there an individual discerned elements of value even in the life and tradition of his people's persecutors. Similarly, centuries earlier the prophet Isaiah had seen his tiny country being ground between the two mighty empires, Assyria and Egypt, that were battling for world supremacy. Nevertheless, he looked forward to the day when the Lord of Hosts would say, "Blessed is My people Egypt, and the work of My hands Assyria and My inheritance Israel" (*Isa.* 19:25). Such spirits are rare.

By and large, the influence of these leaders and teachers was unable to transform the basic attitude of mutual antagonism, which prevailed among most devotees of both religions, being nourished by countless instances of persecution and violence. Among the masses there was little or no recognition of a religious and ethical heritage held in common by Jews and Christians.

It was not until the eighteenth century that a far-reaching change in the mutual attitude of the two faiths became widespread. However unsettling the ideas of the Enlightenment proved to traditional religion, they had the positive influence of creating a spirit of mutual tolerance among the great faiths. Lessing's famous drama, *Nathan der Weise* ("Nathan the Wise"), highlighted the new spirit. The drama, which had a Mohammedan Sultan and a Jewish sage as its protagonists, contained the famous parable of "The Three Rings." These rings, which were identical in appearance, had been fashioned by a father for his three beloved sons, because he could not bear to give the priceless ancestral heirloom to any single one. The overt message of the parable was clear. The three rings symbolized the three monotheistic religions of Judaism, Christianity, and Islam, all of which represented an expression of God's love for His creatures and of the reverence they owed Him in return. Scarcely beneath the surface were two other implications. The three faiths were not totally different from one another, as some devotees might insist. They resembled each other at least as much as they differed from one another, because they shared a common kinship. Moreover, none of the three faiths could reasonably insist that it alone represented the true revelation of God and should therefore be granted a privileged position in a free society.

The process of interreligious understanding, which became manifest in the eighteenth century, was substantially advanced in the nineteenth. Matthew Arnold popularized the idea that the two great sources of Western culture were

Hebraism and Hellenism. By Hebraism he meant the totality of values and attitudes derived from the Hebrew Scriptures, which were preserved in Judaism, and were basic to Christianity as well.

It was in the first half of the twentieth century that the concept of "the Judeo-Christian tradition" or "the Judeo-Christian heritage" came to flower. As is almost always the case in the history of ideas, objective conditions favored this development. First was the widespread irruption of group tensions in America after the First World War. As a result, a group of outstanding Americans was moved to launch what was originally called the "good will" and later the "interfaith" movement. In seeking a basis for their efforts to create a climate of mutual esteem and respect among the disparate elements of the American population, the spokesmen began to stress the common religious and ethical elements of the various traditions. Thus the concept of the Judeo-Christian heritage became current.[1]

The second factor was at least equally decisive. In the years following the economic debacle of 1929, communism seemed to many to be "the wave of the future," scoring impressive victories at home and abroad. The democratic way of life, as it had evolved in Western Europe and preeminently in the United States, now found itself confronted by the massive challenge of a new philosophy which spoke in the name of justice and equality and which did not hesitate to describe itself as representing an authentic "people's democracy." This threat from within and without challenged equally all the major religions of the West as well as the secular cultures they had nurtured. If the far-flung battle against the communist foe was to be won, there was an imperative need for a countervailing ideology, a system of values that could evoke the passionate loyalty of democratic peoples. Hence politicians as well as spokesmen for religion fell back in increasing measure upon the concept of a Judeo-Christian tradition.

The third factor was the growing recognition that religious pluralism was not merely a reality in modern life but an ideal to be cherished in a free society. We have scarcely begun to understand that the full significance of pluralism lies in the future. Only pluralism can serve the needs of the emerging world community of the future, which will include countless varieties of religious belief and unbelief. In any event, the existence of pluralism on the American scene stimulated the quest for the common factors in Catholicism, Protestantism, and Judaism which would justify describing them as "the religions of democracy" [2]

The confluence of these factors gave widespread currency to the doctrine of a Judeo-Christian tradition and incidentally served to give the three major faiths a symbolic as well as a measure of practical equality in American life. Among the beneficial consequences has been the larger measure of recognition which has come to the minority faiths and the enlarged opportunities afforded their devotees in the economic area, the academic life, and the general culture.

The concept of a Judeo-Christian tradition, arising as it did in response to practical needs, tended to be expressed in popular terms. As a result, its precise content was rarely spelled out and its implications and limits were scarcely explored. In its heyday, the concept encountered little opposition, its validity being regarded as self-evident. After all, did not Jews and Christians believe in one God and did not both revere the Hebrew Scriptures or the Old Testament as the Word of God? As a result, two assumptions were made, implicitly rather than explicitly, to be sure: first, that the two partners in the Judeo-Christian tradition were agreed on important issues; and second, that where they disagreed, the issues were not important.

Of the two propositions in this working theory, the first was correct or at least tenable—there are substantial elements of agreement. Perhaps because they are so evident, they are at times disregarded, in accordance with the psychological principle to which Edgar Allan Poe called attention in "The Purloined Letter," that the obvious is easily overlooked. On the other hand, the second assumption—that the differences are unimportant—was highly dubious.

When the inevitable reactions set in, it was not difficult for some theologians, who are adept in the art of making subtle distinctions, to deny categorically the validity of the concept of a Judeo-Christian tradition and to dismiss it as an imaginary notion concocted to serve apologetic ends or political purposes.[3] Thus a distinguished spokesman for Orthodox Judaism recently argued against the truth of the idea. It is clear that he is deeply worried lest a recognition of a bond between the two faiths lead to the disappearance or the attenuation of the older and less numerous religion. A few other Jewish thinkers, including, paradoxically enough, some who have been most strongly influenced by Christian theology, have also insisted that there is no significant common ground between Judaism and Christianity.[4] The concern for the survival of Judaism is thoroughly legitimate and indeed necessary, but the future of the tradition is not advanced by a refusal to face the facts.

It is not strange that some theologians have found it possible to deny the link between Judaism and Christianity. They have a natural penchant for drawing up formulations of abstract dogma, divorced from the background of history and culture, and isolated from the context of human experience. Juxtapose the *Thirteen Principles of Judaism* as formulated by Maimonides and the *Athanasian Creed* of Christianity and the differences will appear vast and unbridgeable. But observe these articles of belief within the context of the living communities in which they arose, and the points of contact and similarity will become evident.

When the concept of a Judeo-Christian tradition is examined on its merits, it becomes clear that neither position, be it an all-out affirmation or a total negation, is valid. That both approaches have their proponents testifies to the fact that each contains elements of truth and error.

For nineteen centuries the relationship between Judaism and Christianity has been subtle and shifting. This ambivalence can perhaps be expressed by recourse to the Hebrew lexicon. In Hebrew, the verb meaning "to embrace" (*habhak*) is phonetically related to the word meaning "to wrestle" (*'abhak*). Modern psychology has also familiarized us with the intimate connection between love and hatred, friendship and hostility. The polarity between the two faiths, far from disproving the bond between them, testifies to its reality.

What is needed is an understanding of the elements of identity and similarity on the one hand, and of difference and opposition on the other. The elements of agreement make possible a consensus of outlook without which a viable society cannot be maintained. The elements of divergency create the conditions for a fruitful and stimulating dialogue on the perennial issues of God, man, and the Universe. Since even the wisest of men are granted only a partial glimpse of the truth, every approach to reality gains by being challenged and chastened by views of a divergent character.

The differences between Judaism and Christianity are genuine and profound. That both Judaism and Christianity are rooted in the Hebrew Scriptures and share many other elements of a common background is undeniable, but even the same sources have developed far-reaching variations. Truth, Renan reminds us, lies in the nuances. Given subtle differences in emphasis and in timbre, a new individuality emerges. While the Hebrew Scriptures, to be sure, are sacred to both religions, Judaism accords primacy to the Torah over the Prophets, while Christianity stresses the Prophets. For Judaism, the Prophets are a vital commentary on the Torah, which is the fountainhead of the life of faith. For Christianity, the Law has been superseded by the New Covenant and it is the Prophets that constitute the most significant element of the Old Testament.

This difference may be sharpened still further. For classical Judaism, obedience to the Law is the unique and indispensable instrument for the fulfillment of the will of God. On the other hand, classical Christianity, in the formulation of Paul, is strongly antinomian, denying the validity and authority of the Torah. Indeed, Paul argued that the Law served to increase the consciousness of sin and thus contributed to the sinfulness of man.[5] The rabbis, on the other hand, declare, "The Holy One, blessed be He, wished to add merit to Israel. Therefore He increased for them the Law and the Commandments, as it is said, 'God was pleased for the sake of His righteousness to magnify the Torah and make it glorious.' "[6] While Judaism regards the Law as the pathway to God, Christianity substitutes the person of Christ, belief in whom constitutes the road to salvation.[7] No matter how much one may reduce the importance of loyalty to the Law in Judaism and stress the value of law in Christianity, a substantial margin of difference will remain.

Closely linked to this far-reaching difference is the divergent role of the Messiah in the two religions. Both the Hebrew word *Mashiah* and the Greek *Christos* mean "anointed," and it is true that the Christ of Christianity derives from the Messiah of Judaism. Indeed, several additional links in the process of transmission may have been supplied by the recently discovered scrolls of the Dead Sea sectarians.

Nevertheless the two concepts are poles apart. Traditional Judaism sees in the Messiah the future redeemer, who will succor the Jewish people from exile and mankind from oppression and violence, ushering in the reign of universal justice, brotherhood, and peace. In the words of the Talmudic sage, Samuel, "There is no difference between the present order and the days of the Messiah except the removal of the oppression of kingdoms (*shi'bbud malkhuyoth*)." [8] For Christianity, the Savior offers redemption to the individual soul that would otherwise be doomed to damnation because of Adam's primal sin. Moreover, in Christian thought, the Savior has no special function to perform for the Jewish people.

There is a third fundamental difference. Christianity regards itself as the heir of Old Testament Judaism, and legatees generally inherit only after the death of the testator. It is needless to add that the Jewish religion has never agreed that it is moribund and therefore in need of an heir. On the contrary, it has continued to maintain its existence and, though its two daughter-religions are considerably more numerous and powerful, it has never surrendered its conviction that Judaism would some day be the universal faith of mankind.

These differences are far-reaching and enduring, and by that token they guarantee the individuality and distinctiveness of the two faiths. Yet even here the link between them is unmistakable. It inheres not only in the history of Israel from which Christianity takes its point of departure. The fact is that the Jewish position on these basic points of issue has never been totally expunged from Christian consciousness.

Thus it is true that Paul sought to negate the Law as being a source of sin and to substitute the "spirit" as the arbiter of human action. Nonetheless, Christianity has continued to be exercised by the problem and has recognized the need for law in a stable society, as is clear from the rich development of Church law in the centuries after Paul. So, too, while calling itself "the new Israel," the Christian church has in practice recognized that the old Israel still lives on and has sought to reckon with it as a reality. Nor has the Church been impervious to the appeal of the Jewish concept of the Messiah as the redeemer of human society and not merely as the savior of the individual. This has created the doctrine of the Second Advent of Christ, destined to establish the Kingdom of God on earth. That the historical Jesus did not succeed in achieving this goal was emphasized with telling effect by Jewish polemists in the religious disputations that were forced upon Jews in the Middle Ages.

These are the primary differences between Judaism and Christianity, but there are others only a little less significant. Even where both traditions accept the validity of a given passage, the varying stress accorded it often becomes significant. In Judaism, the call "Hear O Israel, the Lord our God, the Lord is One," known as the *Shema*, which precedes the commandment to love God (*Deuteronomy* 6:4–9), holds a central place. This is the classic affirmation of the fundamental Jewish doctrine of the unity of God. It is accordingly recited at the close of the Day of Atonement and by each Jew on his deathbed as the Confession of Faith. Jesus as a professing Jew assigned to it the same importance. According to *Mark* (12:28–34), he quoted the verse when answering the question as to which is the greatest commandment. The *Shema* holds no such central position in Christianity; and, in the version in *Matthew* (22:35–40), Jesus' reply to the same question does not include this verse.

On the other hand, the Adam and Eve narrative in *Genesis* has served as the source for the central Christian concept of the Fall of Man, which has been elaborated with incredible depth in twenty centuries of Christian thought. In traditional Judaism the paradise tale is, of course, familiar and famous, but aside from a few minor references it has developed no theological significance.

Traditional Christianity has always made much of the seventh chapter of *Isaiah*, in which it found a prophecy of the Virgin Birth of the Savior more than seven centuries after the period of the prophet. That a palpable error in translation underlies this view of the passage has long been recognized by virtually all Christian scholars. This error, incidentally, may not inhere in the Septuagint, as is generally believed. In classical Greek the word *parthenos* usually means "virgin," to be sure, but it also has the meaning of "young woman," without regard to her marital status. It thus corresponds very well to the Hebrew *'almah*. The new Revised Standard Version now correctly renders the Hebrew word *'almah* in *Isaiah* as "young woman." But this fact has little affected the use of the verse in contemporary Christian life. Nor has the significance of this passage for Orthodox Christian believers been appreciably diminished.

Similarly the fifty-third chapter of *Isaiah*, which depicts the Suffering Servant of the Lord, has been regarded in traditional Christian circles as a prophecy of the career of Jesus. It has therefore played an incalculable role in Christian thought. When the Dead Sea Scroll containing the text of the book of *Isaiah* revealed a variation of one letter in one word (in 52:14), it generated a literature of massive proportions, because some Christian scholars thought it suggested a reference to the Messiah.[9]

In Judaism the moving figure of the Suffering Servant of the Lord was equated with the Jewish people—a view shared by most modern scholars. Nevertheless it never became equally basic in the traditional Jewish world view. Thus, practically none of the beautiful "Servant Songs" were chosen for the *Haftarot*, the prophetic readings in the synagogue liturgy for the Sabbaths and Festivals of the year.

Nor are the differences between Judaism and Christianity limited to proof-texts. The early Christian church, to be sure, took over the body of Jewish ideas and a mass of Jewish practices which were current in first-century Jewish Palestine. This legacy, however, was subjected to a very complex process. The ritual practices were largely surrendered, especially when Gentile Christians began to predominate over the Judeo-Christians in the ranks of the new church. But much of Jewish ritual observances remained, as the festivals of Easter, Pentecost, and Christmas attest. For these characteristically Christian festivals preserve unmistakable links with their Jewish prototypes, the holidays of Passover, Shavuot and Hanukkah.

With regard to the ideas taken over from Judaism, there were elements which Christianity accepted but many which it modified, others which it discarded or overlooked, and still others which it reinterpreted or replaced entirely. Such Christian doctrines as the Fall of Man, Original Sin, the superiority of asceticism, and vicarious atonement are, it is true, slightly adumbrated in Judaism, and some few passages may be adduced to support them from Jewish sources. But the student who is truly at home in Judaism recognizes that they are not in the mainstream of the tradition, being secondary in character. In addition, there were of course many basic dogmas which became uniquely characteristic of the Christian faith, such as the Virgin Birth, the Incarnation, and the Passion. These beliefs, which have no counterpart in Judaism, have added immeasurably to the individuality of Christianity.

On the other hand, Judaism retained and developed various insights of its own. These are to be found less often in abstract formulations of creed than in the context of legal practice and institutional forms. Throughout its history the

Law has been the life of Judaism, interpreted and developed in the pages of Scripture, the discussions of the Talmud, the formulation of the Codes, and the decisions of the *Responsa*—a process of growth and development still going on today.

It has been one of the great merits of Christianity to focus attention upon the fate of the individual and the means available to him for his salvation. This is not to deny the existence of a deep and ongoing interest in the needs and problems of society. Conversely, while the individual soul has certainly never been lost sight of in Judaism, the genius of the tradition has placed at the heart of its concern the destiny of the group, be it the family, the nation, or the human race. As has been noted, this is one of the basic differences between the Messianic doctrine in Judaism and Christianity.

It is therefore by no means accidental that the Founding Fathers of the United States found inspiration for a free society of equals primarily in the Old Testament rather than in the New. A century later, the proponents of "the social gospel," of whom Walter Rauschenbusch was probably the most influential figure, called for social justice as a categorical imperative of their Christian faith. They found the basis for their social idealism primarily in the Hebrew prophets and in the social legislation of the Torah, rather than in the *Gospels* or the *Epistles* of Paul, who generally acquiesced in the political and social conditions of the Roman Empire.

The ethics of Jesus as transmitted in the New Testament are, to be sure, frequently invoked as an ideal. But it is abundantly clear that their focus is basically upon the individual. Moreover, as Albert Schweitzer and others have demonstrated, they are motivated by imminent eschatology, by a vivid conviction that the existing social and political order will shortly be destroyed by the miraculous intervention of God. It follows that such burning issues as foreign domination, poverty and wealth, slavery and the status of women are not of genuine concern to a man who seeks to achieve his salvation in the brief interval before the Divine cataclysm sweeps the world away.

When this expectation failed to materialize, the Church no less than the Synagogue needed a viable system of ethics for a perdurable society of normal men. The need is equally vital today, when the accepted standards of morality, individual and collective, seem to be crumbling before one's eyes. In his quest for an ethical outlook, twentieth-century man is more likely to find a source and inspiration in the concrete laws of the Pentateuch, the idealistic aspirations of the Prophets, and the realistic insights of the Hebrew Wisdom writers, than in the New Testament. *What cannot be stressed too strongly, however, is that when Christians turn to the Hebrew Scriptures, they are not going out of the bounds of their own tradition but are utilizing the resources of the Judeo-Christian heritage, which has been theirs for two millennia.*[10]

In view of these differences between Judaism and Christianity, both basic and secondary, palpable and subtle, is it still possible to speak in meaningful terms of a "Judeo-Christian tradition"? I believe that the answer is in the affirmative.

In the first instance, the historical fact that Christianity is rooted in Judaism is more than a fact of history. No matter how far the two faiths may diverge, they share the same constellation of heroes, honor the same patriarchs and prophets, cite the same Scriptures, and share many of the same ethical ideals.

That is not all. A tradition is neither monolithic nor motionless. The validity of the concept of the Judeo-Christian tradition becomes clear when it is seen not merely as a body of abstract thought but as the embodiment of living communities of men.

The warmth with which the concept of a Judeo-Christian tradition has been affirmed and denied testifies to the fact that the emotions, and not merely the intellects, of men are involved.[11] But much of the controversy derives from the failure to consider some basic principles which must be reckoned with, if we seek light and not merely heat on the issue.

A. *A religion is more than a body of theological dogma, and tradition is more than religion.* Tradition includes an entire pattern of life, a complex structure of thought and emotion, a heritage of shared experiences, a body of common cultural and ethical values, a fund of memories and aspirations.

At first blush Judaism and Christianity would therefore seem to be thoroughly at variance here, for a shared experience from different positions does not produce a common ideal or even a similar viewpoint. Quite the contrary. The Crusades, for example, even when stripped of the romanticizing tendencies of earlier historians, are properly regarded as a positive factor in history, which advanced the progress of Christian Europe by exposing it to new cultural influences. But for the Jews, the Crusades represent a calamity of major proportions. In their wake came the annihilation of the flourishing Rhineland communities and the beginning of increasing isolation for European Jewry, which culminated in the widespread establishment of the ghetto.

Christians and Jews lived on the same continent from the fall of Rome to the French Revolution, yet their destinies were almost diametrically opposed. For Christian Europe the earlier centuries, summarily called the Dark Ages, gave way to the Middle Ages, which were marked by ever broader horizons of thought and action. This positive trend resulted from the Crusades, the voyages of Marco Polo, the arrival of Greek scholars in Western Europe after the fall of Constantinople in 1453, the Renaissance, the voyages of exploration, and the Reformation. For the Jews the process was tragically reversed. The earlier period, when they had far closer and friendlier relations with their Christian neighbors, was followed by a progressive deterioration in their status and their growing alienation from the mainstream of Western culture.

Nevertheless, throughout the Middle Ages there were similar forces at work in both communities which led to similar phenomena, of which the proponents themselves were not necessarily conscious. The religious revival of the Franciscan order had its counterpart in the pietism of Rabbi Judah he-Hasid (1146-1217) and his school.[12] Indeed, there were cases of outright borrowing of religious practices. Such important elements of contemporary Judaism as the *Yizkor*, or Memorial Service, were influenced by early German pietism. The word *Yahrzeit*, the anniversary of the day of death, is still retained in its German form in modern Judaism.

It is scarcely accidental that the Spanish city of Avila, later famous as the home of the great Catholic mystic St. Theresa (1515-82), was the domicile of the anonymous Jewish "Prophet of Avila," author of a long treatise called *The Book of Wondrous Wisdom*,[13] which proclaimed the advent of the Messiah for 1285. It was in Avila, too, that Moses de Leon (1250-1305) the author-compiler of the Jewish mystical classic, the *Zohar*, lived for some time.[14] The anonymous Kabbalistic work *Ra'aya Mehemna* ("The Faithful Shepherd"), composed near the end of the thirteenth century, shows striking affinities with the Spiritualist movement of the Franciscan order.[15]

The leading historian of Spanish Jewry, Yitzhak Baer, calls attention to the potentially great significance of the thirteenth century both for Judaism and Christianity and to their common climate of thought and emotion: "The mystically oriented pietist movement, which had been active in Spain since the second quarter of the thirteenth century, aspired, consciously and by implication, to a thoroughgoing reform of all aspects of Jewish social and religious life. Similar forces were operating also in the Christian Church during the thirteenth century. Students of medieval Christianity point out quite correctly that the thirteenth century was fraught with potentialities for a social and religious reform more genuine and more pervasive than that effected in the sixteenth century by the Protestant Reformation. Jewish history did not parallel the history of the Christian Church in every respect, but the historians' evaluation of thirteenth-century Christianity can be applied with equal truth to contemporary Judaism." [16]

The millenarianism that swept Christian Europe in the seventeenth century was well aware of the Jewish Messianic movement associated with Shabbatai Zevi (1626–76). For all their genuine differences, the seventeenth-century Christian mystic, Jakob Boehme, reflects the response to the same human needs which found expression in Rabbi Israel Baal Shem Tov and the Hasidic movement in Jewish circles a few decades later.

B. *Religion cannot be isolated from culture, of which it is an indispensable element.* Religion influences the other segments of culture and in turn is influenced by them. If it is conceded that "the concept of a common tradition uniting two faith communities has relevance under a historico-cultural aspect," it must also be meaningful for the religious content of both communities, for religion never exists in isolation from all other human concerns.[17] On the contrary, men inevitably express their religious faith in cultural forms and institutions. This is particularly true in such areas as the study of the Hebrew Bible, which was cultivated in both the Jewish and the Christian communities, as we have seen.

At times the lines of influence are striking and unexpected. Thus, James Boswell prefaces his great *Life of Dr. Samuel Johnson* with a quotation in the name of the medieval Jewish scholar, Rabbi David Kimhi, who cites a rabbinic utterance, "Even the idle talk of great men is worthy of study." It is therefore not altogether too far-fetched to describe this great masterpiece of English literature as an extended commentary on a passage in rabbinic literature!

C. *A living tradition is never monolithic, but will always contain currents and crosscurrents, and even strongly antagonistic tendencies within itself, which nevertheless are authentic components of the tradition.* Of this truth, the recent history of Roman Catholicism has forcefully reminded us. To cite the history of Judaism, its first creative period produced the Bible. The overarching unity of the Scriptures which modern readers may find within it did not exist during the biblical period itself. To put it into Hegelian terms, the Bible represents a synthesis emerging out of the thesis and antithesis of conflicting attitudes, ideas, and emphases that were expressed by the Hebrew priests, the prophets, and the sages.[18]

In the days of the Second Commonwealth, when the foundations both for rabbinic Judaism and for Christianity were laid, the interplay of sects was fierce and unrelenting. The Pharisees represented normative Judaism, but they were challenged on the right by the Sadducees and on the left by a cluster of Essenic sects, who, for the first time in recorded history, now speak to us directly out of the Dead Sea Scrolls. Each group undoubtedly tended to regard the others as beyond the pale of the "authentic" tradition.

Today religious adversaries are rarely, if ever, destroyed physically by their opponents, though one has the uncomfortable suspicion that this may be due to lack of power rather than to lack of will! Religious controversialists are quick to read their opponents out of the fold. Instances of this tendency are plentiful, even among contemporary Christians and Jews.

Nevertheless, the antagonists are all within the same tradition, as history reveals time and again. In the eighteenth century, the hostility between the *Hasidim* and their opponents, the *Mitnaggedim,* was so intense that the greatest rabbinic authority of the age, the Gaon, Elijah of Vilna, was prevailed upon on two different occasions to excommunicate the new sect. Today both are compatible components of Orthodox Judaism.

It is the function of the objective historian and the careful observer to recognize that such conflicting strands constitute part of a larger pattern. This is true within both Christianity and Judaism and within the wider context of the Judeo-Christian tradition.

We in the West who are identified with either Judaism or Christianity are acutely conscious of the divergences between them. However, the impression that would be borne in upon an Oriental observer would be radically different. To a Chinese Confucianist, a Japanese Taoist, or an Indian Buddhist, Christianity and Judaism would appear as basically two versions of the same religious tradition. A man raised in a Far-Eastern culture would find the points of identity and similarity between the two Western religions far more significant and numerous than the elements of difference. He would be struck by the fact that both Judaism and Christianity share in large degree the same Scriptures, revere the same sacred history, believe in a personal God of righteousness, adhere to an activistic ethical code stressing personal responsibility and observe a body of rituals with strong affinities and resemblances. Quite properly, he would see the Western monotheistic religions standing together in marked contrast to the Oriental religio-philosophic tradition, which also appears in a variety of forms.

D. *Even where genuine divergences exist between Judaism and Christianity, the contrast is often not total but one of emphasis and relative importance. An element which is dominant in one tradition nearly always exists in the other, albeit in secondary form.* Hence aspects of minor significance may, as a result of new insights or new conditions, gain in importance. Even in dormant form, these elements constitute a resource available for use when the need arises. A few instances will help to elucidate the point.

The biblical and rabbinic tradition is fundamentally life-affirming. It sees in the phenomena of the natural world the abundant signs of the Living God. Hence it does not look askance at the physical aspects of existence. This attitude is demonstrated by the multifarious details of rabbinic law, which regulate every aspect of life, including diet, dress, the family, business, and etiquette. While hedonism is frowned upon, Judaism is basically unsympathetic to asceticism, regarding it as a mark of ingratitude toward the Giver of all blessings. Nevertheless Judaism developed substantial ascetic tendencies, particularly in the Middle Ages, the roots of which may be found in earlier periods.

In classical Christianity, asceticism occupies a central place. Yet it is clear that Christianity is far closer even in this respect to Judaism than to Oriental religion. Hence it is possible for some Christian teachers and many more Christian laymen today to negate the ascetic strand in their tradition, without feeling any sharp sense of strain.[19] Even in earlier times and in circles that cultivated asceticism as the highest good, Christianity never carried the tendency as far as Buddhism, which dismissed the entire fabric of the material world as an illusion and declared that the highest goal of life is to attain a level where all desire is absent.

Individual exceptions aside, Western man, be he Christian or Jewish, is not likely to find the quietism of Nirvana acceptable as an all-encompassing philosophy of life. The overwhelming material problems that afflict India—its poverty, disease, and overcrowding—may be charged not unfairly to the nonactivistic, antimaterialistic world view that is dominant in India's creeds. Yet as a critique of the excesses inherent in the pursuit of the world's physical blessings, the spirit of Hindu thought is perennially valuable. Western religion, reflecting as well as affecting the temper of the civilization in which it functions, is predominantly activistic, but this trait easily passes over into useless bustle and the fever of motion for its own sake. The strain and struggle of achievement often mask little more than acquisitiveness and greed, so that life is robbed of all serenity and peace. Here Oriental religion, with its stress upon the contemplative life as the *summum bonum,* supplies a much-needed balance to the perils of activism. The "truth" lies neither with the West nor with the East, but in a creative tension between the two. What is true of such widely disparate traditions as that of Oriental and Western religion is even more true of the two components of the Judeo-Christian heritage.

E. *In a free and open dialogue, each member of the Judeo-Christian tradition can serve to enhance, and if need be, to correct the other for the mutual benefit of both.*

Thus we have noted that in Judaism ascetic tendencies occupy a lesser place in the hierarchy of values than in Christianity. Yet the enjoyment of life's pleasures can easily be distorted into hedonism and materialism and degenerate into license and irresponsibility. Here the correctives of discipline and of asceticism are needed to emphasize the virtues of self-restraint and moderation, and to stress the insignificance of the material aspect of existence. Such a counterbalance is to be found in the ascetic tendencies which exist in all religions to some degree, but which are stronger in classical Christianity than in Judaism.

From the days of St. Paul, Christianity has underscored the truth that "the letter killeth, but the spirit giveth life" (*II Cor.* 3:6). Yet always there is the grave danger of a vague spirituality expressing itself in emotion, but finding no concrete manifestation in life. Here the emphasis upon works and not merely upon faith, which characterizes Judaism, is a valuable corrective. The stress upon conduct embodied in law, which Judaism has exemplified through the ages through the development of the *Halachah*, is today increasingly recognized as an essential ingredient of an endurable society.

Judaism is a faith intimately linked to an ethnic group, though its universalistic vision encompasses all men. Christianity takes pride in knowing no ethnic boundaries, but it sets up standards of belief as essential to salvation. Christianity can help safeguard Judaism against weakening its universalistic aspect. Judaism can remind Christianity that national loyalty is neither irrelevant nor hostile to the good life and that granting freedom of thought to those who differ with us is entirely compatible with a strong commitment to one's own faith.

The Christian doctrine of original sin, particularly as reinterpreted by some contemporary thinkers, has already influenced the thought of many exponents of Judaism. It has served to reveal the dark depths within the human soul which an easy and superficial optimism has tended to overlook. Traditional Judaism, on the other hand, takes a realistic view of human nature, without accepting the doctrine of original sin. From this vantage point it is able to offer guidelines for dealing with the agonizing problems of family life, race relations, religious differences, and national loyalties within the context of a world community.

The dialogue between the two faiths might well address itself to such themes as the tension between law and freedom, the relationship of the material and the spiritual, the dichotomy between the letter and the spirit, issues with regard to which there is a difference of emphasis in Judaism and in Christianity.

F. *Finally, given the common origin and the abundance*

of similar elements in both traditions, it is clear that new insights and changing historical circumstances can serve to bring the traditions even closer, not to a point of identity but to a position of greater similarity of outlook. Consider the most central area of theological conflict. On the one hand, classical Christianity claims to be the sole avenue of salvation through the faith in Jesus as the Savior. On the other, Judaism insists on the election of Israel, and the eternal validity of the Mosaic Revelation as embodied in the Jewish tradition.

Neither doctrine has been abandoned, but a change of emphasis and mood has undoubtedly taken place. The Catholic doctrine, *Nulla salus extra Ecclesiam*, "No salvation outside the Church," has been interpreted in recent years far more broadly than in the past. Contemporary Catholic thinkers include within the concept of the Church all men and women of good will and character who seek to live in accordance with their consciences. Several years ago Cardinal Cushing made it clear that this broad view is normative for contemporary Catholicism, as Father Leonard Feeney learned to his cost, when he insisted upon the narrow interpretation.

In Judaism, the concept of the election of Israel has remained central in the belief of most groups: Orthodoxy, Conservatism, and Reform. Only Reconstructionism has officially surrendered the doctrine. Yet even among the upholders of the traditional viewpoint there has been a growing emphasis upon the doctrine as a moral imperative for Jews, a call to *noblesse oblige*, rather than as an instrument for the exclusion of non-Jews. This ethical view of the election of Israel has a long and honorable pedigree. It may be traced back twenty-seven centuries, to Amos, who reinterpreted the folk doctrine of the chosen people to mean adherence to a higher standard of obedience to the Divine Will, "You only have I known of all the families of the

earth, therefore will I visit upon you all your iniquities"
(3:2). From Amos to our own day, the idea has gained in
strength, as in Israel Zangwill's definition of a chosen people as "a choosing people."

As more liberal attitudes toward those outside their respective groups gain increasing adherents, both in Christianity and in Judaism, one more link is being forged in the
chain of the Judeo-Christian tradition, a chain that was ex-
plicit, even if not fully expressed, for centuries.

The doctrine of the Trinity is central to traditional
Christianity. In some quarters today its value has been seriously questioned, as by the Rev. James A. Pike, formerly
Bishop of California, who wrote, "Jesus was in every sense
a human being, just as we are." [20] The Rev. Benjamin
Minifie, rector of the Grace Episcopal Church in New
York, has declared that "the Trinity has never been a very
satisfactory way of expressing the Christian faith in
God." [21] To be sure, this point of view is not the dominant
one among Christian believers. Yet it is probably fair to say
that in increasing measure the Trinity is being reinterpreted
by modern Christian theologians, either explicitly or implicitly. It is the unity of God which is generally underscored in contemporary Christian teaching. Speaking as one
who stands outside the tradition, I have the impression that
if the controversy of Arius and Athanasius were to take
place today instead of in the fourth century, the unitarian
emphasis of the former would not be formally stigmatized
as heretical nor would its adherents be subjected to excommunication.

The Christian doctrine of the Fall of Man and Original
Sin is central to the Christian drama of salvation. In spite of
some assertions to the contrary, it has no genuine analogue
in Judaism. Modern Christian theologians such as Reinhold
Niebuhr have reinterpreted the idea of original sin with
great profundity. Yet in the life and thought of many

Christian believers, it seems to be taken literally only rarely. The concept of human nature with which most contemporary Christian believers operate seems far closer to the Jewish doctrine. According to biblical and rabbinic teaching, every man possesses two *yetzers*, the good impulse and the evil impulse, and is given the capacity to choose the right and reject the wrong.[22]

One of the great issues in Christian theology is the efficacy of faith over works. Basing himself upon what he felt to be the overwhelming testimony of the New Testament, Martin Luther emphasized the efficacy of faith rather than works, thus contradicting the official teaching of the Catholic Church. Today many Protestants would no longer adopt so uncompromising a position. In recognizing the importance of works as the means to salvation, they would be drawing closer not only to the outlook of Catholicism but to the viewpoint of Judaism, which has always declared that observance of the Commandments takes precedence even over the study of the Torah and that works are the touchstone of men's worth. In fact, the rabbis went so far as to declare that God himself mused, "Would that men forsook Me, but kept My law"—adding the afterthought, to be sure, "because the light within it would bring them near to Me." [23]

To one Jewish observer at least, there seems to be growing evidence that contemporary Christianity is moving toward a greater appreciation of attitudes and insights that have always been congenial to Judaism. The new emphasis in Catholic circles on the principle of collegiality and the role of the laity as the people of God, the modification of ascetic practices and the growing involvement of the religious in the problems of the secular world—all these are reactions characteristic of normative Judaism, indeed, of the Pharisaic rather than the Essenic approach. The search for new formulations of doctrine and practice associated with

John Courtney Murray and Hans Kung, Paul Tillich and Reinhold Niebuhr, Bishop Robinson in England and Bishop Pike in America have aroused vigorous conflicting reactions, but it is such differences that are the stuff of meaningful dialogue.

Perhaps the most striking case in point of a growing *rapprochement* between the two components of the Judeo-Christian tradition is to be found in the crucial area of marriage and family relations. The classical Christian doctrine takes its departure from St. Paul, who exalted celibacy and regarded marriage as a concession to human imperfection.[24] In our day, Pope Pius XII felt it necessary to admonish strongly those who exalt marriage above celibacy.[25]

No more diametrical confrontation is conceivable than with traditional Judaism. In every period, from the Bible to the Talmud, through the Middle Ages to the modern age, and in every school of thought, including that of the most rigorous mystics and ascetics, marriage is regarded as man's most sacred estate, and the first of the Commandments. Traditional Judaism frowned upon celibacy and interpreted the technical term for marriage, *kiddushin*, as "sanctification." When Ben Azzai, one of the sages in the Talmud, remained unmarried, he felt constrained to justify his departure from the norm as due to his passionate desire to concentrate upon the study of Torah: "My soul is in love with the Torah." [26] Nonetheless, his practice never became normative in Judaism.

Moreover, the authentic Jewish tradition, both in the Bible and in the Talmud, recognized marriage as possessing not one but two basic purposes, procreation and human companionship. According to rabbinic teaching, the biblical commandment, "Be fruitful and multiply" (*Gen.* 1:28), was fulfilled by begetting two children. The second function of marriage, expressed in the observation, "It is not good for man to dwell alone" (*Gen.* 2:18), served as the basis for the rabbinic insistence that all men should be married, even those incapable of begetting children, either because of physical disability or age.

Protestant Christianity, by and large, found itself in harmony with these two purposes of marriage. The ferment in Roman Catholic circles today represents a growing recognition that the age-old attitudes of the Church need to be revised. On October 11, 1965, a group of eighty-one distinguished Roman Catholic laymen petitioned the Vatican Council to set up a post-council committee "to reconsider the present combination of pastoral duties with celibacy." A more positive appreciation of the human body and of the rights of men has already been influential in the deliberations of the Ecumenical Council, the appeal stated. "These changed views cannot bypass the clergy," it added.[27] When and if such a reinterpretation takes place, Catholics will find the material for a new attitude toward marriage available to them in the Hebrew Scriptural heritage that they share with non-Catholics, Jewish and Christian.

We may now restate our basic thesis. The concept of a Judeo-Christian tradition is no myth. While each component has its own individuality, both in content and in emphasis, there are fundamental elements they hold in common.

The Talmud tells that in some cases of doubt as to the law, the rabbis would say, "Go out and see how the common people are acting." [28] Politics, it has been said, is too important to be left to politicians. It may perhaps be equally true that religion is too vital to be left to its technicians. It may well be that the man in the street, whose knowledge of his specific religious tradition is frequently vague and whose understanding of its implications seems superficial, may have a better vision of the forest precisely because he does not see each of the trees.

Frequently observers of religion on the contemporary scene criticize the current religiosity on the score of its superficiality and vagueness. Though there is substantial justice in the complaint, the criticism may be swallowed too uncritically! One often has the feeling that the critics are objecting to the fact that the masses today do not seem to be interested in the niceties of the theological distinctions to which they, the critics, are committed. But this so-called "undenominational religion," while undoubtedly suffering from many defects, deserves more of a defense than it has generally received. The proverbial "man in the street" would define his religion as love of God and faith in Him, though he might be unable to present a thoroughly elaborated theological position. He would insist that the love of one's fellow man, expressed in decent human relations, is the essence of obedience to the Divine will, no matter what other creedal and ritual demands his specific tradition may make. If the unsophisticated advocates of such a religion possessed the requisite learning, they could easily buttress their position by citing chapter and verse from the prophets and sages of Judaism and from the teachers and saints of Christianity.

As the Western world confronts the challenges of the second half of the twentieth century, it possesses a spiritual resource of incalculable power in the Judeo-Christian tradition, which together with the Greco-Roman heritage has laid the foundations of Western civilization and may yet help to redeem it from catastrophe.

The two elements in the tradition, as we have seen, have differed in greater or lesser degree with regard to many elements of their world view and their way of life. But they have always been at one in their allegiance to the concept of the Fatherhood of God and its all-important corollaries, the brotherhood of man, his inalienable dignity, and his right to justice and freedom as a being created in the Divine image. For Judaism and Christianity, the great commandments are the Decalogue, the Golden Rule, the injunction to love God with all one's heart, and the prophetic formulation of man's duty as "doing justice, loving mercy, and walking humbly with God." [29] If these be overly familiar quotations, the fact testifies how thoroughly the Judeo-Christian tradition has permeated the consciousness, if not yet the conduct, of men.

In the past, the full implications of these doctrines were all too often unrecognized, except by the greatest spirits in both traditions—the prophets, sages, martyrs, and saints. The rank and file of men found it easy to proclaim their allegiance to their religious faith, while holding fast to racial inequality, religious bigotry, social injustice, and war. But the teaching of the tradition, while it could be ignored, could never be wholly expunged from the consciousness and the conscience of men. The biblical word could be misinterpreted; it could not be blotted out.

Today the biblical heritage that Judaism and Christianity hold in common, deepened by the shared experiences of nineteen centuries of struggle, defeat, and aspiration, constitutes an inexhaustible fountain of guidance, inspiration, and courage for modern men. Much has been granted to our generation, but all too often we have lost the alpha and the omega, our roots in the universe and our sense of purpose in life.

The Judeo-Christian tradition is no mere exercise in semantics or a device of apologetics. Men need to recognize the validity of the concept, in order to explore its dimensions and to be aware of its limits. The dialogue between the two component elements in the tradition will chasten and deepen both, while the recognition of the unity of the tradition will bring men a new sense of fellowship and a reassurance of victory.

Life has always been the matrix of thought. Undoubtedly the concept of the Judeo-Christian tradition has emerged in our day because men are moved by a greater sense of urgency than ever before in meeting massive problems both at home and abroad. But the truth of the idea is not impugned by the fact that it was long obscured by blindness and bigotry, by narrowness of vision and the lust for power. One cannot halt an idea whose hour has come. In the painful and heartrending struggle to enlarge the boundaries of justice, freedom, and peace for all men, those who have been nurtured by the Judeo-Christian tradition will be sustained by their common faith that it is the will of their Father in heaven that His Kingdom be established on earth. To this basic enterprise, which alone endows man's life with meaning, the Jew and the Christian will each contribute insights and attitudes, derived from his specific background, that will benefit the other. They are not identical twins; it is enough that they are brothers.

CHAPTER EIGHT

INTERMARRIAGE
AND THE JEWISH FUTURE

IT IS SURELY obvious that this volume represents a partisan approach to the problems confronting the Jewish tradition, for it is dedicated to its meaningful survival. As we have seen, when the opportunities and temptations of the modern age broke in upon the medieval world of the ghetto, undermining the structure of the Jewish community and the authority of Jewish tradition, there was no single, monolithic response to the challenge. With few exceptions, the Jews of Western and Central Europe accepted with enthusiasm the offer of political citizenship and its accompanying civic, cultural, and economic opportunities. At the same time most modern Jews, with varying degrees of conviction, to be sure, wished to retain a sense of continuity with their past and a feeling of Jewish identity in the present. The various responses to the challenge of the Emancipation and the Enlightenment—religious, cultural, and nationalist—discussed in the opening chapters of this work, differed sharply from one another. Yet what they had in common was more significant. They were all survivalist in philosophy, regarding the preservation of the

Jewish identity as a good, and seeking to maintain a link with the Jewish tradition, which they each interpreted according to their lights.

It is from this survivalist position that the present work is written, out of a conviction that the individual Jew, the Jewish group, and the world will gain by the preservation of the Jewish heritage; and conversely, that the disappearance of Jews or the decay of Judaism would be a tragedy.

Nonetheless, it has been pointed out that from the inception of the modern age another viewpoint, that of assimilation diametrically opposed to survivalism, has been widespread and powerful. Though assimilation is to be met with in virtually every period of Jewish history, it was not until the modern age that it became a dominant factor. In the ancient world, cases of willful defection were few. One of these rare instances was the nephew of the Jewish philosopher Philo, Tiberius Alexander. He became a pagan and served as Roman procurator over his unruly former brethren in Palestine. Later he helped Vespasian and Titus in the siege and final destruction of Jerusalem in the year 70. A more equivocal case was that of the historian Josephus, who betrayed the Jewish cause during the war against Rome and became a client of the Roman Flavian family, whose name he adopted. From his comfortable berth in the imperial capital, he spent the closing period of his life writing his indispensable works on Jewish history and defending his people against the anti-Semitic detractors.

In the Middle Ages cases of conversion to Christianity and Mohammedanism by men seeking a broader field for their talents than the ghetto provided were by no means unheard of. Nevertheless, these phenomena of total assimilation were relatively few in number and limited in impact.

It was in the modern age, when the mass movement of Jews out of the ghetto into the general life of the Western world gained momentum, that total assimilation became a widespread phenomenon. Heinrich Heine declared that the baptismal certificate was the passport to Western society. In his own life, to be sure, it proved to be an admission card to second-class citizenship. Nonetheless, the stream of defections from the Jewish community to the brave new world beckoning outside continued to grow in intensity from the end of the eighteenth century to the present.

At the threshold of the modern period the Jewish philosopher and spokesman, Moses Mendelssohn, had declared in his passionate plea for equality and freedom, *Jerusalem*, that if equal rights were offered to Jews at the cost of the surrender of their Judaism they would reject the rights. He was unduly optimistic. After his death all his children, except his oldest son, were themselves converted to Christianity, either in its Catholic or its Protestant version.

As the nineteenth century wore on, another technique of assimilation became more prevalent than outright conversion. Intermarriage had the advantage of avoiding some of the moral problems connected with conversion. Intermarriage did not require professing another faith on the part of men and women who had little or no religious convictions of any kind. Nor did it entail the sense of guilt involved in overtly deserting an ancient and honorable tradition for which one's ancestors had suffered and died through the centuries.

Finally, intermarriage could be justified on idealistic grounds. It offered the means for achieving a "nonsectarian" society in which the divergences between Jews and Christians, a distinction without a difference—so it seemed —would be obliterated. Thus the promptings of desire and of personal advantage were powerfully reenforced by an idealistic vision of a world in which prejudice would be reduced, if not totally eliminated.

In sum, the growing integration of all elements of the

population in the free society, reenforced by these varied motivations, has made intermarriage the royal road to defection from the Jewish community.

Intermarriage, which may be defined as a marriage in which the bride and the groom are of different religious backgrounds and neither has converted to the faith of the other, has been studied statistically for over a century. By and large, the data is fullest for Germany and less adequate for other communities.[1] In Germany the percentage of Jewish grooms and brides marrying outside their faith rose from 8.9 and 7.6 respectively for the years 1900–05, to 27.6 and 17.4 respectively for the years 1927–33, the half decade before Hitler's accession to power. German Jewry represented an old established community going back for centuries. In Canada, largely peopled by recent immigrants from Eastern Europe, the percentage of Jewish grooms and brides intermarrying rose from 3.5 and 1.7 respectively for 1927–33, to 11.0 and 5.4 respectively for 1960–62, virtually a fourfold increase.

For the United States, data was both fragmentary and inexact, being based largely on estimates and unsatisfactory techniques of research. Erich Rosenthal's epoch-making study of intermarriage in Iowa and in Washington, D.C., obviously dealt with special, atypical situations.[2] Iowa possesses a very small, thinly scattered Jewish population. Rosenthal found that the Jewish brides and grooms who were married in Iowa in 1953–59 had an out-marriage rate of 15.0 and 35.6 respectively. Washington, D.C., on the other hand, has a highly mobile, intellectualized Jewish population largely employed by government agencies. In Washington Rosenthal found the overall figure of religiously intermarried Jews to be 13.1.

Undoubtedly the figures for these two communities are higher than for the American Jewish community as a whole. Yet they are not as much out of line as some would believe. Thus, 14 percent of Jewish high school seniors in Boston and 21 percent of such students in St. Louis were children whose fathers or mothers were not Jewish. Among Jewish high school seniors in Omaha and Denver the percentage of children of mixed parentage was 23 and 27, respectively. A survey of a small sample showed that 12 percent of Jewish husbands and about 11 percent of Jewish wives had non-Jewish spouses.[3] The conventional figure of 6 percent for Jewish intermarriage in America, which has been quoted for decades, is far too low, as the present writer has long maintained. I believe that it is far closer to 10 percent today and is constantly rising.

This conclusion is demonstrated by two of Rosenthal's most significant findings. His figures reveal that intermarriage rises with each succeeding native-born generation, as every fair-minded observer has noted. His figures for Washington give the first generation of foreign-born American Jews an intermarriage rate of 1.4 percent, the second generation, native-born children of foreign-born parents, a rate of 10.2 percent, and the third generation, native-born offspring of native-born parents, a figure of 17.9 percent.

The second significant factor in his study was the evidence that a college education doubles the rate of intermarriage. Thus in the third generation the figure rose from 17.9 percent to 37 percent. With the rapid expansion of college education for American Jews, the prospects are grave indeed, unless the trend is halted or reversed.

Finally, the comfortable notion that intermarriage brings as many into the Jewish fold as it takes out cannot be sustained. Children of mixed marriages are raised as Jews only where there is a formal conversion of the non-Jewish partner to Judaism and these cases are generally not included in statistical studies of intermarriage. In the vast majority of instances of intermarriage, the children are lost to Jewish life—70 percent in Rosenthal's figures, approximately 75 percent in pre-World War Germany.

In sum, intermarriage represents virtually the most extreme form of de-Judaization. It therefore constitutes the major threat, though not the only one, to the survival of the Jewish tradition, because if unchecked, it will spell the decline and ultimate disappearance of the Jewish community as a recognizable entity. Indeed, several mass circulation media, drawing upon recent statistical studies, have focused attention upon intermarriage as presaging "the vanishing American Jew."

Homilies and laments on the subject are plentiful but are not likely to prove very helpful. There is need for additional research on the facts, and even more, for a careful analysis of all the factors entering into intermarriage, so that constructive steps may be taken for meeting this major challenge to the Jewish future.

At the outset it should be recognized that intermarriage is a complex phenomenon and that any attempt to think in terms of a unitary solution is therefore doomed to failure. Any statement on the subject couched in such terms as "The answer...", or "the only answer," is, *ipso facto*, wrong. Any given course of action may be useful in dealing with one or another element of the problem, but it cannot possibly be the total, definitive answer.

A second, inescapable conclusion is that intermarriage is part of the price that modern Jewry must pay for freedom and equality in an open society. However unpleasant the prospect may be, it is clear that intermarriage can never be totally eliminated or even drastically reduced in a democratic social order.

The idea was recently advanced by a distinguished social scientist that a higher birth rate among Jews would solve the problem by compensating for losses due to attrition.

This is hardly convincing. One can easily imagine a situation in which a much larger birth rate would be accompanied by a larger degree of intermarriage. Catholics have the highest birth rate of any major religious group in America, yet they also exhibit the highest rate of intermarriage. There are several reasons to explain why they seem less concerned about the problem than the Jewish community. In many cases the Church retains the intermarried young Catholic in the fold by achieving the conversion of the non-Catholic partner. Failing that, the Church is often able to insist upon the Catholic upbringing of the children. In other words, Catholics who intermarry often assimilate their non-Catholic partners into the community. Moreover, even the Catholics who leave the Church when they intermarry are still within the Christian community. In cases of Jewish intermarriage, all statistical studies bear out the results of personal observation that the Jewish partner and the children of the mixed union generally assimilate out of the Jewish community.

To revert to our basic contention, living in a free and open society exposes the Jew to assimilation, the most striking and widespread form of which is intermarriage. Since it cannot be eliminated completely, the Jewish community should direct its efforts toward reducing the price it must pay for the status of equality enjoyed by its members. In this respect much can be done.

In order to define the dimensions of the problem and attack it successfully, the factors in intermarriage should be divided into two main categories:

A. *Factors that are not susceptible to Jewish communal action and control. The first is, of course, the personal factor.* Young people meet, become friends, and fall in love, and the emotion becomes the all-powerful influence in their lives. Often it is so strong that it overrides every other consideration. Love conquers all—even a deep commitment to faith and community on the part of the young people themselves, and a genuine concern for the anguish they cause their parents. In a democratic society marked by a progressively greater degree of acculturation, these personal factors will continue to operate in ever larger degree. Attractive young men and women will be meeting each other in school, in business, in the culture realm, in the social sphere, and in public life, unless Jews are prepared to ghettoize themselves—and no one has suggested this course of action.

While this first factor is highly personal, the second is impersonal, ubiquitous, seemingly almost automatic. In our society there are *strong, well-nigh irresistible pressures on our youth to achieve personal advancement in the economic and political areas.* This requires a substantial measure of social integration into the dominant group, if not complete absorption into it. In our Christian or post-Christian civilization, there still are tremendous liabilities involved in being a Jew. Prejudice may not always take on the grosser forms of earlier years when there were restrictions in such basic areas as college admissions and employment. Today the pressures are subtle, particularly as they affect the upper class and upper middle class, but they are nonetheless real and potent.

It is no accident that it is precisely the higher social and economic groups that are most responsive to these social aspirations and consequently are most vulnerable to intermarriage. Thus a very high proportion of marriages involving Jews that are chronicled in the society pages of the Sunday *New York Times*, perhaps half the instances reported, are cases of intermarriage. These people are not suffering from overt discrimination. It is the subtler forms of social acceptance which they are seeking, consciously or unconsciously, and intermarriage offers a less painful form of "passing" into the major group than outright baptism. The higher incidence of intermarriage among the richest elements of the Jewish community is no novelty. The same situation prevailed in prewar Germany, France, and England, as well as in the Czarist Empire.

The various kinds of subtle disability which still affect and afflict these Jews induce in them a marked sense of inferiority. Jews represent not merely a minority group but, with the exception of the Negro, the most conspicuous minority in the Western world. To be sure, the Negro has suffered grievously because his color makes him an easy target. On the other hand, the Jew has suffered discrimination and persecution for two millennia, much of which has been perpetrated "in the name of God" and other lofty ideals. In sum, the vast complex of pressures on Jews to desert the Jewish community that we may call "anti-Semitism" must be included among the factors about which the Jewish community can do little or nothing. For in this area Jews are far more acted upon than active. In this sense, anti-Semitism is a Christian, not a Jewish problem.

The third category of elements not susceptible to Jewish communal activity consists of the *psychological and psychopathological factors.* In his classic work, *Juedischer Selbsthass,* Theodor Lessing collected a large number of examples of Jewish self-hate that have characterized important figures in the German culture-sphere, the most creative of all modern Jewish communities. These brilliant men and women were eaten through with pathological hatred of self because of their Jewish origin. We have already noted some striking illustrations not only in Europe but in America as well.

Selbsthass, like every pathological phenomenon, takes many forms, from the trivial to the tragic, from small vulgarities to major psychoses. The importance even of tiny little slips has been highlighted by Sigmund Freud in his *Psychopathology of Everyday Life.*

Jewish self-hatred in all its forms exists in modern society as a reflex of the age-old anti-Jewish prejudices of the non-Jewish majority. Though not the only cause, it supplies a powerful drive toward intermarriage. Where this state of mind exists, there is little that can be done. By the time the case of incipient intermarriage comes to the attention of the parent or the rabbi, the social worker or the psychologist, the situation is generally beyond remedy. Even if we meet with the young man and woman in question, we talk past them, not with them or to them. They already are enclosed in a protective shell which shields their neurosis or psychosis and cannot be penetrated. Any discussion concerning the proposed intermarriage will deal with superficial and irrelevant aspects of the problem. On the underlying realities there is no communication.

Another psychopathological factor is the phenomenon of *rebellion against parents or against the entire social structure.* At every hand we see the breakdown of family authority, which is closely linked to the collapse of moral standards among parents. Intermarriage has been described as one strand in this pattern of maladjustment and conflict within the contemporary family. That family conflict is more characteristic of Jews than of others is by no means certain, but these strains and stresses are undoubtedly widespread.

What is particularly frustrating is that this rebellion against parents often occurs where there is no objective reason in the attitudes and behavior of the parents. This type of revolt can be documented with many instances.

I recall an older couple, gentle, cultivated, and pious folk, whose son was a graduate of one of the best Hebraic collegiate institutions in New York. The son would tell his father, "Dad, you won't need to worry in the future. My home will always be kosher." A few years later the son married out of the faith. He was now a professor at a Midwestern university, where it was not even known that he was a Jew. Finally his heart-broken parents prevailed upon him to meet with me. He rejected any suggestion to discuss with his wife the possibility of raising his children as Jews.

In cases such as these there is no tangible fault to find with the behavior of the parents. The motivations for alienation and intermarriage are psychopathological, with no genuine link to objective reality. Obviously, there are other instances where the actual conduct of parents evokes justified hostility on the part of children. When this resentment takes the form of self-alienation through intermarriage, it is pathological.

Another widespread phenomenon that prepares the groundwork for intermarriage is *name-changing*, the shedding of recognizably "Jewish" names for "Anglo-Saxon" surnames. Names are no longer a clue to the personal background of young people. When youngsters begin to "date" they naturally do not begin their acquaintanceship by asking, "Tell me, what is your religion?" By the time that question arises, the initial bond of love may have been forged between them. Perhaps it is purely an accident, without any significance, that virtually the only biblical names popular among "modern" Jews are drawn from the New Testament: Matthew, Mark, John, Paul, Stephen, Thomas, and Peter.

Another vital sociological factor making for assimilation and intermarriage is *the disappearance of the older Jewish areas of settlement* and their replacement with new areas of residence for Jews. Once there were Jewish neighborhoods; today there are only neighborhoods in which Jews live. Undoubtedly a positive identification with Judaism is of great importance as a deterrent to intermarriage. Yet it is obvious that most people do not choose their wives or husbands out of a conscious religious commitment, but because of the social contacts which neighborhood life fosters. To be sure, there are cases where a young man says, "I am looking for a Jewish girl because I want to be a Jew!" But for every such instance, there are a score where Jewish young men marry Jewish young women simply because of physical propinquity. Living in Jewish areas of settlement, they come into contact with one another and ultimately find a Jewish marriage partner. The breakdown of the Jewish neighborhood opens the floodgates to intermarriage.

These causes of intermarriage, whether operating separately or in combination, are often disguised. The real reason frequently does not come to the surface because it is overlaid with the patina of *rationalization*, ideological or personal, or both. It is by no means rare to have a Jewish young man present a long catalogue of unattractive traits that he attributes to all Jewish girls. Conversely, some Jewish young women will insist that Jewish young men as a group are repositories of virtually every fault and possess few redeeming features. Stereotypes are the raw material from which prejudice is constructed; once lodged in the mind, they can almost never be dislodged, for they are not susceptible to objective observation or rational analysis.

The same consideration applies to the various ideological rationalizations which are used to defend intermarriage and to dismiss objections to it as mere prejudice. College youngsters sometimes justify intermarriage on the ground that "all men are created equal." Having taken courses in logic, they know perfectly well that the argument is an outrageous *non sequitur*, of which they would not be guilty in another context. That the point is advanced time and again here is evidence that not reason but rationalization is at work.

Similarly, with regard to the frequent complaint that

young people are dissatisfied with the quality of the Jewish life around them in the synagogue and other institutions. This contention is not to be dismissed lightly, and we shall return to it shortly. Yet very often the explanation is an excuse and the dissatisfaction an alibi for defection.

This formidable list of factors, which can perhaps be augmented, embraces those elements of contemporary Jewish life that are not readily amenable to control or even to major amelioration on the part of the Jewish community. By and large, these aspects of contemporary life need to be endured because they cannot be cured.

B. *The second category of factors making for intermarriage consists of those which are susceptible to Jewish communal action and control.* These may be further subdivided into two classes. The first consists of *measures which affect the structure and character of the Jewish community* and would make Jewish adherence more desirable and significant. The second consists of *steps directly affecting Jewish individuals and families.*

It cannot be denied that there are major ills in the Jewish community which often serve to alienate from Judaism many young people, not to speak of their elders. One such phenomenon is the *growth of intensified denominationalism in the Jewish community.* It is a tragic paradox that precisely when the American environment is shaping the attitudes and mores of most American Jews along the same lines, so that their similarities are growing, organizational rivalry and factional competition are on the increase. In the absence of substantive grounds for loyalty to one cause rather than to another, the lowest standards of the marketplace have been imported into Jewish religious and communal life.

As we have seen, there are far-reaching and significant differences in the content and the approach to the Jewish tradition that are embodied in the varied philosophies of

Judaism. Reform, Conservatism, and Orthodoxy each possesses areas of concern and achievement that could enrich and stimulate the others, if a genuine dialogue were to take place among them. Unfortunately, institutional interests rather than ideological commitments frequently lie at the base of these divisions of the Jewish community. The problem is not that there are differences among Orthodoxy, Conservatism, and Reform, but that the Orthodox are not Orthodox, the Conservative not Conservative, and the Reform not Reform.

Today the concept of *Kelal Yisrael,* "the totality of Israel," is honored in the breach rather than in the observance. Not merely the phrase but, what is more significant, the concept has practically disappeared from the written and spoken utterances of the last few years. This divisiveness makes it more difficult for young people to attach themselves to the Jewish community, especially when they do not have clear-cut commitments to one or another group but are seeking identification with their people as a whole.

Another critical area is *the high cost of Jewish affiliation.* The resplendent structures, gleaming in glass and chrome, that house our synagogues, centers, and other institutions, represent capital investments of many hundreds of millions of dollars. As a result, families of limited income and particularly young people at the bottom of the economic ladder find themselves unable to meet the dues and assessments and therefore often remain outside the purview of organized Jewish life. Human nature being what it is, these families often tend to rationalize their nonaffiliation into total hostility toward the goals and ideals of the institutions in question. For it is a fact of life that if we cannot have what we want, we end by not wanting what we cannot have.

In the case of Jewish youth, this argument against the *status quo* may begin as a rationalization of their rebellion, but it has too much objective truth to be dismissed out of hand. When the youngsters grow up and marry, they often find themselves outside the inner circle of communal leadership. At best, they adopt a minimal affiliation. They may join a synagogue for a few years while their son goes to Hebrew school. After his Bar Mitzvah or Confirmation, which generally marks the end of his Jewish education, they drop their membership. Even if they remain affiliated, they remain on the periphery, unable to attain positions of prestige and influence in the Jewish community, which are basic requirements for self-respect and self-fulfillment. It is ironic that these Jewish families seeking to find their place within the Jewish community make the same wry discovery as those who try to flee from Judaism by joining the majority—"It isn't being kept out that hurts; it's being let in and made to feel out!"

Closely related to the swollen budgets of our institutions, only a fraction of which are dedicated to the authentic purposes for which the institution was created, is the growing *impersonalization* within their walls. To maintain these large institutions, vast membership rolls are required, which in turn lead to the creation of elaborate staffs. The most dedicated rabbi or social worker finds himself overwhelmed with the problems of administration and major policy. There is all too little time or energy left for the "minor concerns"—which are almost the only significant ones—such as personal relationships. Preaching from the pulpit, particularly when the congregation is only sparsely represented in the pews, or lecturing from the platform to large audiences, cannot replace the intimate give-and-take of a rabbi and a congregant, of a youngster and a Center worker, of a teen-ager and a youth leader. The impact which the Hasidic movement has made even upon our assimilated and sophisticated society today derives in large measure from the fact that it seeks to establish this personal relationship, working not with masses but with individuals, whom it draws within the orbit of its influence by direct contact. In an age when, to borrow Buber's insight, the "I-it" approach is becoming universal, human beings hunger for the "I-thou" relationship. Our institutional structure rarely makes this possible.

Another widespread ill of the Jewish community is *the absence of recognizable goals for Jewish life in America* that are worthy and significant. It is certainly untrue that low cultural and ethical standards are universal in our institutions and in their leadership, widespread complaints to the contrary notwithstanding. There are, of course, professionals in Jewish service who are merely "professional Jews," to whom their life's work is merely a "job," but they are a minority. Indeed, it would be difficult to find a cadre of professionals in any field with a sense of dedication superior to that of the generality of rabbis and Jewish teachers. Today there is also a great deal of genuine Jewish concern among Jewish social workers and Center executives. They may not have all the answers to the manifold problems besetting Jewish life, but many of them are genuinely involved in the quest.

However, the degree of Jewish commitment among the so-called lay leadership of the community often leaves much to be desired. Here, too, there are many thousands of dedicated laymen on every level who serve the Jewish people with self-effacing sincerity and deep devotion. But there are far too many others for whom organized Jewish life is a pastime, who seek to advance their position or prestige through community "leadership," who constantly propel themselves into the public prints in an insatiable thirst for publicity. In this age of public relations, our youth and their elders read of "leaders" who are "Guests of Honor" at the innumerable testimonial breakfasts, lunches, dinners, and suppers that crowd the calendar of the Jewish community, but they see little evidence of high or even acceptable cultural, religious, or ethical standards among them. On the contrary, the personal qualities of far too many "outstanding citizens" are not calculated to inspire young people to meaningful Jewish commitment.

In order to overcome the conditions in Jewish communal life that contribute to alienation and ultimately to intermarriage, no single program will suffice. A beginning, at least, must be made toward setting true standards for leadership in the Jewish community, even at the risk of a loss in popularity and in support. The truth needs to be emphasized that a "good Jew" is not one who gives but one who lives as a Jew. In view of the centrality of Torah in the hierarchy of Jewish values, a good Jew is a learning Jew, not necessarily a learned Jew, because only what one learns is alive; what one knows from the past may be dead or dying.

It becomes clearer each day that the meaningful survival of American Jewry depends upon what should become its major enterprise—*education in the broadest sense of the term*. It requires a pooling of resources and an intensification of effort by such traditional institutions as the home, the synagogue, and the school, as well as such new agencies as the Community Center and the summer camp, that have arisen in the American milieu.

Equally important, the all-but-total concentration upon the Jewish education of young children must be abandoned. It is teenagers and adolescents who represent the "dangerous age." Strenuous thought and effort should be directed to intensifying their education, both formal and informal. Adult education must cease being the hobby of a few and become a major enterprise of all institutions and movements dedicated to meaningful Jewish life.

The deepening of the Jewish educational process for every age in the community is not to be limited to the classroom, the lecture platform, and the pulpit. There is need for an intensification of the informal education of the Jewish club for children, young people, adults, and "senior citizens." Therein lies the importance of the Jewish Community Center.

There have been some recent developments in the *Jewish Center movement* that are disturbing. In some quarters the doctrine of "nonsectarianism" is being proposed as a guiding philosophy for these institutions. Several years ago, in the wake of the Janowsky Report, a noticeably increased stress upon the Jewish character of the Center movement became evident. Now a reaction has set in. In part it may be induced by the removal of many Jews from the older Jewish neighborhoods and their replacement by non-Jewish residents. As a result, the local Center leadership finds itself with a building and facilities which it wishes to utilize and so a nonsectarian program is introduced. In some instances, the nonsectarian emphasis may be chosen in order to avoid "competition" with synagogue centers and other Jewish community organizations. In others, it may stem from a lack of Jewish knowledge and commitment on the part of the professional and lay leadership.

Whatever the motivations, the end results of the process are clear. The near or total elimination of the Jewish program means watering down the Jewish loyalties and interests of the members which the Center was originally designed to further. Moreover, if Jewish Centers become places for interreligious social gatherings of young people, we are directly stimulating the process of intermarriage.

There is a world of difference between Jewish Community Centers where non-Jews are sincerely welcomed at specific functions as guests, and Community Centers where non-Jews are officially members of the institution. Institutions of the latter type can succeed only in achieving the total denudation of Jewish values for the majority of Jews whom they serve, and the acceleration of the process of alienation among Jewish youth. Jewish survival is endangered by interdating and doomed by intermarriage. The Jewish community is not yet prepared to underwrite the cost of its own destruction.

We cannot overestimate the importance of multiplying Jewish social contacts for our young people. One of the most important values of the Jewish Community Center and of the synagogue center lies in the fact that they serve to bring Jewish young people together. One would prefer to have them meet under Jewish auspices for a Jewish program, but it is better to have them meet under Jewish auspices without a Jewish program than not at all. There is no need to be apologetic about the fact that one of the principal objectives of the Center is simply to create a wholesome social milieu for the meeting of Jewish youth. Generations may come and go, but the role of the *Shadchan* ("marriage broker") goes on forever.

In addition to the School and Center, another instrument has recently been forged that seems full of promise. The past few decades have seen the growth of a network of Jewish *summer camps* that have been called into being by the various cultural, religious, fraternal, and Zionist agencies. A very high percentage of the young people who feel themselves committed to Judaism have been inspired by the experience of Jewish living and learning in camp. Often they are influenced toward Jewish loyalty, not by the ten months of the year they spend at home but by the eight or ten weeks they spend in summer camps. There is need for expanding the number of Jewish summer camps tremendously. If American Jews are not yet able to create a natural and enjoyable Jewish atmosphere in their homes and communities, they can, at any rate, do so in the summer period.

Finally, there is the element that might logically have appeared at the beginning—*the strengthening of Jewish religious loyalty*. It is generally recognized that there has been a growth of attachment to Jewish religious adherence among many young people today. To be sure, the practices which are being retained or revived tend to be those which are unique and nonrepetitive in life. On the other hand, the regular observances, like the dietary laws and Sabbath rest, continue to lose ground except in certain limited though increasingly articulate groups. *Pari passu* with these tendencies, there has been a significant growth in synagogue attendance on the Sabbath and the festivals. This is insufficient for a religiously committed Jew, but it is a starting point.

In a war for survival, strategy is important. In order to attach our young people to Judaism, it is necessary to seek out those practices that they can be persuaded to observe. When a young father names his baby daughter during a synagogue service, he is linking his personal life to his people and faith. When and if great occasions of human life are associated with Judaism through ritual, they achieve a group, indeed a cosmic, significance that transcends the individual's destiny and hallows it. The ritual takes on—to borrow a term from the Christian tradition—the character of a sacramental act. In the language of the Jewish tradition, a custom has been elevated to the level of a *Mitzvah*, "a divine commandment." The *rites de passage* at birth, puberty, marriage, and death transform the great turning points of human experience from the natural to the holy.

The proposals we have thus far discussed are designed to remedy and ameliorate some of the ills of contemporary Jewish life. Their effect upon intermarriage will necessarily be long-term and indirect.

1. Several constructive steps, however, may be taken vis-à-vis Jewish individuals and families, which can have a direct impact upon the problem of intermarriage. There

is need of a network of *Family Counseling Centers* in the larger urban centers, at least, properly staffed with competent social workers, psychologists, and rabbis. These counselors would need to possess not only the requisite technical skills but more elusive gifts—a genuine human sympathy coupled with an insight into human nature which only the untranslatable Hebrew term *sekhel* ("good sense") can convey. Finally, they would be men and women who are not indifferent to Jewish life but believe in it and want it to survive. Today there are many rabbis who are equipped with the broad perspective that we traditionally associate with the social worker, and conversely there are many social workers who have a sense of commitment to the Jewish heritage. The Family Counseling Centers should, in a word, be manned by rabbis and laymen who would place at the center of their concern the well-being of the individual and his family, while not ignoring the needs of the community.

The character of the staff is extremely important. Not every rabbi and not every social worker has the requisite personality, background, and sense of commitment to deal adequately with the complex problems involved in alienation. There is another reason. Several years ago a Jewish refugee from Nazi Germany who was converted to Catholicism published his autobiography. In his book the author claimed that when he was wrestling with agonizing spiritual problems, he could not find a rabbi in Germany with whom he could discuss his difficulties. Whatever the truth of his contention, American rabbis are much more harried than their confreres were in Germany. Many young people today are convinced that there are no rabbis to whom they can talk and no place to which they can take their problems. Or they may be unwilling to go to their family rabbi, precisely because he knows them and their family too well.

The creation of a Family Counseling Center in New

York and the other great centers of Jewish population would seem an absolute necessity, if any headway is to be made in meeting the threat of intermarriage. By the concrete help that the Jewish community would be giving to its young people it would prove it has a genuine concern for their well-being, recognizing that they are important for themselves, for the Jewish people, and for the heritage which only they can preserve and transmit to the world.

These counseling services extended to individuals and families would underscore the truth that a sense of rootedness, a feeling of belonging, is essential to spiritual health, and that the objective should be the positive goal of spiritual health, and not merely the negative one of minimizing the symptoms of disease.

The psychic well-being of the individual is impossible without his moral well-being. The fact should be emphasized again and again that in very many cases of intermarriage more than intermarriage is involved. There are many moral ills that come in its wake—self-deception, alienation from the roots of one's being, self-seeking careerism, often a lifetime of living a lie, of Jewish anti-Semitism, directed against oneself as well as one's fellow Jews. There are moral sins involved in intermarriage, over and above the religious transgression.

Moreover, intermarriage and defection from the Jewish tradition almost always lead to the spiritual impoverishment of the individual as well. It means cutting oneself off from the millennial tradition, rich in wisdom and idealism, that possesses extraordinarily valuable resources for meeting the challenge of modern life. It cannot be emphasized too strongly that Judaism is not a Jewish version of Christianity. It contains insights and ideals that are either lacking or insufficiently clear in the dominant religion. In the areas of group relations, national, racial, and religious, Judaism has its own distinctive and life-giving message for the world. In the field of personal morality, of sex, marriage, and the family, the Jewish tradition at its best has wise and sympathetic guidance to offer its own children and all men. Some of these social and ethical values and insights of Judaism have been elucidated in these pages and elsewhere by this writer and other interpreters of the Jewish tradition. Nevertheless, much more needs to be done to bring these spiritual riches into the life of our generation.

When young people are contemplating abandoning their people it is only fair, for the sake of their personal well-being, that along with all other elements of the problem they be made aware of the resources they and their unborn children would lose by their defection. Even if Jews do not agree wherein the essence of the Jewish heritage resides, they all feel that there is something infinitely precious in it. This has been recognized even by many Jews—such as Heine and Berenson—who have wandered away from their people and yet have continued to feel some link with the tradition they have discarded. Surely those Jews who have not deserted the ship can explicate, with conviction and without rancor, the viable and valuable elements in the Jewish tradition.

In meeting with young people contemplating intermarriage, I have had occasion to say to them, "Your ancestors died for Judaism. We are asking you to live for it. You are being called upon to make a great sacrifice for your people and your faith, for love is precious and painful to surrender. It is hard for me to ask and harder for you to obey the call. But a hundred generations of your ancestors have lived and struggled and created, so that you might carry on the unbroken chain of Judaism and bring Jewish children into the world to live on after you. And as for the young Christian that you love, Christianity puts an identical claim to its children—they have an obligation to preserve and transmit the Christian heritage to generations to come."

It is undoubtedly true that those who were not prepared to listen to the rabbi generally did not come to see him. But there were many who came, and some who heard what was being said—and understood. What is needed is a genuine human sympathy for the situation of troubled young people, coupled with a sense of dedication and a readiness to fight for the life of the Jewish people and its tradition.

Emphasizing the welfare of the individual means much more than giving statistics on intermarriage, the higher number of divorces, or the low fertility rates of intermarried couples. It means highlighting the injury to their psychological health and to their moral standards which is involved in forsaking their own people. It means revealing the intellectual and spiritual impoverishment of their lives entailed by intermarriage, which generally cuts them off from the Jewish heritage. When the young people say to me, "Well, our parents do not know Judaism themselves," the answer should be, "All the more reason why you must explore it for yourself before abandoning it."

Another observation may be added. It often happens that a youngster contemplating intermarriage says, "I don't know why my parents are so disturbed. They never gave me a Jewish education. They do not practice the Jewish religion in the home. They were never the least bit interested in Jewish culture and now they're hysterical. They don't know why they object. They are either hypocritical or prejudiced or both. They are thoroughly unreasonable. I do not see why I should give up something precious to me." The contention is highly reasonable—but it fails to reckon with what lies beyond reason. The response would be somewhat as follows: "It is true your parents do not know what to say to you. But behind their apparently irrational attitude is something far deeper than logic. What is involved here is one of the basic drives of human nature, the dread of annihilation, the passionate desire for immortality. Whether or not we believe in immortality beyond the grave, we all know that we attain to immortality in this world through our children. When your parents contemplate the possibility of your marrying outside the fold, and realize that their grandchildren will no longer be Jews, it is the end as far as they are concerned. If they sound hysterical, it is because they are faced by the specter of their own extinction. They cannot put their fear into words for you, they are not even consciously aware of what impels them, but it is as deep as the instinct of self-preservation. There lies the source of their agony."

Experience testifies that in several instances this approach made an impression on sensitive young people, who were made to realize that their parents were not merely expressing some narrow prejudice or indulging a dislike or contempt for the alien. It suddenly became clear to them that they literally held their parents' lives in their hands.

Whatever the value of these specific approaches, a network of broadly based Counseling Centers on Intermarriage and Family Problems is a basic element in the program for meeting the probem.

2. Another proposal is undoubtedly more controversial, but one that I believe to be essential. Parents and Jewish leaders have a right and a duty to do everything in their power to prevent intermarriage. But when all efforts fail and the intermarriage cannot be prevented, *the Jewish community must make the effort to bring the non-Jewish partner into the community through conversion to Judaism.*

This approach is justifiable from the standpoint both of Judaism and the Jewish people. Basic to it is the conviction that Judaism has significance for mankind, and not only for those who are born Jews. That Judaism will ultimately be accepted by all of mankind is basic to the vision of the future in the Jewish tradition in its most creative periods, and

in the thinking of its greatest exemplars. Every Jewish service ends with the *Alenu* prayer which concludes with the
words of the prophet Zechariah, "On that day, the Lord
shall be one and His name one"—not merely that God will
be one, but that His name will be one, that the faith of Israel will be the faith of mankind. This hope, it seems to me,
enjoins upon Jews at the very least the obligation to bring
into the household of Israel those of God's children who
are contemplating or have already established intimate
bonds with Jews through marriage.

There is every justification for the traditional insistence
that a person should not be accepted into Judaism who
seeks conversion for ulterior motives. But all too often this
concept of sincere conviction is construed far too nar-
rowly. We need a much more sympathetic insight into the
meaning of sincerity and genuine conviction. Human motivation is almost never unilinear, but rather a complex of
factors. In the Bible itself Ruth, the prototype of the ideal
proselyte, became a Jewess out of love for her mother-in-
law. For Ruth says to Naomi, "Where you go, I will go.
Where you lodge, there I will lodge," and only then does
she add, "Your people shall be my people, and your God
my God."

If a person of non-Jewish background, after an extended
period of discussion and study followed by a solemn ritual
of conversion, accepts Judaism and takes upon himself and
his children the responsibilities and the disabilities of Jewish
belonging, he should be welcomed warmly by the family
into which he enters and by other Jews. Even if the original interest in Judaism came from the wish to have a religiously harmonious and unified home for the children,
this is no real ground for doubting the sincerity of the
act. Even if memories and vestigial habits of thought persist in some degree in the proselyte, this is only to be expected. At the very least, the children will have been born

and raised as full-fledged Jews. A convert may be compared to a naturalized citizen, whose offspring are native sons. When thoroughly successful, conversion is "a new birth," a life-transforming experience. Even when it is less, it is still worth undertaking as a "salvage operation," designed to advance harmony and happiness.

When the proselyte throws in his or her lot with Jews, the community should welcome them warmly and not continue to regard them as outsiders. When the non-Jewish partner is made to feel at home, he can become truly integrated into the Jewish community and the entire family can be saved for Judaism and the Jewish people. Rabbis can testify out of their experience that when the conversion fails "to take," the fault often lies with the Jewish partner and his family and associates, who persist in regarding the proselyte as "outside the pale."

3. Finally, the Jewish community should establish an ongoing *Institute on Intermarriage and Family Problems,* in which sociologists, psychologists, rabbis, and communal leaders would continue to explore all facets of the problem, many of which need considerably more study. The Institute would also consider the various methods available for meeting this crucial problem of life and death for the Jewish people.

In the face of this massive problem there is one additional cause for genuine optimism. Throughout its history, German Jewry was confronted by the same problem of intermarriage. Yet there was no conscious, organized communal effort to deal with the problem. It was treated purely on an individual basis, which is to say, it was scarcely treated at all. In the face of the threat, German Jewry was divided— and was conquered.

The widespread communal concern with the problem manifested by American Jewry, the ongoing effort to analyze its components and to devise programs of action for meeting it, represent a new and hopeful departure in the strategy of Jewish survival in the modern world. The road ahead is not easy, but the readiness is all. Though total success is impossible, it is well to recall the wise words in *The Ethics of the Fathers:* "The task is not for you to complete, but neither have you the right to desist from it."

CHAPTER NINE

DIRECTIONS OF
THE AMERICAN
JEWISH COMMUNITY

THROUGHOUT THIS BOOK our primary concern has been with ideal goals—with the values that may be found in the Jewish heritage and with the hope that modern Jews can be won for meaningful Jewish commitment. But how realistic is this hope? What are the prospects for the survival of the Jewish people and its tradition in the closing third of the twentieth century?

Any effort to delineate, let alone forecast, trends in the American Jewish community is exposed to many hazards. In the first instance, we must reckon with the infinite variety of human nature and the incredible complexity of human behavior. The refractory and stubbornly individualistic character of the data with which we must deal explains the difficulty in establishing valid generalizations in the social sciences. As a result, the practitioners of the natural sciences have often been loath to recognize the social sciences as thoroughly scientific disciplines.

Our problems are increased when we turn to the Jewish group. The Jewish community is *sui generis* in its history, its character, and its structure. As we have seen, any effort to place Jews in such sociological categories as a "nationality," a "religious denomination," or by that most bloodstained and meaningless of terms, "race," distorts the face of reality and leads into blind alleys and disaster. The only term that can be used at all is "people," because it is the least specific and is largely free from the connotations of political allegiance, or geographical contiguity, or cultural homogeneity.

That the Jewish people is "a people dwelling apart, not to be reckoned among the nations" is one of the fundamental insights of biblical thought. The uniqueness of the Jewish group, emphasized time and again by the Torah, the prophets, the historians and the sages of Israel, is sober fact. We may explain it as we will, either in naturalistic terms as the result of the extraordinary historic experience of the Jewish people for which there is no parallel elsewhere, or in theological terms as the result of Divine election. For me, both explanations are true and complement each other. Be this as it may, what is clear is that Jews cannot be placed upon the Procrustean bed of accepted sociological norms unless we are prepared to perform a major amputation upon the patient.

Finally—and this truth has been ignored both by articulate Jewish leaders and thinkers in the State of Israel and elsewhere—American Jewry finds itself in a novel situation unparalleled even in its own unique historic experience in the past.

A half century ago the Hebrew thinker and essayist, Ahad Ha'am, contrasted the large, concentrated, deeply Jewish communities of Eastern Europe with the small, assimilated Jewish communities of Western Europe. In the Jews of Germany, France, Italy, and England, who were increasingly assimilating into the general community and who generally lacked any deep roots or sense of commitment to the Jewish heritage, Ahad Ha'am saw signs of deep-seated inferiority, even of Jewish self-hate, vis-à-vis the Christian religion and the dominant culture. Accordingly, he stigmatized Western Jewry as living in '*abhdut betokh heruth*, "slavery within freedom," in spiritual bondage under conditions of relative political and economic equality. On the other hand, the deeply conscious Jewish masses of Czarist Russia were living in *heruth betokh abhdut*, "freedom within slavery," being spiritually self-respecting and free, in spite of their political disenfranchisement and their social and economic isolation.

As I have pointed out in greater detail elsewhere,[1] American Jewry, which is large, populous, politically free, economically integrated, and yet strongly conscious of its Jewish character and deeply concerned with preserving its Jewish identity, constitutes a *novum* in recent Jewish experience. If we borrow Ahad Ha'am's nomenclature, American Jewry can only be described as living in *heruth betokh heruth*, "freedom within freedom," being spiritually at liberty to develop its own group life within the context of American equality.

At the same time American Jewish life is beset by major, even critical problems.

One source of doubt and fear regarding the future lies in the deep abyss that yawns between the official stance of the Jewish community and the personal attitude and reaction of individual Jews. In its corporate life, its organizations and institutions, American Jewry is overwhelmingly committed to Jewish survival. Individually, however, many Jews are indifferent and even negative toward their Jewish survival and that of their children in any meaningful sense.

Much ink has been spilled, for example, on the question as to whether "American Jews are in exile." Obviously, American Jewry is not in exile, if we compare its deep and growing integration into American life with the position of

East European Jews who were virtually excluded from all
the areas of the national life in their respective countries.
At the same time, in a very genuine sense American Jews
are not completely at home even in America, in spite of the
fact that officially they possess full political, social, economic, and cultural equality. It is a truism of contemporary American life that while there are close and friendly
relations between Jews and non-Jews in America during
the business day, there is "a five o'clock shadow" which de-
scends at nightfall, when the gates of an invisible "evening
ghetto" close. As a rule, the free and uninhibited social
intercourse which takes place in the leisure hours of evening is largely limited to members of one's own group.

This may be disputed with great warmth by those who
insist that "some of my best friends are Jews (or Gentiles)," as the case may be. There are, of course, many exceptions, but in general those who make these passionate
avowals seem to me to protest too much to be wholly convincing.

To cite a trivial yet significant experience, again and
again in discussions with young American Jews of enlightened views, one hears them say, "We don't want our children to associate only with Jews. It is so narrowing."
Rarely, if ever, does one encounter the parallel reaction
among Christians. By and large, non-Jews find it not
merely comfortable and natural but eminently desirable to
associate with others of their own religious and ethnic
background, and are quite unconscious of any narrowing
effect. There are few rabbis indeed who, at one time or another, have not been informed by the principals before a
wedding ceremony, "Rabbi, there will be some Gentiles
present at the service." I doubt that many Catholic priests
or Protestant ministers have ever been given the same
kindly "warning" with regard to Jewish guests at wedding
ceremonies in their churches! These instances are too

minor to qualify as examples of Jewish self-hate, of which there are, unfortunately, too many examples available. They do, however, reveal a widespread sense of inferiority and a measure of psychological insecurity, which is very real.

We may now proceed to a more specific analysis of the present character of the American Jewish community, before attempting to forecast its trends in the future.

In the *social and economic spheres,* the process of Jewish integration has been proceeding steadily and has achieved notable success. Today, seventy percent of American Jewry are native-born. It is clear that ours will be a second-, third-, and fourth-generation native-born community within a few years. American Jews will also qualify as far and away the most educated segment of the American people. While there were 15,000 Jewish college students in 1919, the present figure is in excess of 275,000 and will reach a peak of 400,000 by 1970. In another generation the vast majority of American Jews will be college-educated. This phenomenon is the result of the interplay of two factors—one contemporary, the other historical. American Jewry is a community largely oriented to the free professions. This has helped to preserve a strong attachment, though in secularized form, to the high value set upon education by the Jewish tradition.

The *social and cultural integration* has been nearly as effective as the economic. The immigrant and the first native-born generation are passing from the scene, and with them goes the characteristic phenomenon of the Jewish ghetto or neighborhood. The East Side of New York, the West Side of Chicago, the South Side of Philadelphia, are part of a receding background, but only for the middle-aged and the older members of the community. They evoke neither memory nor emotion in their children.

To be sure, new Jewish neighborhoods have emerged as

part of the trek to suburbia. In part, this is the result of the pressure to social exclusion against Jews still effective in many areas. In even larger degree, it is a reflex of the desire of Jews to live in proximity with "their own" people and raise their children in contact with other Jewish children with whom they are more "comfortable."

There is, however, a significant qualitative difference between the old Jewish communities and the new. Perhaps the most obvious change, which is generally overlooked, is the rapid decline of Yiddish. This distinctive tongue, drenched in religious and cultural values that were garnered through centuries of Jewish experience, rich in the earthy wisdom of the folk, yet echoing to the heights of faith in an unseen Presence, fashioned every nook and cranny of the Jewish personality. The use of Yiddish unquestionably served as one of the most potent factors, as it was the most universal, in creating Jewish consciousness among traditionalists and radicals alike, as well as all the groups between. Its virtual disappearance represents a giant step toward assimilation. In the old ghettos, the streets themselves were filled with the sounds and smells of Jewishness. The odors of Jewish cooking, the sound of the Sabbath Eve Kiddush, the light of candles aglow in the windows on Friday evening and on Hanukkah, the ramshackle Succoth built in backyards and on roofs, the echoes of prayers from the hundreds of synagogues, the funeral processions through the streets, the carrying of Torah scrolls at dedication ceremonies, the presence of bearded patriarchs in the streets—all these impinged on the consciousness of Jews both young and old, who might themselves rarely if ever cross the threshold of the House of Prayer.

Today the Jewish experiences of even Jewishly committed families fulfill, almost to the letter, the old slogan of the Maskilim, "Be a Jew in your tent but a man in your going forth." The nineteenth-century Haskalah did not, of course, recognize that there is no such thing as a generic "man" and that if one is not a Jew in the public arena, he is, perforce, a non-Jew, with no "no-man's land" between.

The social and cultural integration of American Jews has marched *pari passu* with their increasing diversification and growing integration *in the economic sphere*. A generation ago the gifted Zionist leader, Chaim Arlosoroff, who visited the United States, wrote a series of perceptive papers on American Jewry in the Hebrew quarterly, *Hatekufah*. He pointed out that in spite of the vaunted sense of equality in which American Jews gloried, they were largely excluded from the basic and stable industries that were fundamental to the American economy, such as the utilities, the railroads, steel and iron, and banking. The sectors into which Jews had penetrated were largely the liberal professions and the industries of high risk and secondary importance, such as retail merchandising, the textiles and clothing, and the then burgeoning radio and electronics field. Some forty years later the picture has not been totally transformed, but it has been radically modified. There are still significant areas in the American economy that are *judenrein*. But even these bastions of prejudice are being breached.

A new factor of great cultural and economic significance is the penetration of Jews into American *academic life*. Two generations ago, Jews in teaching were almost exclusively limited to the elementary and high school levels. Only a handful of the most gifted and outstanding of Jewish teachers and scholars attained to professorial rank. Today our colleges and universities are filled with Jewish faculty members. By virtue of their creative abilities, their intellectual attainments, and their influence upon the spiritual life of America, they offer an opportunity of the greatest possible significance for building a creative and meaningful Jewish life in America, if we can retain the loyalty of these gifted sons and daughters of our people. At the same time, Jewish academicians also constitute a major challenge, since they often exhibit, although fortunately not always, a lack of Jewish knowledge and a sense of alienation from Jewish life, which may be expressed in intellectual terms but frequently has deep psychological and social roots.

In sum, the dominant trend in the social-economic sphere is integration. The secondary or recessive trend, that of exclusion, still operates significantly but with slowly diminishing power.

In the field of *religious and cultural life*, the trends are not easily measured and are even more difficult to evaluate. One conclusion that I believe can fairly be drawn from the past two decades is that there has developed a greater degree of acceptance of Jewishness on the part of American Jews in general and of Jewish youth in particular. Several factors have played their part. With the growth of the second and third native generation, adherence to Judaism is no longer equated with alien status. So too, the greater acceptance of religious loyalty as a normal characteristic of the American scene, coupled with the recognition of Judaism as one of the "three major faiths," has been highly important. Finally, the emergence of the State of Israel, the heroism of its birth and its brilliant achievement during its young history, have brought a new sense of self-respect and prideful identification to untold numbers of American Jews.

This widespread acceptance of Judaism is best pictured in the form of a pyramid. The lowest and broadest level may be denominated *Jewish association*. It includes the vast number of American Jews whose personal and social life is spent largely in association with other Jews and who anticipate that in the normal course of events their children will marry within the Jewish fold. Their lives otherwise are largely lacking in any positive Jewish activity, except perhaps for a sporadic contribution to a Jewish charity. Their Jewish souls tend to be warmed by the reflected glow of the flame of Jewish activity indulged in by their neighbors. At the outside, three million Jews are officially members of congregations, Orthodox, Conservative, and Reform, and of other Jewish institutions and organizations, and the actual figures may be lower. This leaves two and a half million Jews without any formal mark of Jewish identification, whose relationship to Jewish life is exhausted by their association with other Jews.

The next layer in the pyramid, small in compass but still very extensive, may be described as that of *affiliation*. It consists of the three million or more Jews who express themselves Jewishly by some form of Jewish affiliation, be it the synagogue, the community center, the B'nai B'rith, the branches of the Zionist movement, or other Jewish organizations. They contribute of their means to these causes and in return are influenced by them, in greater or lesser degree, through the activities in which they participate, by the literature emanating from the central agencies, and by their efforts on behalf of these causes.

The phenomenal growth of congregations within the last two decades and the vast building programs which have dotted the landscape with magnificent temples from Maine to California gave rise a few years ago to the optimistic announcement that this was the Jewish counterpart to "the revival of religion" in America. Critics were quick to point out that the basic motivation for this "edifice complex" here was social rather than spiritual, the desire to establish one's identity as a member of a recognized group.

Now while this diagnosis is true, it is not the whole truth. It fails to ask a further, significant question: Why is it that with the growth of suburbia and the desire for affiliation, it was not the community center or the P.T.A., the political club or the civic association which became the nuclear group around which people clustered? Why did young couples, coming into new areas where there were no established patterns of group behavior, almost instinctively organize congregations to provide for Jewish education and public worship? The social impulse undoubtedly has predominated on the conscious level, but the subconscious motivations, the quest for roots, cannot be ignored. If we seek to forecast the wave of the future, we must keep in mind that many American Jews wanted more than they knew they wanted.

At the peak of the pyramid—and at its narrowest—are the individuals and families whose lives reflect *conscious commitment to Judaism.* They are concerned with Jewish values and practices. From varying religious and cultural points of view, they seek to preserve the Jewish way of life, for themselves and their children.

Several observations are in order with regard to this elite group in American Jewry. By and large, they reflect a greater interest in Jewish knowledge than in actual Jewish practice; they are more concerned with understanding their background than in adopting a contemporary pattern of Jewish observance. This trend has led to the proliferation of Judaic instruction on the university level. A generation ago there were literally no academic positions in biblical and Semitic studies open to Jews. Today there are scores of Chairs in Judaic Studies and Religion at colleges and universities throughout the United States which are either filled by or are looking for Jewish scholars. Increasingly, Ivy League schools are adding young Jewish scholars to teach Bible and Judaism. One of these colleges specifically asked for a Jewish scholar who "is himself committed to the tradition." During a decade of teaching as Professor of Religion at Columbia University, I saw the enrollment in the courses on Judaism rise from a handful to several hundred. While the class roster included a sizable minority of non-Jewish students, the vast majority, quite naturally, were young Jews who recognized the need for some understanding of their Jewish heritage if they were to be truly educated.

Yet even with regard to Jewish observance, there has been a noticeable increase among younger Jews. It has, however, been largely concentrated in those rituals which are associated with special occasions, such as circumcisions, the *Pidyon Haben*, the Bar Mitzvah, the Bat Mitzvah, and Confirmation, the *Aufruf*, and the more recent ceremony of the Blessing of a Bride. There has also been a significant growth of synagogue attendance on the Sabbath and the festivals. On the other hand, there has been far less acceptance of the daily regimen of Jewish life. The strict observance of the Sabbath and of Kashrut (in spite of the growing number of food products bearing the hallowed "U" sign) continues to lose ground, except for certain limited though increasingly noticeable groups. In short, there has been not so much a revival of Judaism as a revival of interest in Judaism among a significant minority of American Jews.

In sum, there has been a growing acceptance of one's Jewish origins by American Jews ranging from passive acquiescence to active participation. Simultaneously, however, an opposite tendency has been making itself felt—a growing trend to assimilation and total absorption within the minority group. Even among the Jews who marry within the fold, who tell their children that they are Jews and have their associations largely with other Jews, alienation from Jewish life is widespread. It runs the gamut from mere indifference to strong hostility, manifested toward the historic tradition or to contemporary Jewish life, or toward both.

The most obvious and disquieting symbol of Jewish alienation lies, of course, in the phenomenon of *intermar-*

riage, already discussed in the previous chapter. Intermarriage is the most prevalent form of defection, but it is not the most extreme. Far more pervasive than intermarriage and outright conversion has been the widespread *alienation* from Jewish values characteristic of many creative and intellectual Jews. A striking case in point is afforded by one of the most gifted of contemporary dramatists, Arthur Miller, who, as far as I know, is a Jew. Nevertheless, the values and concerns of his powerful play *After the Fall* derive from Christian theology, but without the saving grace of its affirmations. The title of the play itself reflects the central role which the Adam and Eve narrative in *Genesis* occupies in the Christian drama of salvation, where it serves as the prelude to the advent of the Savior.

The evidence for Miller's alienation from Judaism, however, goes far beyond the title. In several of his plays, Miller reveals a growing conception of sex as inherently evil. Maggie in *After the Fall* becomes the symbol of sex as infinitely alluring and infinitely sinful. This is far removed from the normative Jewish teaching on sex and marriage.[2]

Even more central is the obsession of the hero, Quentin, with the search for "purity" and "innocence." Since by their very nature these virtues do not exist in men, Quentin comes to the conclusion that all men are involved in guilt and hence the criminal and his victim are both equally sinful. Thus when Quentin, who is himself Jewish, sees the barbed wire of the Nazi concentration camp, he says, "My brothers died here . . . but my brothers built this place." He has learned that "We are dangerous . . . the wish to kill is never killed." All we can do is "forgive it; again and again . . . forever?" Not being a formal Christian, Miller does not go so far as to offer the answer of Christian theology that the grace of Christ forgives and atones.

Like so many Jewish intellectuals, Miller has ceased

being a Jew without becoming a Christian. And how much has been lost in the process of alienation! The voice of the Hebrew prophets, their faith in the right and their moral passion, the painstaking endeavor of rabbinic law and practice to build a just society, all this has been silenced in the comfortable profundities that lie "beyond good and evil." Quentin muses over his past: "I look back to when there seemed to be a kind of plan, some duty in the sky . . . the world so wonderfully threatened by injustices I was born to correct! How fine! Remember? When there were good and bad people? . . . Like some kind of paradise compared to this." He thus validates the abdication of moral decision and the surrender of moral judgment, and in effect justifies the refusal to undertake any action against evil.

The attractions of this position are manifold, but its perils are self-evident. Were Arthur Miller spiritually and intellectually Jewish, he would have recognized that the legitimate goal of human striving is the concern not for "innocence" but for "righteousness" and that discrimination and judgment in the ethical sphere are essential and indispensable aspects of the human condition.

It is the same blurring of ethical judgment which is the crucial defect of Hannah Arendt's controversial treatment of the Eichmann trial in her *Eichmann in Jerusalem*. As one wades through her meticulous analysis of the various bureaus, divisions, and offices of the Nazi apparatus, the whole hideous enterprise becomes vastly impersonal and the living victims disappear from sight in the process. She finally arrives at the conclusion that the Jews are at least as guilty of their destruction as the Nazis—if not more so!

It is noteworthy that a generation or two ago, Jews were in the forefront of movements for social justice. Today they tend to take refuge in the murky profundities of existentialism and in the generalized conviction of all men's sinfulness, so that they are committed to no course of action and are free from the intellectual and moral obligation of judgment.

Our concern here is with these attitudes as manifestations of Jewish alienation. Being profoundly convinced that the Jewish world view is of the greatest value, I see this estrangement of our creative sons and daughters from the sources of their Jewish existence as a threefold tragedy. It robs the Jewish community of some of its potentially most valuable human resources. It deprives these creative spirits of the insights and values of the Jewish heritage that could help and enrich their own work and thought. And by the same token, it impoverishes the life of modern man, who could benefit enormously from the outlook of the Jewish world view—at once wise and humane and courageous.

These major phenomena in the life of contemporary Jews do not exhaust the challenges confronting the Jewish future. Perhaps the greatest peril lies in the unsavory aspects of organized Jewish life, which we have already noted. These include the intensified denominationalism which divides the Jewish community without enriching it. There is the high cost of Jewish affiliation, which keeps many families of modest means, particularly young people, out of the membership ranks. Finally, there is the growing impersonalization and lack of genuine human contact within these mammoth institutions. These ills, to be sure, characterize American life, and indeed modern society as a whole, but that is scant comfort for the observer concerned with the quality of Jewish life and its prospects for the future.

Finally, the American Jewish community, as its units of organization, religious, cultural, fraternal, and social service increase, is confronted by *a growing and critical shortage of personnel*. The rabbinate, the social service profession, and Jewish education are all greatly handicapped by the absence of sufficient recruits. At present there is a grave shortage of rabbis who are barely reproducing their numbers, an even larger lack of social and group workers, and a tragically declining pool of manpower in the field of Jewish education, where our Teachers' Training Institutes do not suffice to replace those who are removed either by death or retirement.

In this respect, as in so many others, Jews are like other people, only more so. The ministry, teaching, and social service appeal, by their very nature, to those possessing a sense of social idealism, an urge to serve others. Obviously, status, salary, and other working conditions play a part which cannot be ignored. Yet precisely when it was felt that the urge to serve others had all but disappeared in America, along came the Peace Corps. Already thousands upon thousands of young and middle-aged Americans have demonstrated that the wells of idealism have not yet run dry, even in our materialistic civilization.

What conclusions emerge from this fragmentary survey of the American Jewish community today? It is clear that the Jewish group is here to stay and that barring some major catastrophe which would engulf American society as a whole, there will be men and women in the millions who will be identified as Jews. In spite of very genuine threats to its physical survival, the danger lies not in the vanishing American Jew, but in the decaying American Jew, in the preservation of Jewish identity without Jewish content.

In the open society where Jews are increasingly integrated, socially, economically, and intellectually, the hazards of defection are real and growing. The American Jewish community must anticipate that the phenomena of alienation, intermarriage, and conversion will endure and even increase. In spite of these perils, however, it is clear that American Jewry, with few and insignificant exceptions, is unprepared to adopt a path of isolation from the general American community and that it will fight to maintain its civic, political, and cultural equality. Since, however, American Jewry is almost equally determined to preserve its Jewish identity in significant degree, and keep "the price-tag of acculturation" as low as possible, it must do all in its power to battle against these forms of defection.

Since neither isolation nor legislation nor physical force is a deterrent to assimilation, the only effective weapon lies in education. In our child-centered age, we are frequently told that education is derived from the Latin *ēdūcō*, "lead out," and that therefore "education" means the drawing out of the child's faculties and interests. The eminent philologists, Greenough and Kittredge, insist that this is an erroneous etymology, that the root of the noun is *edŭco* with the basic meaning of "leading or bringing up, as from the egg to the chicken, or from infancy to mature years." These two proposed etymologies are not necessarily far apart. They suggest that education means more than bringing out the latent capacities of the child, although it includes it. It is also essential to lead him up toward a tradition and bring him up to a sense of values and a way of life, which is obviously not part of his hereditary endowment or of the general environment and toward which he must be led gently but firmly. Left to his own devices, a child growing up in twentieth-century America would not evolve the standards and ideals which are precious to Jews, and which are needed by the world. The fulfillment of the child's own inner qualities and the satisfaction of his desires are, to be sure, legitimate objects of concern, but they must not be allowed to constitute the be-all and end-all of education. The youngster must also be brought into contact with the complex of religious insights, ethical attitudes, and cultural values which exist in Judaism and are organically related to one another.

If we are to achieve this high purpose, our present educational structure is tragically inadequate. Because of the ubiquity of the Bar Mitzvah and Confirmation rites, Jewish education tends to be limited to the pre-teen-age years. It is hardly likely that this state of affairs can be totally overcome by changing the age of the Bar Mitzvah rite, for example. What we need is an ever greater emphasis on Jewish education during the adolescent rather than the childhood years. It is in the teen-age period that the youngster begins to mature, that the all-pervasive influence of his home is reduced, that he establishes meaningful contacts with the outside world. The optimistic statistics with regard to Jewish school enrollment need therefore to be realistically evaluated. What is truly significant is the number of children receiving a Jewish education on the high school level and the larger number of teen-agers who can be involved in informal programs of Jewish education.

These are the years of doubt and questioning and rebellion, of trying one's fledgling wings, of exploring the mysteries of a great, unfamiliar, frightening, yet endlessly fascinating world. If our young people are to be led toward positive Jewish commitment, the rabbi, the Jewish teacher, and the social worker must be given the time and the leisure to establish personal relations with our youth.

I should like to suggest what may seem a heretical notion on both sides of the fence, that the social worker and youth leader must become "lay rabbis." This proposal should really be a tautology, since the rabbi, unlike his Christian counterpart, has historically been a layman, distinguished only by the greater measure of his Jewish learning. If I may press on to another heresy, I believe that the youth leader and the social worker can, in several respects, be more effective than the contemporary rabbi in winning youth to Jewish commitment. Indeed, every sincere worker has an obligation to recruit young people for Jewish service. In the first instance, group workers are not hampered by the denominational divisions which plague adult Jewish life and which, especially at the youth level, appear to be of secondary significance. In the second, the aura of ecclesiastical status, which inevitably envelops the rabbi in our "three major faith" culture, often creates a chasm between the rabbi and youth which not all rabbis are capable of overcoming. Youth leaders can bring to this task a refreshing absence of ecclesiasticism and denominational loyalty, an openness to problems and challenges and a willingness to experiment with new forms that are all too often lacking in the "Establishment."

Finally, the rabbi's manifold activities leave him too little leisure or energy for these personal relationships, however eager he is to establish such contacts. I am suggesting that the youth worker should therefore be preeminently a teacher of Jewish values and an advocate of Jewish living, utilizing the nonformal, voluntary setting of a club room, the camp, the Center.

I should like to add that this transformation of function will be of the greatest benefit to the social worker as well as to the Jewish cause. Careful surveys have indicated that the biggest problem of the Jewish Community Center today is the continuous decline in membership of the young people between the ages of 18 and 24. Since 1947, young adult members have dropped from 23 percent of the total Center membership in the United States to less than 6 percent. In 1947, there were approximately 105,340 Center members in this age category. Within twenty years their number has declined to approximately 34,600. Undoubtedly many factors enter into the picture. Nevertheless, on the basis of these figures as well as from my own experience with group work among children, young people, and adults, extending over three decades and more, I believe that this decline in affiliation demonstrates that a strictly recreational program is insufficient to maintain the loyalty and participation of youth. Recreation is today available in many sectors of American life, and the Jewish Community Center cannot compete with more attractive auspices that make less demands upon our young people—if all we offer is "a good time."

In the decade and more since the Janowsky Report, the Jewish Center movement has become increasingly aware of this truth. What is even more significant, the Jewish Community Centers have, by and large, recognized that their primary *raison d'être* is the building of Jewish identification through meaningful Jewish experiences for their youth and adult membership. Nevertheless, much more remains to be achieved in translating this recognition into concrete programs.

There is also another consideration of far-reaching importance involved. When Jews band together for non-Jewish purposes, simply because some people of ill will and narrow vision exclude them from their gatherings, they are building a ghetto. When Jews unite for specific Jewish purposes, they are not creating a ghetto but a voluntary association for the enrichment of some aspect of life, like the members of a symphony orchestra, a theater group, or an art league. It is paradoxical but true that here de-Judaization means ghettoization.

Perhaps another heresy will be pardoned along with the others. Today stress is being placed on Jewish songs, arts and crafts, and dancing as instruments of Jewish self-identification and self-expression. I yield to no man in my love for these manifestations of the Jewish spirit. Yet historically, Jews have been "the people of the Book"—and it is in literature, in the written word, that the Jewish spirit has found its primary expression. I suspect that the relative popularity of the nonliterary arts is not unrelated to the popularity of "non-books" and television in an age where genuine reading is fast becoming a lost art.

We need to recall the basic truth expressed in the slogan, "He who doesn't read is no better than he who can't." If the Jewish school and the Jewish group worker can halt or reverse this process toward illiteracy, a major contribution to the general personal development of our youth will have been made. As far as Judaism is concerned, Jewish literature is its royal road, both for its intrinsic beauty and interest and as the source of the Jewish values we wish to inculcate. This goal implies a positive commitment to the worthwhileness of the Jewish tradition as a source of guidance if not of governance, of inspiration if not of direction.

Another resource of inestimable value resides in Jewish humor at its best. There is no happier instrument for communicating the wisdom, the humanity, the optimism, and maturity of the Jewish vision of life than authentic Jewish humor, much of which is available in English already.

Out of an instinctive recognition of the truth of the mystic utterance, "God, Israel, and the Torah are one," American Jews have, in growing numbers, created not merely community centers but so-called synagogue centers. Here the religious services and the educational activities are amplified by a social, cultural, and athletic program for children, adolescents, and young adults.

Unfortunately, the Center program in many of these institutions has been minimal and not overly successful. It requires the guidance and direction of professionally trained workers. Using the terms in the broadest functional sense, I believe that *a synagogue which is no center is as inadequate as a center which is no synagogue.*

In the decades that lie ahead, we may anticipate the reduction of the dimensions of anti-Semitism in America and perhaps throughout the world. We may hope for a growing degree of self-sufficiency on the part of the State of Israel. We can foresee the continued expansion of welfare services by governmental and communal agencies in America. Thus the decks are being cleared for a radical restructuring of values and goals in the institutions and agencies of American Jewry.

The practical problems of assuring physical survival, economic self-sufficiency, and group defense have preempted much Jewish energy, talent, and substance in the eighty years since the Czarist persecutions of the 1880's. Today these problems are by no means solved, but they are receding in importance. For the first time in modern history the Jewish community can devote its considerable abilities to the task of building its spiritual ramparts.

We may now briefly retrace the path we have trodden in our survey of the past and present of the Jewish tradition and in our effort to analyze its future. The major threat of assimilation will continue as long as the Jewish people survive. The problem will be more obvious and pressing in the Diaspora, but it will be nonetheless real, though more subtle, even in the State of Israel.

On the other hand, the Guardian of Israel neither slumbers nor sleeps. Within the Jewish community are powerful forces of regeneration, marshaled by a strong will to survive. The modern age has drastically weakened the power and authority of the Jewish tradition and has destroyed the structure of the self-contained, self-governing traditional Jewish community. To meet this challenge a variety of regenerative movements came into being in the areas of culture, religion, and nationalism.

Jewish culture experienced a new florescence in the last century and a half. It expressed itself in the birth and development of the Science of Judaism which, for all its weaknesses and blind spots, has made possible an understanding of the Jew and Judaism and their role in history. The revival of Hebrew and the flowering of Yiddish literature have enriched immeasurably the content of Judaism. All these manifestations of Jewish culture, coupled with the extraordinary contributions by Jews of talent and genius to all aspects of the life of modern society, have demonstrated anew the boundless fecundity and creative power of the Jewish spirit.

The Jewish religious tradition was confronted by major challenges from modern life and thought. It suffered major blows, but did not succumb. Instead, its spokesmen evolved a variety of responses to the impact of the modern age, conventionally subsumed under the principal rubrics of Orthodoxy, Conservatism, Reform, and Reconstructionism, but with many other tendencies and subcurrents in evidence.

Finally, the Jewish will to survive put forth a supreme effort and, from the ashes of the Nazi crematoria and extermination camps, created the newborn State of Israel as a member of the family of free nations. Largely because Jewish nationalism was in harmony with "the spirit of the age," it registered the most striking success.

Every mountain peak conquered is merely an opportunity for facing a new challenge. These positive achievements in the areas of Jewish culture, religion, and national rebirth have obviously not solved all problems; on the contrary, they have created new ones. These issues cannot be coped with successfully unless we have a true understanding of the nature of Jewish identity, which is without parallel in the modern world and therefore not susceptible to the usual sociological categories. Only if the unique character of Jewish peoplehood is fully grasped, may we hope for Jewish unity and creativity in the new era that has already begun.

The will to maintain the Jewish tradition derives from the conviction that it has significant insights to offer modern man in a difficult and confused age. One such contribution lies in the Jewish doctrine of freedom of conscience for all men. This concept is all the more remarkable because it arose in a religious tradition that did not doubt for a moment that it alone was the authentic revelation of God. The attitude of tolerance in Judaism toward other faiths, notably toward Christianity, is therefore of considerable interest. Of even greater practical importance is the attitude of the dominant faith toward Judaism. The complex yet intimate relationship between the two religions and their devotees during two millennia imposes a moral and an intellectual obligation upon Christian leadership to undertake a broadly based program for the understanding of Judaism and Jews among Christian teachers and laity. Thus the Christian world can do more than lament and repent. It can begin to undo the wrongs of centuries which have made the people of Christ the Christ of peoples.

The bitter memories of persecution and suffering have been a barrier to a recognition of the elements that Judaism and Christianity have in common. An examination of the nature and content of both faiths demonstrates not an identity, to be sure, but the reality of the existence of a Judeo-Christian tradition, within which both Judaism and Christianity have their own strongly marked individuality. The recognition of the existence of the Judeo-Christian tradition and of its scope and content holds great promise for the spiritual growth of Western man in the future.

The preservation of Judaism as a vital factor in civilization requires the survival of Jews as a living people. The free society which affords the individual Jew rich opportunities for self-fulfillment tends to weaken his sense of attachment to his people. Intermarriage is the most noticeable, as it is the most dramatic, threat to Jewish survival. When the various factors in intermarriage are realistically analyzed, it becomes clear that while it cannot be eliminated in an open society, it is possible to reduce its extent and consequently its impact upon the future of the Jewish community. Intermarriage is not the only form of spiritual alienation today. Nevertheless, it constitutes the principal threat to the meaningful survival of the Jewish tradition in America and the world.

If American Jewry is to minimize its losses through assimilation, it will need to mobilize its resources for strengthening Jewish loyalty by building a voluntary community dedicated to organic Judaism. Thus the circle will come complete and the basic characteristic of the natural and compulsory Jewish communities of earlier eras will be renewed—with one fundamental difference: While the organic character of Judaism must be restored, allegiance to the Jewish community must be voluntary and not compulsory.

This new stage in the evolution of the Jewish community will not emerge tomorrow or the day after. Indeed, the organizational problems are at present insuperable. But the lineaments of this voluntary community dedicated to organic Judaism may be set forth as an ideal, if not yet as a blueprint. Its base will be the recognition of the unique character of the Jewish people as an *'am 'olam,* both "a world people" as well as an eternal people. It will underscore the centrality of the State of Israel as the spiritual homeland of world Jewry, *pari passu* with its faith in the survival of American Jewry as a vital, active, and potentially creative center for Jewish life. It will, at the same time, reaffirm wholeheartedly the role of American Jewry as an integral element of the American people, since group loyalties morally conceived and culturally expressed are not mutually exclusive.

It will actively encourage all manifestations of Jewish creativity in art, literature, music, drama, philosophy, and scholarship. Yet it will recognize the centrality of the Jewish religion as the heart of Jewish expression and of Jewish brotherhood. At the same time, it will emphasize the right of all Jews, which is confirmed by the Jewish tradition, to fellowship in the Jewish community, however far removed they may be at present from an affirmative attitude toward Jewish tradition. Accordingly, it will welcome all individuals and groups who may be unable to give their assent to Jewish religious beliefs and practices, but who wish to participate in some positive phases of Jewish life that elicit their concern and interest.

The voluntary community dedicated to organic Judaism will underscore the body of ethical and universal ideals which its religious teachings and national consciousness have sought to perpetuate and intensify. It will therefore emphasize the duty and destiny of the State of Israel, and of world Jewry, to advance the Messianic ideals of the One God and of the one humanity, embodied in a world order of social justice, individual and group freedom, and universal peace. It will need to evolve an approach to the dominant religious culture of the Western world, which is basically Christian or post-Christian, that will make it possible for Judaism to engage in fruitful cooperation, while safeguarding its own individuality.

To achieve these goals, the voluntary Jewish community of the future will give, in deed and not merely in word, the highest priority to Jewish education for children, adolescents, and adults, conceived in the broadest terms and based on the three pillars of faith, culture, and peoplehood.

From the three-thousand-year-old experience of his people, the modern Jew has inherited a rich tradition which has been shattered into fragments. His tragedy is that he does not know what to do with it; his glory is that he is unwilling to do without it. By striving to restore its wholeness of spirit and making it relevant to the world, contemporary Jews will not be laboring for themselves alone. They will help build the world community of tomorrow, which will be dedicated to the enhancement of life for each human being. This requires freedom for every man as an individual and for the group from which he derives his cultural and spiritual values. Thus, American Jews will demonstrate the truth of Bernard Lazare's great affirmation, "Being a Jew is the least difficult way of being truly human."

NOTES

CHAPTER ONE

1. This classification was first proposed by the writer in *The Jew Faces a New World* (New York, 1941), pp. 12–31. Cf. also my papers "Toward a Creative Jewish Community in America" in *Proceedings of the Rabbinical Assembly of America*, 1949, and "Creating an Organic Community" in *Commentary*, 1950, pp. 23–33. See my *Judaism For the Modern Age*, pp. 21ff. and *passim*.

2. Two instances are known to us from the Greco-Roman period, aside from the Hellenizing priests of the pre-Maccabean era. Tiberius Alexander, the nephew of Philo of Alexandria, who became a pagan, served as Roman procurator of Judea (until 48 C.E.), and later advised Vespasian in the siege of Jeursalem. The historian Josephus defected to the Romans during the war and settled in Rome, where he wrote his *Antiquities, History of the Jewish War,* and his tract, *Against Apion,* a defense of Judaism against the attacks of a contemporary anti-Semite. These writings of Josephus point to his pride in his heritage and his identification with his people, which impelled him to try to justify his weak, if not traitorous, behavior during the war against Rome.

3. On the history and development of the types of Jewish community and the variations among them, cf. S. W. Baron, *The Jewish Community* (Philadelphia, 1942), 3 vols., A. A. Neu-

man, *The Jews in Spain* (Philadelphia, 1942), and Fritz Baer, *Die Juden im christlichen Spanien*, 2 vols. (Berlin, 1929, 1936). The two volumes have appeared in an English translation under the title of *A History of the Jews in Christian Spain* (Philadelphia, 1961, 1966).

4. We owe this term to the seminal thinking of Mordecai M. Kaplan. Cf. Mordecai M. Kaplan, "The First Step Toward Organic Community," in *The Reconstructionist*, vol. 15, No. 7 (February 18, 1949), "The Conference on Organic Community." *ibid.*, No. 2 (March 4, 1949), and his book, *The Future of the American Jew* (New York, 1951). See also Carl Alpert, "Toward an Understanding of Organic Community," *ibid.*, vol. 15, No. 8 (May 27, 1949). Kaplan's influence stimulated the application by Max Kadushin of this concept to the study of rabbinic Judaism; cf. his *Theology of Seder Eliahu* (New York, 1932), pp. v, vi, 17–32; *Organic Thinking* (New York, 1938), pp. v–x, 1–15; *The Rabbinic Mind* (New York, 1952).

5. *Idra, Zohar.*

6. See *Palestinian Talmud, Hagigah* 1:7.

7. See *Emunot Vedeot*, chap. 3 (Leipzig, 1851, photographic edition New York, 1947, p. 80). Curiously, the text uses the plural, *torotheha*, "its Torot, teachings."

CHAPTER TWO

1. For a detailed discussion of the Science of Judaism, see the following chapter.

2. The fullest treatment of the history of Reform Judaism in its earlier "classical" phase is David Philipson, *The Reform Movement in Judaism* (New York, 1907). See also Emil G. Hirsch in *Jewish Encyclopedia*, vol X, *s.v.* Reform Judaism. For the subsequent history of the movement and its newer tendencies, the *Yearbooks of the Central Conference of American Rabbis*, published annually, are an invaluable and indispensable source. The basic documents are collected in W. Gunther Plaut, *The Rise of Reform Judaism* (New York, 1963).

3. See Max Wiener, *Abraham Geiger and Liberal Judaism* (Philadelphia, 1962).

4. Cf. the Introduction to the valuable work of S. B. Freehof, *Reform Jewish Practice and Its Rabbinic Background* (Cincinnati, 1944), vol. 1; vol 2 (Cincinnati, 1952); *idem, Recent Reform Responsa* (Cincinnati, 1963).

5. See Hermann Schwab, *The History of Orthodox Jewry in Germany*, translated by I. R. Birnbaum (London, 1950).

6. An English version of *The Nineteen Letters of Ben Uziel*, translated by B. Drachman, appeared in New York in 1899. A revised translation, prepared by Jacob Breuer, was published in New York in 1960. During the last decade many others of Hirsch's works have been translated into English.

7. Among earlier works on the movement, Saul Phineas Rabinowitz' Hebrew biography of *Rabbi Zechariah Frankel* (Warsaw, 1898) may be cited. More recent works concentrating on the American scene include M. Sklare, *Conservative Judaism* (Glencoe, Ill., 1955), which is primarily concerned with the socio-economic background of the movement; R. Gordis, *Conservative Judaism, A Modern Approach* (New York, 1956); M. Davis, *The Emergence of Conservative Judaism* (New York, 1963); H. Parzen, *Architects of Conservative Judaism* (New York, 1964). See also notes 15 and 16 below.

8. Cf. *Orient*, 1842, nos. 7, 8, 9.

9. B. *Berakhot* 13a.

10. Cf. *A Religious and Social History of the Jews*, 1st edition (New York, 1937), pp. 393f.

11. Cf. *Studies in Judaism* (Philadelphia, 1896), Series I, pp. xi–xxv, and Bernard Mandelbaum, *The Wisdom of Solomon Schechter* (New York, 1964).

12. Cf. R. Gordis, "Authority in Jewish Law" in *Proceedings of the Rabbinical Assembly of America* (1942–47), which was published also as two papers in *The Reconstructionist*, November 13 and 27, 1942, and *Judaism For The Modern Age* (New York, 1955), pp. 127–85, esp. pp. 166ff.

13. Two studies of the Williamsburg Community have recently appeared: Solomon Poll, *The Hasidic Community of Williamsburg* (Glencoe, Ill., 1962), and Gershon Kranzler, *The Hasidim of Williamsburg* (New York, 1963). A study of the New Square settlement is now in process by Edith Freedman.

14. A prime source for the outlook of this predominant group in Orthodoxy may be found in the journal *Tradition*, published by the Rabbinical Council of America.

15. In addition to many papers by M. M. Kaplan, see the basic presentation of his outlook in *Judaism As A Civilization* (New York, 1934), which has been followed by many other important works, notably *The Meaning of God in Modern Jewish Religion* (New York, 1937); *The Future of the American Jew* (New York, 1948); *The Greater Judaism in the Making* (New York, 1960); and *The Purpose and Meaning of Jewish Existence* (Philadelphia, 1964). Other expositions of Reconstructionism

are to be found in the writings of Eugene Kohn, Milton Steinberg, and Ira Eisenstein.

16. For a collection of papers by many of the contemporary leaders of the movement reflecting its philosophy, see the excellent volume edited by Mordecai Waxman, *Tradition and Change: The Development of Conservative Judaism* (New York, 1958), which contains a valuable introduction. The reader may be referred to the varied writings of Israel Friedlander, Solomon Schechter, Louis Ginzberg, Solomon Goldman, Louis Finkelstein, Max Kadushin, Max Arzt, Simon Greenberg, Jacob Agus, Robert Gordis, Ben-Zion Bokser, and others, for varying interpretations of the basic viewpoint of Conservative Judaism.

17. On assimilation as a response to the modern age, see chaps. IX and X below. For a classification of the assimilatory process under seven categories see Milton M. Gordon, *Assimilation in American Life* (New York, 1964). The implications of this study for Jewish group survival in America are trenchantly analyzed by Marshall Sklare in "Assimilation and the Sociologist" in *Commentary*, May 1965, vol. 39, pp. 63–67.

18. On intermarriage, see chap. IX below. This phenomenon, which is more amenable to statistical investigation than conversion or "alienation," is the subject of a growing literature. Cf. Hershel Shanks, "Jewish-Gentile Intermarriage," in *Commentary*, vol. 16, October 1953; Erich Rosenthal, "Studies of Jewish Intermarriage in the United States" in *American Jewish Year Book*, vol. 64, 1963; Werner J. Cahnman, ed., *Intermarriage in Jewish Life, A Symposium* (New York, 1963); the volume *Intermarriage and the Future of the American Jew*, proceedings of a conference sponsored by the Commission on Synagogue Relations of the Federation of Jewish Philanthropies (New York, 1964); and Albert J. Gordon, *Intermarriage* (Boston, Beacon Press, 1964).

Chapter Three

1. See his *Liberty and Letters—The Thoughts of Leopold Zunz* (London, 1959), pp. 8–9.

2. *B. Shabbat* 112b.

3. Cf. *Midrash Ekhah Rabbati* on *Lam.* 2:9.

4. Cf. *Die gottesdienstlichen Vorträge der Juden historisch entwickelt* (1882) and *Der Ritus des synagogalen Gottesdienstes geschichtlich entwickelt* (1850).

5. Wallach, *op. cit.*, p. 18. It should, however, be noted that Zunz regarded the Science of Judaism, which he created, as a "swan

song" rather than as the announcement of a new dawn. He saw it as the end rather than as the beginning of Jewish life. Here Zunz based himself on Hegel's assumption that the rise of science is always coupled with the downfall of a people. *Op. cit.*, p. 19.

6. Cf., for example, his *A Century of Jewish Life* (Philadelphia, 1944), p. xxxvii.

7. Cf. his essay *"Hokmat Yisrael"* in *Debir* (Berlin, 1924), vol. 1, pp. 1–16.

8. Cited in Max Wiener, *Abraham Geiger and Liberal Judaism* (Philadelphia, 1962), p. 90.

9. See, for example, *Midrash Shemot Rabbah* 47:1.

10. Max Scheler, *Moralia* (Bonn, 1923), p. 110ff., cited by Wallach, *op. cit.*, p. 28.

11. See *B. Kiddushin* 40b and parallels.

CHAPTER FOUR

1. On the varying positions in rabbinic law concerning the status of Jewish converts to other religions, see R. Gordis, "The Status of the Jewish Convert" in *Congress Weekly*, March 4, 1963, pp. 7f.

2. On the doctrine of the uniqueness of the Jewish people, see R. Gordis, *Judaism for the Modern Age* (New York, 1955), pp. 30–45, 118f.

3. Cf. B. J. Bamberger, *Proselytism in the Talmudic Period* (Cincinnati, 1939), W. G. Braude, *Jewish Proselyting in the First Centuries of the Common Era* (Providence, R.I., 1940); *Universal Jewish Encyclopedia*, vol. 9, pp. 1–4, *s.v.* Proselytes.

CHAPTER FIVE

1. On the Chazar kingdom, see A. B. Pollok, *Khazaria* (Hebrew), Tel Aviv, 1951; D. M. Dunlop, *The History of the Jewish Khazars* (Princeton, 1954). For a brief account, see M. L. Margolis and A. Marx, *A History of the Jewish People* (Philadelphia, 1927), pp. 525f.

2. Cf. his provocative book bearing the same title, *Secularism is the Will of God* (New York, 1954).

3. We have developed the theme of the relationship of ethics to religious faith in *A Faith for Moderns* (New York, 1960).

4. Thus some time ago, a furore was created in the State of Israel when members of the ultra-Orthodox community of Me'ah She'arim in Jerusalem sought to prevent vehicular traffic on

the Sabbath by stoning and even burning the cars coming through the Mandelbaum Gate. When the police arrested the leaders of the group, their sympathizers in New York demonstrated in front of the Israeli consulate carrying banners in the name of "the Committee for Religious Freedom in Israel."

On December 18, 1964, the *New York Times* reported that the Most. Rev. Luis Alonso Munoyerro, titular Archbishop of Sion and Catholic Vicar-General for Spain's armed forces, gave an interview to the newspaper *ABC* in Madrid in which he denounced full religious liberty for Protestants in Spain as part of an international conspiracy that was seeking "to make Catholic unity disappear from our fatherland." The archbishop urged Spaniards to learn from history to be "circumspect" and not to "join the chorus of those champions of liberty who judge the success of the Vatican Council by whether it produced the enslavement of the conscience of Catholic peoples, and among them the Spanish people."

It is of course well known that the Soviet Constitution guarantees "freedom of religion and the right of antireligious propaganda." This right to "freedom of religion" is felt to be entirely compatible with the heavy disabilities visited upon virtually all religious institutions and leaders, the prohibition of religious education for the young, and the all but complete suppression of Judaism.

5. Cf. the judicious comments on the subject of the role of the Maccabees in Christian thought in T. K. Cheyne. *The Origin and Religious Content of the Psalter* (New York, 1895), p. 29.

6. Cf. Josephus, *Antiquities* XII, 9:1; 11:3.

7. Cf. A. B. Ehrlich, *Die Psalmen* (Berlin, 1905), pp. v, vi.

8. The literature on the religious movements in the Judaism of the two centuries B.C.E. is enormous. For a brief presentation of some of the differences among the sects, see R. Gordis, *The Root and the Branch* (Chicago, 1962), pp. 34f.

9. Cf. *B. Sanhedrin* 88b, *Shabbat* 17a.

10. Cf. *Mishnah Eduyot* 4:8.

11. Cf. *Mishnah Sanhedrin* 10:1.

12. Cf. Maimonides, *Mishneh Torah, Hilkhot Teshubah* 3:7 and the comments of RaBaD *ad loc.*

13. On the uses of the ban in medieval Judaism and the famous, though atypical, excommunications of Uriel Acosta and Benedict Spinoza, cf. R. Gordis, *Judaism for the Modern Age* (New York, 1955), pp. 292–306.

14. The validity of this observation deserves to be examined through a study and analysis of the historical evidence.

15. On this fundamental aspect of Judaism, cf. *The Root and the Branch*, pp. 23–27.

16. This contention has been a staple in the thinking of Arnold Toynbee. The same view is set forth by Leo Feffer, who cites the same commandment. Cf. his paper "Church and State—A Jewish Approach" in Jacob Fried, ed., *Jews in the Modern World* (New York, 1962), vol. 1, p. 210. This is particularly astonishing since, aside from Feffer's general knowledge of and insight into Judaism, he himself cites Roger Williams, who utilized the Decalogue which includes this commandment as the foundation for his theory of religious tolerance. Cf. *op. cit.*, pp. 219f.

17. Cf. *B. Sanhedrin* 56a–60b; *Tosefta, Abhodah Zarah* 8:4–8.

18. Cf. *Yalqut Shimeoni* on *Judges*, sec. 42.

19. Cf. *Galatians* 3:38.

20. On the history of Gentile-Jewish relationships in Christian Europe, see the excellent study of J. Katz, *Exclusiveness and Tolerance* (Oxford, 1961). On religious tolerance in Judaism, see also A. Altmann, *Tolerance and the Jewish Tradition* (London, 1957).

21. The texts of many of these disputations are assembled in J. D. Eisenstein, *Otzar Vikkuhim* (New York, 1928), albeit in uncritical form. Cf. also Katz, *op. cit.*, pp. 106ff. and the bibliography there cited. The most recent study of the subject is that of O. S. Rankin, *Jewish Religious Polemic of Early and Late Centuries* (Edinburgh, 1956).

22. The modifications of the Talmudic laws by great legal authorities in the early Middle Ages are analyzed by J. Katz, *op. cit.*, pp. 12–36.

23. Cf. Katz, *op. cit.*, pp. 102ff.

24. Cf. the moving passage in his *Sefer Mitzvot Hagadol* (Venice ed., 1547), pp. 152c-d, cited by Katz, *op. cit.*, p. 104.

25. Cf. *Tosefta, Sanhedrin* 13:2.

26. Maimonides, *Hilkhoth Melakhim*, 8:11; *Hilkhoth Teshuvah*, 3:5; *Hilkhoth Eduth*, 11:10; the *Commentary on the Mishnah*, *Sanhedrin*, 10:12; *Teshuvoth Ha-Rambam ve-'Iggerothav*, Leipzig, 1859, part 2, p. 23b.

27. Cf. his *Kuzari*, 4:23.

28. Cited in Bezalel Ashkenazi, *Shittah Mequbbetzet*, 1761 ed., pp. 78a, 178, 6c.

29. His descriptive phrase, *'ummoth bageduroth bedarkhei hadath-ot*, means literally, "nations restricted by the ways of religion." Cf. Katz, *op. cit.*, pp. 114-15, for a careful and well-balanced treatment of Meiri's views.

30. Cf. *Tosafot* on *B. Sanhedrin* 63b.

31. Cf. *Mishneh Torah, Hilkhoth Melakhim* 1:4.

32. Cf. *Mishneh Torah, Abodah Zarah* 9:3; *Commentary on the Mishnah, Abodah Zarah* 1:3.

33. Cf. *Emunot Vedeot* 2:5.

34. Cf. Moses Rivkes, *Be'er Hagolah* on *Shulhan Arukh, Hoshen Mishpat* 525, 5.

CHAPTER SIX

1. W. D. Davies, "In What Way Does Christianity Depend upon and Profit from Its Jewish Heritage?" a paper presented at a conference on "Judaism in the Christian Seminary Curriculum" convened in Chicago, Ill., by the Divinity School of the University of Chicago and the Bellarmine School of Theology of Loyola University on March 24-25, 1965.

2. For an elaboration of these conclusions, see the writer's "The Significance of the Dead Sea Scrolls" in *Jewish Frontier*, April, 1957, pp. 17-24.

3. We have sought to expound some of these viable and significant elements of the Jewish tradition in *Judaism For the Modern Age* (New York, 1955) and in *The Root and the Branch: Judaism and the Free Society* (Chicago, 1962).

4. "I Believe in the Bible" (published by the Congregational Christian Church), p. 7.

5. In a paper read at the Conference referred to in note 1, entitled "The World Council of Churches and Judaism."

6. Wilder, *op. cit.*, pp. 7-8.

7. *Op. cit.*, p. 11.

8. Rabbi Eugene B. Borowitz, "A Jewish-Catholic Colloquy" in *Congress Weekly*, March, 1965, pp. 7-8.

9. In his review of Hans Küng's new book, *Justification: The Doctrine of Karl Barth and a Catholic Reflection*, in the *New York Times Book Review*, March 7, 1965, p. 18.

CHAPTER SEVEN

1. Cf. e.g., Morris S. Lazaron, *Common Ground* (New York, 1939); S. S. Cohon-H. F. Rall, *Christianity and Judaism Compare Notes* (New York, 1927).

2. This is the title of a volume, with the subtitle *Judaism, Catholicism, Protestantism in Creed and Life,* by Louis Finkelstein, S. Eliot Ross, and W. A. Brown (New York, 1943).

The bearing of religious teaching on the democratic world view is explored from the Catholic side by John Courtney Murray in *We Hold These Truths* (New York, 1960), and from the standpoint of Judaism by R. Gordis in *The Root and the Branch: Judaism and the Free Society* (Chicago, 1962).

3. Similarly, Milton Himmelfarb points out that some Zionist thinkers oppose the concept of a Judeo-Christian tradition as an attempt by Diaspora Jews, particularly in America, to establish a rationale for their permanent status outside of the State of Israel. See his excellent paper "On Reading Matthew" in *Commentary,* vol. XL, October, 1965, pp. 56–65.

4. Among those who questioned the validity of the concept, there were important differences of standpoint. Cf. Trude Weiss-Rosmarin, *Judaism and Christianity—The Differences* (New York, 1943); A. H. Silver, *Where Judaism Differed* (New York, 1956); and the interchange between Paul Tillich, who defended the concept (in *Judaism,* vol. 1, April, 1952, pp. 106–09), and Bernard Heller, who opposed it (*ibid.,* vol. 1, July, 1952, pp. 257–61).

5. Cf. *Romans* 4:15: "The law worketh wrath, for where no law is, there is no transgression." See *Romans, passim,* esp. chaps. 4, 6, 7.

6. *Mishnah, Makkot* 3:16.

7. Cf. *Gal.* 2:16: "A man is not justified by the works of the law, but by the faith of Jesus Christ."

8. See *B. Berakhot* 34b and parallels.

9. Cf. D. Barthélemy in *Revue Biblique,* vol. 57, 1950, pp. 546f., who maintains that the Jews expunged Messianic references from the original text of the Hebrew Bible—as though the Messianic faith did not exist in Judaism! His view is rightly rejected by W. H. Brownlee, who suggests instead that the Dead Sea Sectarians deliberately altered the Hebrew text in order to produce a Messianic passage. See his studies in *Bulletin of American Schools of Oriental Research,* nos. 132 (1953) and 135 (1954); *New Testament Studies,* vol. 3, October, 1956, and April, 1957; idem, *The Meaning of the Qumran Scrolls for the Bible* (New York, 1964), pp. 204–15.

10. This contention is a basic theme in the writer's *Politics and Ethics* (Center for the Study of Democratic Institutions, Santa Barbara, 1961) and *The Root and the Branch: Judaism and the Free Society* (Chicago, 1962).

11. See J. B. Soloveitchik, "Confrontation" in *Tradition*, vol. 6, Spring-Summer 1964, pp. 5–28, as well as the strongly worded paper by Steven Schwarzschild, "Judaism, Scripture and Ecumenism," in *Judaism*, vol. 13, 1964, pp. 269–73.

12. Cf. F. Y. Baer, "The Religious-Social Tendency of the *Sefer Hasidim*" in *Zion*, vol. 3, 1938, pp. 4–6; Katz, *op. cit.*, p. 93.

13. Cf. Yitzhak Baer, *A History of the Jews in Christian Spain*, vol. 1 (Philadelphia, 1961), pp. 277–81.

14. Cf. Baer, *op. cit.*, p. 198.

15. Cf. Baer, *op. cit.*, pp. 270–77. We believe that other Christian influences on this work have not been fully investigated.

16. Cf. Baer, *op. cit.*, p. 305.

17. The words in quotation marks are cited from J. B. Soloveitchik, *op. cit.*, p. 22.

18. On the principal strands of biblical thought and their overall synthesis, cf. M. L. Margolis, *The Hebrew Scriptures in the Making* (Philadelphia, 1922), and R. Gordis, "The Bible as a Cultural Monument" in L. Finkelstein, ed., *The Jews*, 3rd edition (New York, 1962), pp. 457–96.

19. In a sermon delivered at Grace Episcopal Church in New York and quoted in *The New York Times*, November 16, 1964, the Rev. Benjamin Minifie urged the revision of the phrase in the baptismal vow in which the candidate renounces "the world, the flesh and the devil." "As it stands that is a very misleading statement. . . . It seems to be saying that the Christian is not in favor of the world or of the body, that they are synonymous with the devil, that they are evil, and this is complete heresy and absolutely contrary to what we really believe."

20. In a forthcoming book, *What Is This Treasure?* The quotation is taken from a prepublication newspaper article.

21. In the sermon quoted above from *The New York Times*, in another passage he asked, "How, for example, could we explain the Trinity to a man from Mars?"

22. For a brief presentation of Jewish traditional teaching on the subject, see R. Gordis, "The Nature of Man in Judaism" in *Judaism for the Modern Age* (New York, 1955), pp. 225–36.

23. Cf. *Jerusalem Talmud, Hagigah* 1:7, reading *ma'or* (instead of the meaningless *se'or*), with most authorities.

24. Cf. *I Corinthians*, chap. VII *passim*.

25. According to *The New York Times* (September 21, 1952), Pope Pius XII "severely censured" those "who be they priests or laymen, preachers, speakers or writers, no longer have a

single word of approbation or praise for the virginity devoted to Christ; who for years, despite the Church's warnings and in contrast with her opinion, give marriage a preference in principle over virginity."

26. Cf. *B. Yebamot* 63b.
27. *The New York Times*, October 18, 1965.
28. Cf. *B. Erubin* 14b and often.
29. The biblical references for these classical passages are *Exodus* 20:1–17; *Deuteronomy* 5:6–18; *Leviticus* 19:18; *Micah* 6:8.

CHAPTER EIGHT

1. See the comprehensive survey by Nathan Goldberg, "Intermarriage from a Sociological Perspective," in *Intermarriage and the Future of the American Jew* (New York, 1964), pp. 27–58, which contains a valuable bibliography on statistical studies of the subject.
2. See Erich Rosenthal, "Studies of Jewish Intermarriage in the United States," *American Jewish Year Book*, vol. 64, 1963, p. 37, as well as his earlier studies, notably "Acculturation Without Assimilation? The Jewish Community of Chicago, Illinois" in *The American Journal of Sociology*, vol. 66, November, 1960.
3. Goldberg, *op. cit.*, p. 43.

CHAPTER NINE

1. On the uniqueness of the Jewish group, the character of American Jewry, and the various historic types of Jewish community, see R. Gordis, *Judaism for the Modern Age*, especially chaps. 1–3.
2. Cf. "The Nature of Man in Judaism" and "The Jewish Concept of Marriage and the Family" in *op. cit.*, pp. 225–26.

INDEX